T0305466

The Privatization of Israeli Security

The Privatization
of Israeli Security

Shir Hever

First published 2018 by Pluto Press
345 Archway Road, London N6 5AA

www.plutobooks.com

British Library Cataloguing in Publication Data
A catalogue record for this book is available from the British Library

ISBN   978 0 7453 3720 3   Hardback
ISBN   978 0 7453 3719 7   Paperback
ISBN   978 1 7868 0172 2   PDF eBook
ISBN   978 1 7868 0174 6   Kindle eBook
ISBN   978 1 7868 0173 9   EPUB eBook

This book is printed on paper suitable for recycling and made from fully
managed and sustained forest sources. Logging, pulping and manufacturing
processes are expected to conform to the environmental standards of the
country of origin.

Typeset by Stanford DTP Services, Northampton, England

Simultaneously printed in the United Kingdom and United States of America

Contents

Tables

Graphs

Acknowledgements

This book would never have been possible without the help and support of many people who have worked with me over the past five years to turn this project from an idea raised in political discussion to the book in its current form.

My deepest gratitude to my two PhD supervisors, Professor Cilja Harders and Professor Yehouda Shenhav, who have patiently guided me in the long journey from a research proposal to a book, dedicating a great deal of time far beyond my expectations, and sharing their own experiences with me. Professor Harders has not only guided me in my academic process but also in making valuable contacts and inviting me to take part in academic life in the Freie Universität in Berlin. Without her help I would not have been able to find funding for my work nor to find teaching opportunities. Professor Shenhav has expressed faith in me throughout the process, and despite the long distance has made himself available to guide me and offer invaluable advice.

The group of PhD students under the supervision of Professor Harders formed a community and I am exceedingly grateful for all the help that I received from them. Anna Antonakis, Sherry Basta, Naoual Belakhdar, Imad Al Soos, Ebtisam Hussein, Sebastian Neubauer, Eva Schmidt and Allison West have all read parts of my work and have given me useful criticism and priceless advice.

During the years of studying the privatization of security in Israel, I encountered several scholars with a similar research interest. The generosity of these fellow scholars and their willingness to share their findings, empirical data and to recommend literature served my research tremendously. I would like to mention the scholars Galit Gelbort, Wassim Ghantous, Gregor Reisch, Leila Stockmarr and Alaa Tartir.

In addition, five professors have given me guidance during my work. These professors are Gadi Algazi, Shimshon Bichler, Itzhak Galnor, Jeff Halper and Amir Paz-Fuchs. Not only have I learned much from their writings but also from conversations with them in which they explained a great deal about the process of academic writing and about the study of Israel's security sector.

Thanks are also due to Roger Van Zwanenberg. He approached me to write my first book at Pluto Press and also helped me decide on the topic of this second book. I'm very grateful to David Shulman who stayed interested in the topic and was very patient with me, so that I could graduate before turning my dissertation into a book.

My family's mobilization to help me graduate cannot be overestimated. The long conversations I've had about my research with my brothers Tal and Ya'ar, with my father Hannan and my mother Yael, and with my partner Hadas, have transformed my thinking about many of the aspects I write about. My parents have provided me with books and journals which I needed and was not able to access, my brothers helped in dealing with a German-speaking university and its bureaucratic requirements, and Hadas helped with every stage of the project, although she had her own research to worry about. In addition to the direct help with research, my family and especially Hadas have given me tremendous support in overcoming the magnitude of this task, convincing me that it was even possible.

Abbreviations

APC	Armored Personnel Carrier
BOT	Build-Operate-Transfer
CasP	Capital as Power
CEO	Chief Executive Officer
COGAT	Coordinator of Government Activities in the Territories
CPI	Consumer Price Index
CSC	Civilian Security Coordinator
DAT	Differential Accumulation Theory
DOD	US Department of Defense
FMF	Foreign Military Financing
GDP	Gross Domestic Product
IAF	Israeli Air Force
IAI	Israeli Aerospace Industries
IDF	Israeli Defense Force
IMF	International Monetary Fund
IMI	Israeli Military Industries
IPS	Israeli Prison Service
ISA	Israeli Security Agency
MFA	Ministry of Foreign Affairs
MOD	Ministry of Defense
NGO	Non-Governmental Organization
NII	National Insurance Institute
OCHA	Office for Coordination of Humanitarian Affairs (UN)
OHCHR	Office of the High Commissioner for Human Rights (UN)
OPT	Occupied Palestinian Territory
PA	Palestinian Authority
PFI	Private Finance Initiative
PLO	Palestinian Liberation Organization
PMSC	Private Military and Security Company
PPP	Private-Public Partnership
SLA	South Lebanese Army
SOP	Special Operations Police
UAV	Unmanned Aerial Vehicle
UK	United Kingdom
UN	United Nations
US	United States

Preface

Since my university years I have been an activist in joint Palestinian-Israeli organizations for a just peace in Israel/Palestine. In the early 2000s, very few economists were part of those activist circles, and as a fledgling political economist I found an eager audience interested in economic analysis of the Israeli occupation of Palestine, even as an inexperienced researcher. The Alternative Information Center, a joint Palestinian-Israeli organization, gave me the opportunity to combine political activism and research. The topic of security (Hever, 2009) and the topic of privatization (Adut & Hever, 2006; Hever, 2011b, 2013) came up frequently as relevant to my research there (along with other elements), but the idea of privatized security in Israel seemed to me almost unthinkable at the time.

A series of reports culminated in my book *The Political Economy of Israel's Occupation* which was published in 2010. In it I tried to answer with political economic tools the question which perplexed many progressive political activists: Why do most Israelis support such an expensive occupation? Writing the book, however, left me with lingering questions. The role of Israel's military elite, its gigantic security sector and the international military and security corporations in Israel's local and regional politics remained unclear, and I believe these to be key to understanding Israel's economic and political developments in the last decades. The point of interaction between these actors is in the allocation of resources, responsibilities and authority over the manufacture of security. This allocation in Israel favored the state and its public institutions until the 1990s, when reallocation through privatization started to accelerate and reshape Israel's security policies.

This book attempts to offer a comprehensive look at the privatization of security in Israel, with a focus on the last two decades. Privatization of security in Israel accelerated significantly in the 1990s, and the reasons for this acceleration comprise the main argument presented here. A comedy sketch from the early 1990s appeared in the satirical television show *The Cameric Five*, in which a man sits on a toilet and reads his mail. He is angry that he's being called for reserve duty. "It's all because the IDF [Israeli Defense Force] is a monopoly," he laments. "If there was competition between several armies, like they have in Lebanon, they would never dare call us for so long. I'll be able to choose the army which gives the best conditions. We need privatization." The satire was aimed at the government policy of rapid and wide-reaching privatization, which was being launched at that time. Between 1994 and 2006, five out of the ten large concerns owned by the Israeli government were sold to private investors (Hasson, 2006:11–19). The writers used ad absurdum humor as privatization of security was so unthinkable at the time. Today, however, such a joke is no longer so funny to an Israeli audience because privatization of security has become normal.

The transformation which the Israeli discourse on the privatization of security underwent is striking. In 1996 the Israeli government rejected the offer of the US Lockheed-Martin arms giant to buy Israeli Military Industries (IMI), as the company was deemed a strategic asset to the government (Sadeh, 2001:64–77). Twenty years later, the Israeli government headed by the same prime minister struggled to sell the company (so far unsuccessfully), offering billions in taxpayer money to forgive the company's debts in order to make it more attractive (Arlozerov, 2013b).

However, the largest privatization of security in this period did not take place in the arms trade sector, but with the core activity of the Israeli military: the occupation of the Occupied Palestinian Territory (OPT). The establishment of the Palestinian Authority in 1994 to take over the manufacture of security in large parts of the OPT, and the privatization of the large checkpoints in the West Bank and around the Gaza Strip have struck at the core activity of the Israeli security organizations.

This leads us to the most controversial argument in the book. Is the Palestinian Authority nothing more than a subcontractor of the Israeli occupation? I will argue that the goal of the Israeli government was exactly that, but the motives of the Palestinians who established the Authority were different.

Recent events have thrown the future of the Palestinian government into turmoil. Senior Israeli politicians openly call for the annexation of the West Bank and the end of Palestinian autonomy. President Donald Trump took office in the US and announced that he will not insist on a two-state solution. An annexation could mean a roll-back of Israel's largest project of security outsourcing.

1
Introduction

The key to corporate survival resides increasingly in a political or even a cultural capacity; the ability to influence future customers and suppliers. ... The form of this emphasis on persuasion, however, is distinctive to the arms sector, where it is bound up with the prospect of war, the security potential of new technologies, and so on. Companies have power because they can present themselves as possessing unique knowledge of these issues. This is particularly prominent in the current flurry of claims and counter-claims concerning the future of war.
(Lovering, 2000: 170)

In Naomi Klein's book *The Shock Doctrine* (2007), she writes: "The fact that Israel continues to enjoy booming prosperity, even as it wages war against its neighbors and escalates the brutality in the occupied territories, demonstrates just how perilous it is to build an economy based on the premise of continual war and deepening disasters" ... "clearly, Israeli industry no longer has reason to fear war" (Klein, 2007b:428, 440). These claims are both fascinating and unsatisfying. They raise the questions: Who profits from war? And for whom is the war economy perilous?

In *Israel's Occupation* (2008), Neve Gordon developed the idea that the privatization ideology has been implemented in the occupation of the Palestinian Territory, conceptualizing Israel's reliance on the Palestinian Authority (PA) for policing and maintaining the occupation as a form of outsourcing. It was no coincidence that Gordon proceeded from researching the implementation of privatization in the occupation to the study of Israel's arms industry (Gordon, 2009). And yet he did not discuss the connection between the two. The Israeli attack on the Gaza Strip in the winter of 2008/09 is a good example of this nexus. The PA played an important role in enforcing order in the West Bank and allowing the Israeli military to move its troops into Gaza (Human Rights Council, 2009:335–45). Following the attack, the Israeli military held a trade fair in which the technologies used in the attack were showcased and offered for sale (INN TV, 2009). Furthermore, this invasion brought to the fore the role of private economic interests in forming Israel's security policies. In the years that followed the attack, a debate stirred inside Israel about the privatization of security, as evidenced in books by Yael Berda (2012), Yagil Levy (2012) and Erella Shadmi (2012a); in the film *The Lab* by Yotam Feldman (2013); and in a series of reports by the Van Leer Institute (Paz-Fuchs & Leshem, 2012; Paz-Fuchs & Ben-Simkhon-Peleg, 2013, 2014; Havkin, 2014). The political economy tools proposed in *The Global Political Economy of Israel* by Jonathan Nitzan and Shimshon Bichler (2002) are a way to measure who has profited from the privatization of security, who has lost, and how much.

Although Israeli institutions deny the very existence of privatization of security, the inconsistency of this denial is revealed in the "core vs. periphery" discourse which decision-makers adopt. This narrative justifies the privatization by distinguishing between aspects worthy of privatization and those which are not, a distinction between "core and periphery," in which only peripheral functions of the security institutions may be privatized. However, empirical evidence shows that outsourcing started in 1994 of Israel's core security activity: the occupation of the West Bank and Gaza.

1.1 THE QUESTIONS

This book examines the apparent contradiction between, on the one hand, the very strong emphasis on security politics in Israel as a major tool in the hands of the government for the promotion of policy, with, on the other hand, the tendency of the government in recent years to privatize security – and thereby deprive itself of this tool. Existing theories of Israeli militarism have not yet grappled with this phenomenon. The empirical evidence shows that the process of privatization accelerated simultaneously in almost all of Israel's security institutions: the military, the police and the arms industry. Such privatization was considered taboo in Israel's early years, but the resistance to the privatization has weakened in a series of stages.

The main question that I hope to answer in this book is what are the main reasons for privatization of security in Israel beginning in 1994? This question can be broken down into three smaller questions: (1) How allocation of Israeli public resources to security contributes to privatization, and what kinds of privatization were promoted by this resource allocation? (2) How did Israeli military and security policies affect the distribution of responsibilities between the state and the private sector in the application of force? (3) How have international developments in privatization of security (especially in the US) affected Israel's security privatization policy, and how does the private security and military sector in Israel fit into the global market?

Mainstream as well as critical currents among Israeli political science scholars reject the idea that privatization of security in Israel is possible, and very few scholars have acknowledged this trend. Faced with evidence of privatization taking place, three causal hypotheses have emerged to explain it. The first, relying on official statements of government bodies, is that public security institutions fail to address the requirements of the Israeli government, which is then forced to turn to the private sector instead (see for example State Comptroller, 2010:13–38). An alternative hypothesis emerges from critical scholars that privatization of security contributes to the profits of Private Military and Security Companies (PMSCs),[1] and is driven through corruption and lack of public oversight over government decisions (see for example Paz-Fuchs, 2011:62–6). A third alternative hypothesis is that privatization of security is promoted to absolve state institutions of responsibility to human-rights violations committed by security bodies (see for example Gordon, 2002:321–37).

I wish to argue that a political economy perspective in the framework of the Differential Accumulation Theory (DAT) as developed by Nitzan and Bichler, as well as Securitization theory, can offer a different explanation. (1) Allocation of public funds and regular troops to Israel's security missions has become a heavy economic and political burden, and privatization through sale, outsourcing and privatization by default (see below), in line with neoliberal beliefs and practices, shifts the burden to the private sector while weakening the tie between citizenship and military service in Israel. (2) The Israeli occupation of the Palestinian Territory contributed to securitization in Israel and to an accumulation of expertise and prestige among the Israeli security elite. These trends incentivized members of the Israeli security elite to leave the public sector and join the private sector. (3) The close security relations between Israel and the US have created pressure on Israeli public institutions to imitate US policies and even military doctrine, leading to the adoption of privatization of security policies, albeit at a slower rate than in the US itself. Although all three factors contribute to the same trend, each does so in a different way, while overcoming different forms of political and economic resistance.

Institutional political economy emerged as a critique of both Marxist political economy and neoclassical economics by replacing the concept of capital as a physical thing (such as land or machines) with a social concept of capital. As an alternative to understanding capital as ownership over the means of production, institutional political economy views it as a means of assigning value to what has already been produced. Instead of the Marxist emphasis on class relations as the object of study, institutional political economy focuses attention on social institutions.[2] DAT is a new theory (still undergoing development) within institutional political economy, which develops tools to analyze conflict between elite groups. As such, it is especially useful for analysis of policy decisions pertaining to the relations between the public sector and corporations. Pierre Bourdieu and Erella Shadmi, among others, offer useful insights that help us to round-out DAT in areas which are not yet fully developed.

DAT focuses on two objects of study: institutions and elites. It stipulates that decision-makers promote the interests of their elite group by attempting to accumulate capital away from competing elite groups. The point is not to accumulate as much capital as possible, but rather to accumulate faster than the others, hence the emphasis on *differential* accumulation. The size of the pie is secondary, but different elite groups vie to control the lion's share. Wealth is secondary to power.

1.2 PRIVATIZATION

Two key concepts for this study are privatization and security. Paul Starr defines privatization as "(1) any shift of activities or functions from the state to the private sector; and, more specifically (2) any shift of the production of goods and services from public to private" (Starr, 1988:14). Starr deconstructs the terms "public" and "private" as they have come into use in contemporary social theory. The term "public" in his definition means various institutions of the state, and "private" includes both private companies and organizations of the non-profit sector (ibid.:7–8, 39). Starr discusses the various levels on which privatization can take place: (1) the direct sale of public property into private hands; (2) the outsourcing of the production of public services; and (3) the deregulation of sectors in a way that allows private actors to compete with a public monopoly or the withdrawal of the state from providing services (or allowing the quality of the services to deteriorate) which invites private actors to fill the void. The latter will be called "privatization by default" in this text.

The historical context of the term privatization is important. It emerged from an economic and political science discourse embedded n the modern capitalist nation-state. The prevalence of private mercenary groups in pre-modern times (Kinsey, 2006:34–57) does not fall into the concept of privatization in its modern sense. The global rise of neoliberalism has placed privatization at the center of a constant debate over the distribution of roles between the state and the private sector as two distinct institutions. Neoclassical economic theory, the scholarly pillar of the neoliberal ideology, stipulates that privately owned assets would be better managed than publicly owned ones (ibid.:19–32). Therefore, privatization is an essential tool of neoliberal policy, as well as one of the ten recommendations of the Washington Consensus[3] (Harvey, 2005:3, 60–5). Neoliberalism pushed, quite successfully, for massive privatization of government assets in many countries around the world. The neoliberal economic order, however, does not merely mean a decline of the state and the rise of the private sector, but rather a restructuring of the relations between the two. The concept of "governance" as the main function of the state according to neoliberal ideology does not eliminate the state's role but redefines it (Abrahamsen & Williams, 2009:4, 9, 14).

The concept of privatization assumes the existence of institutions which act as agents of their own interests while interacting with each other. James Cockayne uses Principal-Agent Theory to analyze the privatization of security as a decision in which both the state (the "principal") and the private security company (the "agent") engage in negotiation and weigh the pros and cons of entering into a contract with one another (Cockayne, 2007:196–216). Privatization tenders and contracts are written precisely under this assumption. The porous nature of institutions, evident by the fact that state officials may move into the private sector and become employees of security firms and vice versa, undermines this assumption. Privatization, therefore, requires a more careful analysis of the non-homogeneous interests of various elements within the state and of various private agents.

1.2.1 Objects and recipients of privatized functions

If we start with Weber's old adage that the state is defined as the body which wields a monopoly over the legitimate use of violence (Weber,

1970:77–128), then privatization of security is seen as the disintegration of the state. In this view, it is not important to whom is security privatized. However, the privatization of security in the 1990s drew a great deal of interest focused on the companies who undertake government security contracts. Singer (2003), Avant (2005), Krahmann (2010) and others write about privatization of security as the transfer of security operations to privately owned corporations, and focus on case studies in which incorporated PMSCs have been the targets of privatization, such as in Angola, Iraq, Liberia and Yugoslavia. Civil society organizations such as non-governmental organizations (NGOs) can also take over security functions from the state in an act of privatization (Ebo, 2008:143–58), although this phenomenon is much less studied.

A relatively rare view of privatization considers "privatization by default" to exist when the state withdraws from previously undertaken responsibilities, which are henceforth taken over by the citizens as individuals (Barak-Erez, 2008:475–6; Paz-Fuchs, 2011:62–6). This type of privatization is also called "commercialising" by Željko Branović (2011:3–4).

1.3 THE MEANING OF SECURITY

Security is a charged and fluid term, especially in the Israeli context. Diverging understandings of its meaning can alter the entire framework of the discussion. A good place to start is to look at the development of the Hebrew word. The Even-Shoshan Dictionary offers five meanings to the Hebrew word for security, *bitakhon*: (1) a feeling of certainty; (2) a strong faith or trust in God's graces; (3) guarantee or trust (in a legal or commercial context); (4) security of the state; (5) safety installation to prevent accident or failure. In Hebrew and in Yiddish texts up to the early twentieth century, the second definition of the word was the most prevalent, but with the gradual process of secularization of Hebrew, that usage has declined over the years. In contemporary texts of Israeli Hebrew, the fourth definition has become the most widely used.[4]

While the names of the first armed Zionist groups in Palestine were "Hashomer" (in Hebrew: "the guardian") and "Hagana" (translated as "defense"), the word *bitakhon* became prominent when the State of Israel was founded in 1948, and with it "Misrad Habitakhon" ("ministry of security") which is parallel to what is known in many countries as the "ministry of defense." I will refer frequently to the "Israeli Ministry of Defense" (MOD), but one should bear in mind that the Hebrew name of that ministry is actually "ministry of security." Another ministry in Israel is called in Hebrew *Hamisrad Lebitkhon P'nim*, with the official English name "Ministry of Public Security" (actual translation: "ministry of internal security").[5] The distinction between the concepts of defense and security has been obfuscated in Israeli Hebrew.

The distinction between defense and security is important. Defense can be understood as a reaction to an external attack, and a successful defense repels the attack and restores the state of peace. Defense can also be undertaken in preparation for a future or potential threat. Security has a subtly different meaning. It is a state of affairs that signifies an ongoing protection from threats, be they actual or potential. As it includes the notion of deterrence, security can be said to take place even in the absence of attack. Unlike defense, which comes into play in reaction to an external stimulus, security procedures and actions can also take place in complete absence of conflict. In Section 6.2 I will discuss the emergence of the security logic in the US and elsewhere, yet it is important to note that the logic has already been entrenched in Israel's political culture from the founding of the state.

The word "security" also joins together, and thus blurs the distinction between internal and external security. While "defense" is usually understood in the context of defense against foreign attacks, "security" also means a constant effort to locate and remove threats from within. The Israeli army had been tasked with enforcing military rule on Palestinian citizens of Israel until 1966 and on Palestinian civilians in the Occupied Palestinian Territory (OPT) since 1967. Israel's police force has been tasked since 1974 with military-type responsibilities. The Israeli Security Agency operates both with the military and the police, gathering information and suppressing local dissent, as well as countering foreign espionage. The term "security forces" became a frequent expression in the Israeli media to describe an amalgamation of these organizations and of others which straddle both internal and external security (Shadmi, 2012a:142).

The distinction between the internal and external security was further blurred when the Israeli National Security Council, a body which was formed to advise the government on matters of security, decided to dedicate itself to a variety of issues according to a very broad definition of security, from matters regarding the Israeli military to confronting organized crime inside Israel. The council recommended that the Israeli police will be recognized as a security force, and that recruits who enlist in the police in lieu of military service will be allowed to participate both in police as well as in military actions (ibid.:94–6).

The blurring of the line between defense and security has existed in Israel since its very founding in 1948, but is no longer a distinctive feature of Israeli policy. Didier Bigo points out that in recent decades (especially since the 1990s), this blurring of the line has become a global phenomenon. Bigo shows that organizations tasked with maintaining public order increasingly adopt a terminology of warfare in their work, increasingly referring to themselves as "crime-fighters" and framing their work as combat against an "enemy" (Bigo, 2001:91–3, 106).

Israeli officials also use the term "national security" to further differentiate it from something as mundane as merely safety. The term pertains to security on the state level. The Knesset, Israel's parliament, issued a document dealing with the definition of "national security" (Section 2.6.1) which demonstrates the extent of securitization in Israel's political discourse and at the same time the vague and broad understanding of what security means.

The definition of the term "security" is strongly influenced by the security elites themselves (Huysmans, 1998:231–4). The literature on security is peppered with euphemistic terms and justifications for violence. The term "human security" became a key concept in the critical and human-rights discourse as an attempt to circumvent the militaristic connotations of the security literature (Human Security Unit, 2016). Erella Shadmi has shown that the term "security" is used in Israel almost exclusively to refer to the security of Jews. In rare cases in which the Israeli police are deployed to protect Palestinian citizens, such activities are not defined as "security operations." Even routine police work, however, is referred to as "security" when national-based violence is listed among the possible threats against which the police forces are deployed (Shadmi, 2012a:91–4). "Security threats" are commonly described and alluded to in the Israeli media and by Israeli officials as justification for state policies, and for the investment of resources in the security forces. Crime-related threats, safety hazards or economic precarity are awarded secondary importance, less funding and lower prestige to the relevant state institutions (ibid.).

1.4 THE AXIS OF PRIVATIZED SECURITY

To better understand the field in which privatization occurs, I suggest a thought experiment to consider the extreme cases of "maximum privatization of security" and "minimum privatization of security." These are not empirical cases, but hypothetical extremes. A "maximum privatization of security" reality is one in which no nation-state exists, all security services and products are provided by companies, and mercenaries fight for the highest bidder. In comparison, the "minimum privatization of security" extreme envisions a reality in which everything that has to do with security is fully owned and operated by the state, down to the locks on the doors of private apartments. Security guards would all be police officers and private citizens forbidden to carry firearms. This thought experiment demonstrates that an axis of privatization exists, and though neither of the two extremes exists in actual contemporary examples, states can have different levels of privatization on various points along the axis. Accordingly, the process of privatization can be considered as the process of moving along the axis in the direction of maximum privatization. The case of Israel is fascinating not because Israel is closer to one of the two extremes than any other state, but because of the speed in which it has been moving along the axis since the early 1990s.

Privatization of security is a relatively new phenomenon, seen by some scholars (such as Peter Singer, 2003:55–8 and Elke Krahmann, 2010:3–4) as a breakdown of the modern nation-state. If one considers the modern nation-state as built on the republican model of citizen-soldiers and on the Weberian principle of the state's monopoly over the legitimate use of violence, then privatization of security must be seen as undermining the nation-state. However, PMCSs have started to play a major role both in international conflicts and domestic security operations in recent decades, almost invariably under instructions from sovereign governments of nation-states.

Privatization of security occurs at different rates in different countries. In other words, some states are more willing than others to privatize security operations. In Section 6.6 I will compare privatization of security in the United States (US), the United Kingdom (UK), Germany and Israel. The US is the closest example to the hypothetical "maximum privatization of security" extreme, for a number of reasons: it abolished conscription in favor of a professional army, it relies on privately owned military industries, and since September 11, 2001 (hereafter 9/11) it has taken further steps towards reliance on private contractors for security and defense operations (Krahmann, 2008:247–61). The US Department of Defense (DOD) spent nearly half of its budget on private businesses in 2008 (Krahmann, 2010:125), and between 2007 and 2016 private contractors have provided an average of 62.2 percent of the US forces in Afghanistan (Peters et al., 2017: 5–6). Israel is far behind the US in the race for privatization of security. It continues to employ a conscription-based military and the government still owns Israeli Aerospace Industries (IAI), the biggest Israeli arms company. However, rapid efforts to sell government holdings in the arms industry and increasing reliance on private security companies for some of Israel's most important military operations are clear indications that a trend of privatization of security has been adopted as government policy. The policies of privatization of security accelerate despite the long-standing reluctance of the Israeli government to relinquish the policy options made possible by utilizing state security organizations. Starting from a very state-dominated security sector, Israel embarked upon a very rapid privatization process in the 1990s.

1.5 STRUCTURE OF THE BOOK

The book's narrative proceeds along two paths: (1) a geographic path starting in Israel and moving outwards, from Israel in its pre-1967 borders, to the OPT and then to its global relations; (2) a path which moves from the role of Israel's public institutions progressively towards private companies and their role in the process of privatization of security.

Chapter 2 formulates the analytical structure of the research. It discusses the state of the art in the field of privatization of security in the world, and of Israel's security policies, militarism and the military occupation of the OPT. In the chapter I discuss the three theoretical pillars of the book: Differential Accumulation Theory (DAT), Bourdieu's concept of social capital and the concept of securitization, which analyzes the "culture of security." Chapter 2 elaborates on the types of sources used is this study, and on the methodology which I use in order to analyze the sources. Finally, in this chapter I develop a typology to classify privatization of security in Israel and how this typology is applied to the twelve case studies selected for this research.

After establishing the theoretical framework, the context of privatization of security in Israel must be established. In Chapter 3 I present a historical discussion of Israel's military and security apparatus, in which security was strongly monopolized by state institutions. The importance of the military-security sectors to Israel's economic and political structures is discussed here, and also the way in which neoliberal policies have eroded this importance over the years, causing a decline in differential allocation of public resources to security and a decline in conscription to the Israeli military. These developments constitute an ongoing crisis for Israel's security elites, and thus reframing of security as "technology" is a mechanism for coping with this crisis, and a stage towards privatization of security.

Chapter 4 deals with the actual acts of privatization of security. It deals with the main case studies of privatization of security in Israel, and surveys the three forms of privatization of security in Israel: sale (mainly in the arms industry), outsourcing (such as in consultancy) and privatization by default (by encouraging individuals to participate in the production of security). In this chapter I discuss two failed attempts at privatizing security (mainly the failed attempt to establish a private prison). I also discuss how the policy of privatization of security expanded and took hold in Israel's public institutions despite the initial barriers to privatization described in Chapter 3. The chapter concludes with a timeline of privatization of security in Israel.

Four case studies have been intentionally omitted from Chapter 4, and are included in Chapter 5 instead. There I introduce the core vs. periphery dichotomy, adopted by senior Israeli policymakers as a guiding mechanism for the privatization of security in Israel. This dichotomy's failure to explain privatization of security is one of the main arguments of this book. Through the four case studies presented in Chapter 4 I demonstrate that the areas in which privatization of security has advanced most rapidly are in fact at the core of Israel's security operations, namely, the occupation of the OPT. I show that the occupation is the core activity of the Israeli military, contrary to its presentation by the Israeli security elites as peripheral. This chapter concludes the argument which begins in Chapter 3 that the crisis in Israel's security elite accelerates the privatization of security.

In Chapter 6 I discuss the privatization of Israeli security in an international perspective. The arguments on the effect of global trends and of US aid are fleshed out. The privatization of security policy did not emerge first in Israel, but was adopted by Israeli policymakers from the US in a period of rapid globalization. I focus on the US military aid to Israel as one of the triggers for this phenomenon, compare the privatization of security in Israel to that in other countries, and discuss what role the Israeli military and security export plays in redefining the economic role of PMSCs in the Israeli economy and in Israel's foreign policy. The main customers of Israeli security products and services have reasons to buy these from Israeli companies. These reasons then figure into the considerations of Israeli policymakers when formulating security policies.

In the Conclusions, I argue that the Israeli political and security elites have adopted a "core vs. periphery" discourse, legitimizing privatization of security only in peripheral cases. However, the crisis in the Israeli elite has led to the adoption of a "willful ignorance" strategy which falsely defined the occupation of the OPT as a peripheral task for the Israeli security institutions, thereby allowing practices of privatization in Israel's core security operations to proceed with minimal institutional resistance. In this concluding chapter I also review the reasons for Israel's privatization of security which were discussed in Chapters 3–6.

2
Theoretical Framework

While certain countries in Europe or Asia condemned us for attacking civilians, they sent their officers here and I briefed generals from ten countries so they could understand how we reached such a low ratio. There is a lot of hypocrisy. They condemn you politically while they ask you what your trick is, you Israelis, for turning blood into money.
(Major General Yoav Galant, *The Lab*, 2013)

2.1 THE PRIVATIZATION OF SECURITY RESEARCH

The mere concept of privatization of security in Israel is very new, emerging with the outsourcing of the checkpoints in 2005 (although privatization took place also before the emergence of the concept). Israel's economic newspapers: *Calcalist*, *Globes Magazine*, *Ha'aretz* and *TheMarker* all cover the privatization of security as a security policy question or an economic privatization question.

2.2 SOVEREIGNTY AND THE STRONG STATE

Why would the state willingly give away elements of its sovereignty to a private entity? Republicanism, the school of thought based on the writings of Thomas Hobbes, demands a centralized and state-operated security mechanism. According to Max Weber (1970:77–128), the monopoly over the legitimate use of violence is the very definition of the state, although contemporary scholars have moved on from this definition. Indeed, the republicanist nation-state with a conscripted army and a police force answerable to the government is the model of the state prior to privatization of security, but this model was prevalent mainly between the mid-nineteenth and mid-twentieth centuries, and has been in decline ever since.

Charles Tilly described how paradoxically the nation-state with a conscripted army dialectically sows the seeds of disarmament and peace. He showed that recruiting citizen-soldiers to build the national army eventually leads to those citizen-soldiers protesting against war and demanding political limitations on the use of violence (Tilly, 1990:17–35, 122–6).

Proponents of privatization of security argue that privatization does not threaten sovereignty, as long as it is confined to marginal and technical aspects of security. Governments retain their sovereignty even when they contract external actors to perform security and military services, and part of that very sovereignty grants the government the prerogative to choose through which means to exercise its policies, whether through a national military and police force or through private companies (DOD, 1996; Brooks & Chorev, 2008:116–30). Opponents argue that through privatization, external agents exert influence over decision-makers, and that profit considerations interfere with the democratic process. Claiming that the application of violence is the paradigmatic manifestation of state power, opponents of privatization of security argue that the state itself and its sovereignty is fragmented through privatization (Singer, 2003:55–8; Avant, 2005:43; Maoz, 2008; Krahmann, 2010:3–4).

2.2.1 Strategic ignorance and willed ignorance

Despite the prevalent view that privatization of security signifies the erosion of the state's power (Bauman, 1998:65–9; Singer, 2003:55–8), I suggest that state officials promote the privatization of security not just out of weakness, but for more complex reasons. There is a porous border between the state elites and the private sector elites, and those elites dealing with security can be considered as an elite group. Senior policymakers find employment with the very companies which they have contracted and regulated in their previous roles, and senior management in PMSCs is recruited by the public sector to hold high positions.

A reinterpretation of the concept of sovereignty allows for the possibility of state institutions intentionally relinquishing power in order to grant favor to a certain elite group. Mark LeVine described the development of financial interests inside state institutions which transform the relations between the public and the private sector as a "strategic ignorance," a concept which resonates with Roger Owen's concept of "willed ignorance" (Owen, 2007; LeVine, 2012). "Strategic ignorance" or "willed ignorance" is a process in which governments make strategic mistakes which seem to be a result of incompetence, but actually prepare the ground for massive government spending on private companies that offer solutions to the problems caused by the strategic mistakes. The ignorance of the government is not a result of its weakness during contract negotiations as Singer implies (2003:96), but a willingly adopted mechanism in order to allow the government to act in a certain way despite legal and political obstacles.

LeVine points to the example of the US company Stratfor, or Strategic Forecasting. A company which built its reputation by hiring senior retired military officers, and made it known that politicians and military officers who employ Stratfor could find employment in the company later. Stratfor concluded that the Palestinian resistance to the Israeli occupation is a manageable problem, using means such as those that a PMSC can offer (LeVine, 2012). Privatization of security flourishes in a political environment which prefers technological solutions to diplomatic ones, such as the Israeli political approach to Palestinian resistance of "conflict management" (Bar-Siman-Tov, 2007; Ghanem, 2010:21–38), an environment of securitization and policization in which social problems are reframed as security problems (Shadmi 2012a: 65–7, 121–2), and an environment in which "governance" replaces "government" (Loader, 2000:323; Abrahamsen & Williams, 2009:4, 9, 14). These changes are not a collapse of the nation-state, but rather a mechanism for the redistribution of wealth.

2.3 ELITES, NEW CLASS, SOCIAL CAPITAL

My focus is on the role of Israel's political and military elites in public and private security institutions. Most analysts of militarism in Israel (see Section 2.6.1) depict the Israeli elite as a relatively homogeneous group, in which the delineation between military and civilian elites is blurred. Daniel Maman (1988) examines the relations between Israel's military and civilian elites by means of an extensive survey of the second career pursued by retired military officers, in order to find out how porous the elite groups are with one another, making use of C. Wright Mills's framework of ruling elites as a union of three branches: the political elite, the economic elite and the military elite (Mills, 1956:4).

While Oren Barak and Gabriel Sheffer define the "Israeli security network" as a policy network, porous in nature and united by its common interests (Sheffer & Barak, 2013:20–1), the concept of "security elite" focuses on the identity of the group and by its high internal mobility but restricted external mobility (lack of porousness). Senior Israeli security officials are a homogeneous group, dominated by male, Ashkenazi Jews with high military ranks and strong personal connections to each other (although exceptions certainly exist to each of these classifications). It is common in Israel for members of the security elite to find their way into other elite groups: in government, public service, academia or in business. It is, however, extremely rare to observe the opposite path, of academic or business elites finding their way to commanding a battalion, or managing an arms company or a PMSC.

The second career of Israeli officers is a result of the early retirement policy, a means to prevent the aging of the military, as well as of the high status of military officers which enabled them to convert their military experience into positions of similarly high status in the civilian sector (ibid.:25–7). Maman has identified a trend that until 1973, most retired senior officers joined the public sector, but the numbers were already in decline in the early 1980s as more senior retired officers turned to the private sector instead (ibid.:63). He argues that the trend can be partially explained by the shift from an ideological model of military service to a more practical one, as military officers replace the motivation of "calling" with that of "professionalism" in choosing a military career (ibid.:65–6). This exchange can also be described with Bourdieu's terminology as an exchange from social capital to material capital (Bourdieu, 1985:723–44).

The theory of "New Class" can describe the internal changes in Israel's institutions, the rise of certain elite groups at the expense of others. The theory was formulated in the 1940s by James Burnham (1941) and developed by Daniel Bell (1973) and Alvin Gouldner (1979). It describes how a social class (in the Marxist sense) can transform itself, and redefine its characteristics without a revolution and without changing places with another class. Although the theory was developed to study the rise of the managerial class in the US which transformed the structure of US businesses in the first half of the twentieth century, it is strikingly relevant when applied to study the professionalization of the Israeli military elite.

2.4 DIFFERENTIAL ACCUMULATION, CAPITAL AS POWER

Institutional political economy traces its origins to Thorstein Veblen, and especially his books *Theory of the Leisure Class* (1994, originally published in 1899) and *The Engineers, and the Price System* (1921). The concept of Sabotage is key to the distinction between industry (the production of goods and services) and business (the extraction of wealth from someone else's work), for Veblen argues that profit is achieved through restricting production and distribution of goods and services rather than by increasing their production. Those who determine the scarcity can set the exchange value (ibid.:4–18). The military and security sectors, however, produce tools of destruction. How do they fit into the distinction between industry and business, and where does Sabotage come into play?

The Differential Accumulation Theory was developed by Shimshon Bichler and Jonathan Nitzan in the 1980s to offer a theoretical framework appropriate to an economic system dominated by financial capital. Bichler and Nitzan now refer to the theory as the "Capital as Power" theory or CasP (Nitzan & Bichler, 2009). It hinges on a dynamic context of capital accumulation, in which corporations and individuals concern themselves not with the absolute accumulation of capital, but with constantly comparing their rate of accumulation to that of their peers (hence the term "differential"). It focuses on deciphering the interests of the economic and political elites.

By mapping the array of conflicting economic interests between companies, sectors and public-private relations, the theory offers a typology of corporate strategies aligned on axes of breadth and depth. Breadth indicates the expansion of production and expansion into new markets, while depth indicates a stronger hold of existing markets and a higher profit per unit of production. By combining such strategies, companies attempt to balance their goal of expanding their production base with the conflicting goal of using Sabotage in order to gain a differential advantage over other companies (Nitzan, 2001).

Bichler and Nitzan reconceptualize capital as the power which builds and imposes the social structure. They see order as fluid, ever-changing and fragile. Most importantly, power is constantly reallocated among competing actors (Nitzan & Bichler, 2009:312). This has enabled Bichler and Nitzan to study the rise and fall of the Israeli arms industry and compare it with other capital groups and with the Israeli government (Nitzan & Bichler, 2002:120–2, 177–82). They have also studied the rise of privatized security in the US in the wake of the Cold War's Keynesian militarism (Nitzan & Bichler, 2006:9, 25).

They deconstruct the public-private dichotomy which lies at the heart of the privatization discourse, and consider the public sector to be a capital holding group. Unlike the privately owned capital holding groups, however, the government does not seek differential accumulation, and is manipulated by private capital interests. It acts as a "night watchman"[1] over assets (companies) which are to be privatized at a time convenient to the capital holding groups (Nitzan & Bichler, 2002:85–8).

Nitzan developed a theoretical framework of four strategies of differential accumulation which corporations undertake (Nitzan, 2001:226–74). These four strategies are (1) green-field; (2) cost-cutting; (3) mergers and acquisitions; and (4) stagflation. The strategies are divided according to two axes. One is the breadth vs. depth axis, which indicates whether the strategy seeks to generate more net income or to redistribute the existing income. The second is the internal vs. external axis, which indicates whether the strategy applies in the company's own sector or affects the economy as a whole.

The largest privately owned Israeli arms company Elbit Systems (Section 4.2) has demonstrated its pursuit of the "mergers and acquisitions" (internal breadth) strategy since the 1990s by borrowing heavily and leveraging its loans to purchase smaller state-owned or private companies (Hever, 2011a: 151). The company G4S (Section 6.4) follows a "green-field" strategy (external breadth), and has been willing to invest in establishing itself in the Israeli security market despite the heavy political costs associated with this presence. The statement of the Israel Security Association from November 2013, threatening that Israeli companies may go bankrupt unless they allocate a proportion of their running costs to security, is an example of a "stagflation" strategy (external depth) or creating pressure to increase operating costs while carving out a larger share of the market (Weisberg, 2013). The Palestinian Authority under Prime Minister Salam Fayyad (2006–12) has pursued a policy of "cost-cutting" (internal depth), by attempting to meet standards set by international organizations such as the World Bank and the International Monetary Fund (IMF) and thereby gain legitimacy, with mixed success (Section 5.3).

2.5 PRIVATIZATION OF SECURITY IN CONTEXT

2.5.1 The global context

The most prominent observers of privatization of security since the 1990s (Markusen, 2003; Singer, 2003; Avant, 2005; Minow, 2005) have focused their attention on the US, and to a secondary degree in developing countries. They have also focused on privatization to PMSCs.

These authors consider privatization in military contexts, but most of the companies they discuss prefer to define themselves as security companies.

In his widely cited *Corporate Warriors* (2003) Peter W. Singer stresses that privatization of security and the military industry is not merely a return to the model of mercenaries. The corporate identity of PMSCs is an essential element in shaping privatization of security (ibid.:44–8). Singer uses the terms "privatization" and "outsourcing" interchangeably, and does not investigate sale and privatization by default. He mentions only four of the many Israeli PMSCs, and only very briefly (ibid.:13–14). Ann Markusen (2003) and Martha Minow (2005) noted a second wave of privatization of security following the attacks of 9/11 in the US. The wars in Iraq and in Afghanistan became key cases for the study of privatization of security. The growing presence of private security companies in conflict zones has been followed by an increased discussion in the responsibility placed on such companies and the implications of placing such responsibility on private actors (for example, Wolf et al., 2007:294–320). Anna Leander (2005) demonstrated that demand for private security feeds into a sector with an interest to perpetuate conflict.

2.5.2 The neoliberal context

The rise of neoliberal ideology and policies is the context of global privatization of security in general, and in Israel in particular. Even major right-wing thinkers who wish to restrict the responsibilities of the state to a minimum, tend to keep security among the few remaining responsibilities of the state, as a paradigmatic example of a "public good" (Cornes & Sandler, 1996:304, 349, 400). Milton Friedman, the most famous intellectual associated with neoliberal ideology, has contended that security should remain the purview of the state, even when education and health would be privatized (Friedman, 1982:85–107).

Friedman's ideal is Zygmunt Bauman's nightmare. For Bauman, neoliberalism reduces the state to nothing more than a provider of security services to safeguard the property rights of capital's owners (Bauman, 1998:65–69). Bauman warned that a neoliberal society in which everyone is replaceable, and in which individuals are expected to care for their own needs, is dominated by anxiety. Solidarity is replaced with naked self-interest. Therefore, the relation between neoliberalism and the need for security is clearly evident.

Privatization of security enters into neoliberal societies as the demand for security which can be purchased as a commodity becomes yet another responsibility of the individual, who cannot even expect to receive protection from the state (ibid.:22). Advocates of privatization point out that government intervention is not required in every aspect of life, but this argument is rarely used in relation to security and defense. Defense is considered a paradigmatic public good (Cornes & Todd, 1996:10–12, 143–346, 349, 400),[2] and even neoliberals would consider it last in line for privatization.

2.5.3 Neoliberal and US influence over privatization in Israel

Israel was founded as a "strong state"[3] (Hamilton & Stutton, 1989:1–5), using security politics as a major arm of the government to intervene in the economy. Michael Shalev considered pre-1985 Israel as a corporatist state in which the government, the labor unions (under the leadership of the Histadrut, the federation of Israeli labor unions) and the large corporations have negotiated top-down policies for the management of the Israeli economy (1984:362–3). This has changed with the gradual rise of neoliberalism, with the "Stabilization Plan"[4] of 1985 considered to be a turning point (Ehrlich, 1993:270–1; Shalev, 2004:92–7). Privatization is considered an indispensable aspect of this transformation. The integration of the Israeli economy into global markets, especially following the beginning of the Oslo Process in the 1990s, has been understood by neoclassical and by Marxist scholars as a further strengthening of the Israeli private sector and the upper-middle class.[5] As Yael Hasson has shown, there was an acceleration of privatization in Israel from 1985 to 2005, mainly in the financial, infrastructure and transportation sectors (Hasson, 2006).

The US military aid to Israel since 1973, and the emerging "special relationship" between the US and Israel (Little, 2008:77–116) had a profound impact on Middle East politics. Rashid Khalidi has argued that the US used Israel as a proxy to promote its Middle East interests (2009:29, 122–7, 216), an argument which Jeff Halper elaborated in describing Israel's specific role in the pacification of the periphery (Halper, 2015:193–204). Technologies developed by Israeli military companies were directly utilized by the US (Khalili, 2010:413–33;

Graham, 2011:133–52). A consequence of this massive aid has been that it reshaped Israel's security elites and affected Israel's security privatization policies (Chapter 6).

2.6 SECURITY AND MILITARY AND ISRAEL

2.6.1 Militarism in Israel

Israeli militarism is deeply entrenched in the political system, but Israel's version of militarism is one in which security is understood as a widely encompassing term including both external and military and police operations. The Knesset (Israel's parliament) published a text to define "national security," claiming that "national security includes everything which is needed and vital to ensure the existence, survival and defense of the state" including foreign relations and immigration policy. It admits that no clear guidelines exist to enable external criticism on security considerations (Knesset Library, 2003, my translation).

Security, police and defense have been closely guarded assets of political significance from the founding of the state. Even activities such as public health services, education and entertainment, which are normally within the purview of the private sector in most countries, have been partially conducted by the Israeli military (Seidman, 2010). A reciprocal influence developed between the military and the civilian economic sector (Ben Meir, 1995:106–26). This two-directional relationship explains both the military influence over civilian governmental policies, and the civilian considerations which enter into military policies.

In the 1990s, recruits drawn from Israel's lower classes became more prevalent in the army, while those from the upper classes have largely withdrawn from military service, or have focused on specific roles in the army which promise gainful employment opportunities in the future (Levy, 2012:93). This explains much of the transformation of Israel's security elite and the shift into the private sector. The shift in the demographic participation in the military alters the previously homogeneous composition of the Israeli military elites, and transforms the social networks which generate military policies.

A tension exists between neoliberal and militaristic thinking (Klein, 2007b:15). This tension manifests itself in the Israeli case in the debate over cutting the defense budget. Privatization of security is a key element here, as it allows for an increase in resource allocation to security without increasing the public sector.

2.6.2 Securitization and policization

The discourse of militarism in Israel rarely mentions the other security institutions in Israel, especially the police and the ISA. The term "militarism" can draw attention away from the prevalence of other Israeli security institutions, and the lack of distinction between defense and internal security in Israel. As the Israeli police force takes an active role in the implementation of Israel's military-security policies, privatization in the police is an integral part of the privatization of security (see Section 4.3.7).

Taking the various security institutions together, a broader theoretical framework is needed to understand the role played by these institutions in the political sphere. Securitization is the penetration of the security discourse into civilian spheres. It is the process by which social problems are reframed as security problems, and addressed with the application of force and control mechanisms rather than the application of social policy (Shadmi, 2012a). Shadmi also coined the term Policization (ibid.:65–7), a subcategory of securitization, to describe the expanding role of the police in handling social problems arising from poverty and inequality, and borrows the term Culture of Emergency (coined by Matan Vilnai, see Section 3.2) which describes how security considerations become internalized in the public discourse and normalized as an acceptable part of life. Securitization and the Culture of Emergency are parallel terms, describing the adoption of security-based solutions for social problems on the decision-maker level and in public opinion, respectively. Securitisation, Policization and the Culture of Security are phenomena in which an increased emphasis by decision-makers on security can coexist with privatization of security (ibid.:46). They emphasize the connection between the spread of fear and the profits of corporations, legitimizing extreme measures taken by governments, including expensive contracts and foregoing tender procedures (ibid.:41).

Policization grants the police oversight over additional aspects of public life, even as this very oversight is transferred to private companies (ibid.:121–2). Separating the functions of the police from the institution of the police is what Ian Loader calls "a shift from police to policing"

(Loader, 2000:323), one element within the larger shift from government to governance.

2.6.3 Theories of the Israeli occupation

After the second Intifada in 2000 shattered the illusion that the peace negotiations would soon end the occupation of Palestinian Territories, the occupation was extensively researched from various points of view including historical (Segev, 2005), anthropological (Lori, 2008), architectural (Weizman, 2007), demographical (Amirav, 2007), economical (Arnon, 2007), geographical (Amir, 2010), international relations (Destradi, 2010), political philosophy (Azoulay & Ophir, 2013), political science (Gordon, 2008), public administration (Byrnen, 2005), international relations (Cronin, 2010) and others.

When discussing the outsourcing of major activities of the Israeli military in the context of occupation, Neve Gordon coined the concept of "outsourcing violations" (2002:321–37). He differentiated between alliances with independent forces, and the outsourcing of security operations to subcontractors, such as the South Lebanese Army (SLA) and the PA, thereby laying the groundwork for locating the most central policies of security privatization in Israel's history (2002, 2005, 2008). For Gordon, outsourcing of security is a mechanism by which the government avoids accountability for human-rights violations (Gordon, 2002:321–34).

Gordon differentiated between two phases of the occupation. In the first (approximately 1967–86), the Israeli authorities engaged closely with the occupied population in an attempt to influence it politically and win over its loyalty. In the second phase starting with the first Intifada (in 1986), Israel abandoned direct colonial rule over the civilian population in lieu of indirect rule by proxy of the PA, established in 1994, while simultaneously pursuing separation between the Israeli and Palestinian populations. The second phase is the background for the outsourcing of security discussed in Chapter 5. The change between the two phases is called by Gordon the "privatization of the occupation" (Gordon, 2008:169–222). Eyal Weizman has also attributed this change of policy to the logic of separation, and pointed to the policies of the Separation Wall and the withdrawal of the colonies from the Gaza Strip in 2005 (both are policies which were planned in the 1990s and executed in the early 2000s) as prime examples of the new geographic separation policies (Weizman, 2007:10–16). In a later work, Gordon studied the development of Israel's homeland security sector, and how employees in these companies turn the prestige which they accumulated in the Israeli military or police into a marketable commodity in the private sector (Gordon, 2011:156–60).

2.6.3.1 COLONIAL BUREAUCRACY AND THE MANUFACTURE OR UNPREDICTABILITY

While Gordon focuses on the formulation of Israel's occupation policies, Yael Berda's work illuminates the structure of those policies, and the bureaucratic apparatus through which Israeli policies are implemented. She shows that these mechanisms are intentionally left unpredictable and unsystematic, thereby allowing the authorities flexibility which they can use to keep the Palestinian population in a state of constant fear and uncertainty. Indeed, the informal conduct of the Israeli security elite, based on friendship and camaraderie rather than on chain of command, doctrine and procedure, facilitates the production of such an unsystematic security policy (Sheffer & Barak, 2013:36–40). Berda noted that this is what differentiates the colonial model of bureaucracy from the Weberian model, what she calls "manufactured unpredictability" (Berda, 2012:158–64). Berda analyzes Israeli policymaking in regards to distribution of authority and sovereignty, and the use of security forces in the application of force on the Palestinian population.

Berda further argues that only the ISA regularly takes decisions on security without answering to another institution, making it the representative of Israeli sovereignty in the OPT. Other institutions such as the military government, the district coordination offices, the PA's offices, the Ministry of Trade, Industry and Labor, etc. are of secondary importance, which helps in understanding the willingness of the Israeli policymakers to privatize them according to the logic of center vs. periphery (ibid.:18, 33, 57, 164–5). Berda uses the term "privatization," however, in a different sense, showing that Israeli policy since the cancellation of the "general authorization" has forced Palestinians to obtain individual permits, and creating a database of private information on each Palestinian, thereby "privatizing" the occupation, another way of saying that the occupation is being individualized (ibid.:56–7).

Berda disagrees with Weizman and with Gordon, and argues that the change in Israeli policies tightened the control over the daily lives of

Palestinians, rather than indicating a loss of interest in their private lives (ibid.:22–4). She points out that Israeli policies towards the Palestinians became less personal and more comprehensive. A permit system based on personal favors and pleading with regional officers was replaced with an automatic system of permits which are managed from a centralized office. This change has been analyzed by Gordon and Weizman as an indication of a general disinterest of the Israeli authorities with the nitty-gritty of the management of life of Palestinians on the individual level, and by Berda as a more efficient system to do just that (ibid.).

The disagreement stems not from mutually exclusive analyses but from different perspectives observing the same phenomenon. Gordon analyzes the occupation through the perspective of Israeli policy and decision-makers and their willingness to invest time and resources in influencing Palestinians on the individual level. Berda's research is grounded in the experience of Palestinians who appeal to Israeli authorities for permits, and therefore experience a very arbitrary and oppressive bureaucratic apparatus.

2.6.3.2 MATRIX OF CONTROL

A colonial theory of the occupation highlights the centrality to the colonial regime of control over movement and space. Colonial powers put great emphasis on this control, and commodify the ability of subjects to move through space, as demonstrated by the case of Egypt under British colonial rule (Mitchell, 2002:9, 90–1). The privilege of free passgate becomes a valuable commodity, while restriction on movement redistributes wealth and status towards those with that privilege (Veblen, 1921:4–18).

Jeff Halper's (2008, 2009) concept of the "Matrix of Control" is based on the premise that Israeli strategy is not to cover as much territory as possible but to seize key strategic points in order to restrict the movement of Palestinians. Unlike Berda, Halper argues that the Israeli strategy is concentrated in the checkpoints, which control and regulate movement in the OPT (Halper, 2009:31–40). And yet the checkpoints have been mostly privatized through outsourcing. Has the Israeli government relinquished its most important tool of colonial control in the OPT? This is at the heart of the "core vs. periphery" distinction that will be addressed in Section 5.1.

2.7 SOURCES AND THEIR LIMITS

Data on Israel's security policies is scarce. Much of it, and especially the contents of Israel's defense budget, is classified. Large arms companies in Israel are state owned and are not obligated to make their financial reports public. Contracts between the government and PMSCs are also confidential, and the tenders published by the Israeli MOD require security clearance to read (MOD Online, 2016). Even small payments to private companies by the MOD are classified (Coren, 2015). The budgets of certain Israeli security forces, specifically the foreign intelligence agency "Mossad" and the Israeli Security Agency (ISA), also known as the "Shin Bet," are not included in the defense budget and are not published.

The Akevot Institute in Israel found that 99 percent of the Israeli state archive files are not open to the public (Hofstetter & Yavne, 2016:6). In 2013, it was discovered that the Israeli Ministry of Finance used a fake company to mask payments to security investigators in order to conceal the amounts paid to conduct security investigations for the ISA by private companies. The only reason that the story was exposed is that the company name used by the Ministry of Finance, "Limon – Economic Investigations Ltd.," was already the name of a company that was liquidated in 2009 (Levinson, 2013).

2.8 TYPOLOGY OF PRIVATIZATION OF SECURITY

Comparison between different cases of privatization of security across time, in different countries and of different institutions requires a typology. Singer (2003:92–100) formulated the "tip of the spear" typology, differentiating between (1) "military provider firms" which offer implementation and command; (2) "military consultancy firms" which offer advice and training; and (3) "military support firms" which provide non-lethal aid and logistics. These categories follow the demarcation lines traced by the companies themselves. The spear analogy stresses that privatization becomes more extreme and dangerous the closer it gets to the actual combat. Therefore, the manufacture of weaponry is not included in the "tip of the spear" typology at all.

All three of Singer's categories are present in the privatization of security in Israel. Private security companies (Sections 5.4 and 5.5) have played the role of military provider firms for the Israeli government, but so have organizations which are not companies (the SLA and the

PA, see Sections 5.2 and 5.3). Consultancy firms (especially McKinsey) have been contracted to assist in budget management and logistics of military units (Rozner, 2011:24–31), to prepare a reform in the police force (Arlozerov, 2013a) and in providing education services to soldiers (Blau, 2012). Under the third category of military support firms, one can find the outsourcing of health services to soldiers (Paz-Fuchs & Ben-Simkhon-Peleg, 2013:53–7), food and transportation services (Coren, 2014c), as well as the construction of training centers (Director, 2011; Coren, 2013e), among others.

The "tip of the spear" typology is limited in its usefulness when it comes to Israel, mainly because it is one-dimensional. First, Singer does not consider privatization to non-corporate actors such as NGOs. Second, government institutions are not divided according to the three-tier typology, and outsourcing contracts may spread over two or all three tiers at once. In a colonial reality such as exists in Israel, the distinction between control and surveillance, on the one hand, and war and combat, on the other, is constantly blurred. The privatized checkpoints exemplify how Israeli PMSCs defy the "tip of the spear" categories by performing a combination of services which could be classified within all of Singer's categories (Ghantous, 2012:27), making comparisons between them impossible using Singer's typology.

I propose a typology of privatization of security based on a different perspective. Rather than asking, as Singer does, "to whom is security privatized?" I ask, "from whom is security privatized?" This creates one axis of the typology based on the type of government institution which privatizes its functions. The second axis is the type of privatization. The three major types of privatization are sale, outsourcing and privatization by default (Feigenbaum & Henig, 1994:187). Sale occurs when a public institution is converted into a government company and is sold as a whole, or when assets belonging to a public institution are sold. Outsourcing occurs when certain services which a public institution has provided in the past or is expected to provide in the present are sourced from external, non-public agents. Privatization by default occurs when a public institution allows for a certain need which was previously filled by public institutions to go unfulfilled, thereby encouraging private agents to fill the gap themselves (Barak-Erez, 2008:475–6; Paz-Fuchs, 2011:62–6).

Table 2.1 presents the typology and maps twelve case studies which will be discussed at length in this book. It also mentions whether each privatization was successful, unsuccessful or temporarily successful. Success is defined in a binary fashion as either successful or not, based on the relation between the proposed policy (a bill, a tender or an ordnance), as compared with the application of the policy. Minor compromises or changes to the original policy were not taken into consideration in the definition of success, which is intended here in order to create a mapping of the privatization of security policies.

Table 2.1 Institutional Typology of Privatization of Security

	Sale	*Outsourcing*	*By Default*
Military			
Fighting		1: Security of the natural-gas rigs [unsuccessful]; 6: South Lebanese Army (SLA) [temporary success]	10: Killing by default [unsuccessful]
Checkpoints		7: Palestinian Authority (PA) [successful]; 9: Privatization of the checkpoints [successful]	
Military government		4: Consultancy in security planning [successful]	
Logistics		3: Bahad City [successful]; 12: Hewlett Packard (HP) [successful]	
Police			
Crime fighting			
Control of space		7: Palestinian Authority (PA) [successful]; 12: Hewlett Packard (HP) [successful]	8: Private security companies [successful]
Security of public space			8: Private security companies [successful]; 11: G4S [temporary success]
Logistics			
Prisons		5: Private prison [unsuccessful]; 7: Palestinian Authority (PA) [successful]; 11: G4S [temporary success]	
Security ministries			
Arms industry	2: Israeli Military Industries (IMI) [unsuccessful]		

3
Developments in Israel's Military and Security Institutions

Israel is an armed state: tens of thousands of police officers, prisons service people, regular and reservist soldiers. 180,000 citizens hold a license to carry firearms, and take their guns to their homes every day. (Pini Sheef, CEO of the Security Companies Organization in Hasson et al., 2013)

There is a crisis among Israel's security elites that is one of the main reasons for the privatization of security in this country. In order to understand this crisis, it is important first to examine the hegemonic status which the Israeli security elite had in Israel's political and economic decision-making in the past. Although Israeli society remains highly militarized and in absolute terms commands more resources than in 1994, other elite groups have increased their influence and resources even faster, thereby leaving the Israeli security elite with a command over a smaller *share* of capitalization.

This chapter offers a historical context of Israel's political economy of security, preparing the ground for the next chapter in which the empirical evidence of security privatization will be discussed directly. The purpose here is to identify the object of privatization through developments in Israel's military industry, military expenditure and the culture of emergency. The centrality of the security institutions in Israeli politics makes it difficult to imagine that the Israeli government would relinquish direct control over security operations to private actors. Privatization of security weakens the decision-makers in favor of private companies, shifting social and material capital from public elites to the private sector elite.

As the Israeli military operates in areas which in most countries are operated by civilians, it is reasonable to expect that one of the ways in which the Israeli government can adopt a public-private balance resembling Western states is through privatization. For example, the state may choose to rely solely on civilian teachers to teach Hebrew to new immigrants, to sell lands currently used by the military, etc. However, the facts pertaining to the course of privatization of security presented below challenge this hypothesis. The military remains involved in civilian branches of the government, but some of its other functions are undergoing privatization (see also Chapters 5 and 6).

3.1 SECURITY AS A MANIFESTATION OF STATE POWER

3.1.1 Independence and influence of the military elite

The State of Israel was founded amidst conditions of war, and the military forces had a key role in establishing the political culture of the state from its very inception. Israeli state institutions were very strong from their onset (see Hamilton's concept of a strong state, 1989:1–5), and organized in a corporatist system (Shalev, 1984:362–3). The military elite in these early years was highly politicized and permeability between the military elite and the political elite was high (Maman, 1988:64–6). Numerous members of the Knesset (Israel's parliament), ministers, mayors, prime ministers and presidents have been elected or appointed following a long military service. Yoram Peri found that "Since the 1960s, on average, 10 percent of Israel's Knesset members have been high-ranking reserve officers. Furthermore, about 20 percent of cabinet ministers are generally high-ranking reserve officers" (Peri, 2006:81). Gabriel Sheffer and Oren Barak found that the ratio of Knesset members with a significant security background increased steadily from 1955 to 1984 (Sheffer & Barak, 2013:51).

Simultaneously the security organizations themselves (headed by professional officers rather than by politically elected or appointed officials) wielded significant influence over the shaping of government policy (Ben Meir, 1995:106–26; Barak & Sheffer, 2010:19–30). The army, the security services (the ISA and the Mossad) and to a lesser extent the police have been holding an elevated status in Israel's political sphere (Sheffer & Barak, 2010:4–5).

Rather than subordinating Israel's arms trade to the civilian trade authorities, the arms trade is channeled through a parallel system. The Israeli military's independence is demonstrated in departments of the MOD which parallel civilian authorities. The army has its own department for arms export, and negotiates arms deals directly despite official civilian supervision. It also operates a marketing mechanism for the products which it promotes, and maintains a customs system, separate from the general Israeli customs system used for all other forms of trade (Ben Meir, 1995:89–91; Lifshitz, 2002:62–3). Israel's military exports also serve as an alternative diplomatic channel. There are countries with which Israel does not maintain diplomatic relations, but with which Israel can nevertheless hold a dialogue through the channels established through arms trade (Sadeh, 2001:64–77).

The low level of transparency of the Israeli military-security sector contributes to its ability to act independently with minimal civilian oversight. Transparency International (TI) compared corruption levels in different countries around the world and gave Israel the "D+" mark, placing it in a group of high risk for corruption in the defense sector, among Bosnia & Herzegovina, Cyprus, India, Kenya, Kuwait, Lebanon, Mexico, Singapore, South Africa, Thailand, Ukraine and United Arab Emirates (UAE) (TI, 2013:8–11, 13). The Israeli MOD criticized the report as arbitrary and subjective (Coren, 2013c). The report touches nevertheless on a crucial point – the high level of independence of Israel's security organizations and their autonomy in allocating their budget is relatively high in international comparisons.

Conversely, the civilian function and authorities of the army have made the military into a very important and frequently employed tool in the toolbox of Israeli policymakers. For example, as part of Israel's demographic policies and domestic planning, many cases have occurred over the years in which Palestinian-owned land was defined as a "closed military zone," in preparation for using that land to establish Jewish communities (Dahan Kalev, 1999:152). Military-run radio stations (Seidman, 2010:13)[1] demonstrate the special situation in Israel which differentiates it from most developed countries. Should a station be sold to a private company and no longer employ soldiers, it would constitute a simultaneous act of civilianization and of privatization.

Examples of military decisions which involve civilian considerations are the policy to establish military bases with the intention of turning them into civilian communities later (MOITAL, 2009:70–1); military hospitals which served the civilian population that were established in the early years of the state; and military units that were used to teach Hebrew to new immigrants, to grant professional training courses to the public, to execute agricultural and construction projects, to pave roads, to maintain transitionary camps for immigrants and to distribute groceries (Lifshitz, 2000:72–3).

Examples of civilian decisions with a military element include the establishment of agricultural communities close to the border in order to put civilians in locations where they could spot and report hostile activities (Bisharat, 1994:530–1), establishing housing projects for new immigrants in certain neighborhoods close to the border, in which the residential houses themselves were designed as fortifications due to the belief that civilian communities bolster Israel's borders (Newman, 1989:218–22; Oren & Newman, 2006:569–70). The Israeli government publishes an annual list of "priority area communities" which receive special government subsidies and support. The document contains a paragraph on the security considerations, specifying that the Israeli government sees the strengthening of communities near the border as a strategic security objective (Israeli Government, 2013a:70–1). A branch of the military, the "Education Corps," is charged with military-managed education activities aimed both at soldiers and the general populace. However, this corps is also involved in privatization and purchases education services from external bodies (Section 4.1.2).

These close ties between the military and civilian authorities blur the line separating the responsibilities of the military from the responsibilities of the civil authorities. Military decisions contain non-military considerations, and civilian policies contain security considerations. Military and security policies are not only aimed at protecting civilians but also at providing civilians with additional services, altering their behavior and mobilizing their efforts in assisting in security projects (Seidman, 2010:3–8).

The military wields significant authority over the daily lives of the civilian population. This is manifested in the authority of the army to provide and deny permits to travel out of the country and to confiscate civilian vehicles for military use. Until 1966 Palestinian citizens of Israel were subjected to a military government, and starting from 1967 the army established and controlled the civilian government of the territory occupied in the 1967 War (Ben Meir, 1995:7).[2] The army also maintains an array of education, settlement and welfare services in the "developing towns"[3] in Israel (Tuv, 2002:19–21).

3.1.2 Military in civilian roles following the 1967 War

Following the occupation of large tracts of land in the 1967 War, widespread changes have taken effect in Israel's political culture. Shlomo

Swirski argues that the Israeli government began to see itself as a regional power almost immediately after the war and to act accordingly. One of the first policy decisions was to establish a large, state-owned military industry to provide advanced weapon systems to the Israeli army. Swirski sees this decision within the context of an increased militarization of Israel's political sphere following the war (Swirski, 2008). Avishai Ehrlich argued that the involvement of the two superpowers played a key role in convincing the Israeli government to develop the local military industry in the wake of the 1967 War and to increase cooperation with the US military industry after the 1973 War (Ehrlich, 1993:257; Brigadier-General "Yud," 1995:27). Indeed, unlike the wars of 1948 and 1956, in which military spending was reduced after the fighting ended, the 1967 War was followed by an increase in the defense budget (Swirski, 2008).

Consequently, Israel developed its own military-industrial complex after the 1967 occupation. The military industry became a major element of the Israeli economy. In the six years between 1966 and 1972, the workforce in Israel's military industry increased from 14,000 to 34,000, a growth of 143 percent. The workforce doubled again to 63,000 in 1973 (in the wake of the 1973 War), and reached 20 percent of Israel's industrial workforce (Sadeh, 2001:64–77). More importantly, it grew beyond its role as a government-protected and regulated industry designed mainly to outfit the Israeli military, and became an economic sector in which private investors could invest. The term "military-industrial complex" was coined by US President Eisenhower. Eisenhower referred to the business interests of private companies in the arms industry influencing government policy (Gómez del Prado, 2010). The application of this term to Israel does not imply an identical balance between private and public interests. As long as private companies in the arms industry are overshadowed by government-owned companies, the profit consideration cannot fully explain the type of influence which the industry applies to the government. Private companies emerged as actors in the Israeli arms sector in 1967, but this was only the beginning of a process, which is progressing. The military industry remains dominated by government-owned companies.[4]

The emergence of the military-industrial complex, complete with private companies tied by numerous contracts with the MOD and the Ministry of Public Security, created the potential for large-scale privatization. The rapid build-up of large state-owned companies by the Israeli government also attracted capital from private investors who were interested in purchasing them, adding further pressure on the government to privatize. The large Israeli military provided officers, who retire at an early age and can serve as consultants, liaisons and managers for these companies and for investors.

The massive investments in the military industry at a time when military Keynesianism was in decline and the global economy was shifting investments into implementing technological innovations in the civilian sector were among the main causes for the slowdown in Israel's economic growth rate, and for Israel's "lost decade" (from an economic perspective) between the mid-1970s and mid-1980s. Ariel Halperin demonstrated that during the "lost decade," approximately 60 percent of research and development spending was invested in the military industry, and about 55–60 percent of trained engineers were employed by the military industry, thereby starving the civilian industries of research funding and talented workers (Halperin, 1987:990–1010, 1988:3–6). Israel's defense spending as a proportion of gross domestic product (GDP) declined after 1985 (Swirski, 2008) but not as fast as it did in other countries, even compared to countries in the Middle East (Graph 3.1). The MOD not only served the role of regulator, supervisor and sales promoter (like the Pentagon in the US) but also as the owner of most of the companies (Swirski, 2008).

3.1.3 Allocation of state resources to security

The high allocation of public resources to security is among the reasons for neoliberal actors to call for a privatization of security, in an attempt to cut public spending (Sections 4.1.3 and 5.1.2). Joining those calls are those of capital owners interested in investing in the security sector. Security costs have always been a heavy burden on the Israeli economy. The long-term trend in security costs demonstrates that military costs (as a proportion of GDP) were high in many countries around the world until the 1970s and 1980s, during which time a combination of GDP growth and cuts in defense budgets brought military expenditure to lower levels.[5] The large proportion of the Israeli economy dedicated to security demonstrates that the privatization of the security institutions pertains to a major section of the Israeli economy and of Israel's elites.

Data presented by Abu-Qarn and Abu-Bader demonstrates that until 1978, Israel spent a smaller proportion of its GDP on defense than its neighbors Egypt, Jordan or Syria. Egypt reduced its military expenditure

after signing the peace treaty with Israel in 1978, but Israel's correspond-
ing reduction was smaller. Starting from 1988, Israel spent (in terms of
GDP) a greater proportion of its GDP on its military than any of these
three countries (Abu-Qarn & Abu-Bader, 2007). Graph 3.1 shows Israel's
military security expenditure for 1988–2015, compared with those of the
US, the G20 and the Middle East (excluding Israel). For each group of
countries, the graph uses an unweighted average.[6] The graph shows that
Israel consistently spent approximately twice as much as the US, over
four times the G20 and more than the Middle East average on its military.
This does not include spending on internal security (in which Israel is
also a very high spender) and concealed budgets, such as the budget of
Israel's Mossad and ISA[7] (SIPRI, 2015:388–99, 2017). The graph shows
that the burden of security in Israel is declining over the long run, but
continues to be comparatively high.

In 1999 the expenditure in Israel fell briefly below the Middle East
average when peace expectations in Israel and the stabilization of the
Palestinian Authority led to a decline in military spending. In 2015 the
Israeli expenditure again fell below the Middle East average because of
a spike in military expenditure in Middle Eastern countries due to the
raging conflicts in Iraq, Libya, Syria and Yemen.

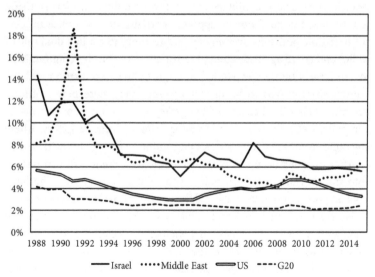

Graph 3.1 Total Estimated Cost of Security (% of GDP)

Source: Based on data from the Israeli Central Bureau of Statistics (ICBS) (2008, 2010,
2013, 2015, 2017).

3.1.4 Military characteristics of Israel's police force

The Israeli police force originally (since 1948) had absolute authority and responsibility over internal security in Israel, according to former major general of the police force Moshe Mizrahi. Over the years this authority has been eroded. When the Israeli government tasked the police with preventing and protecting against terror attacks, in addition to fighting crime, it did not provide the police with additional resources. Instead, the government offered the police more authority, and the right to delegate some of the authority to other organizations.[8] This policy allowed the government to deploy a larger number of security personnel, but an additional consequence of this policy was a blurring of the state's monopoly over the use of violence, and the opportunity for private actors (representing economic or ideological interests) to accumulate enforcement authority.

Shadmi emphasizes the "Enslavement of the [Israeli] police to the building of the nation, and the class-, ethnic-, national- and gender-violence established by the police" (Shadmi, 2012a:14). This interpretation of the role of the Israeli police is enhanced through examples of the para-military nature of the Israeli police, such as the large "Border Police" branch which acts as a military unit and wears military uniforms. Using a 1961 law, the government appoints partially trained police officers for part-time positions over a restricted territory to act in a dual role of police and guard against potential terror attacks in border communities. When Israel's borders expanded through military occupation and the communities ceased to be border communities, these police officers retained their roles because of budgetary reasons, thus compromising the police's effectiveness in addressing crimes in the periphery, where the police continue to operate as a para-military force (Kobowitz, 2013).

After the 1967 occupation, the Israeli police force was drawn further into the grey area between police and military operations. The large civilian population in the OPT and the geographical closeness of the OPT to Israel have shaped the Israeli military-industrial complex in a certain way, with a heavy emphasis on policing, surveillance and perimeter defense (discussed further in the next chapter). It also drew Israel's civilian police into a broader role relating to the enforcement of Israel's occupation policies. After the 1967 occupation the police underwent a series of reforms and changes in which police officers have progressively been equipped with heavier weapons, police units have been dressed in

ISRAEL'S MILITARY AND SECURITY INSTITUTIONS · 37

green, grey and black colors instead of the original blue, and the police have adopted procedures and aims from the military (Shadmi, 2012a:49, 73–4, 100, 136, 142). Israel established a dual legal system in the OPT, in which Palestinians are subjected to military law, and Israeli colonists to Israeli law. The inevitable result was confusion regarding the authorities and responsibilities of police and military officers in the area (Kretzmer, 2013:32–6, 43–4).

In 1974 the Israeli government awarded the police the responsibility over internal security (emphasizing not only crime but also nationally motivated aggression, although Israeli courts distinguish between everyday crime and acts of violence or vandalism committed with national or religious justification). The police established the "civil guard," a voluntary body of armed civilians who help the police in enforcement, especially at night. This body allows private individuals the ability to demonstrate authority normally reserved only for public employees, and therefore can be defined as a minor form of privatization of security, outsourcing a function of the police institution. The police also established a new command center called the "Operations Directorate" (Shadmi, 2012a:19, 43–4). The 1974 reform was criticized in Israel at the time because it diverted resources away from the police's traditional role of fighting crime. The police force itself, however, supported the reform. It created a long-term trend in which police officers enjoyed a certain prestige as part of the "security forces" entrusted with the defense of the country. At the same time, the prestige of the Israeli military suffered because soldiers were required to perform police-like and security tasks, such as conducting arrests, standing in checkpoints, etc. (ibid.:43–4). As part of this process, the police established new units, and redeployed existing units as semi-military units. In addition to the Border Police, which is almost indistinguishable from a military unit, the special patrol unit "Yasam" and the "Yahalom" units were established as the police attack force. These units have used lethal force against Israeli citizens (ibid.:48–9).

3.1.5 Public security in the service of privatization

Among the manifestations of the crisis in Israel's security elite is that in certain cases the production of security is defined by private investors as an economic burden. In such cases privatization of security takes a different path than other kinds of privatization because the investors seek to separate the security from the non-security elements of the privatization, as detailed below. Privatization rarely proceeds smoothly and without obstacles. Especially in the case of privatization of security, the Israeli government had been reluctant at times to give private companies responsibility, and in other cases private companies were reluctant to seek such responsibility. The result was that in the case of the El-Al airline and the extraction of natural gas, among others, the security aspects of the company's operations were separated and kept under state control, even as the company itself was privatized.

This is consistent with the idea of the "state as the night watchman" (Nitzan & Bichler, 2002:85–8). Privatization of security does not always serve the interests of capital's owners. In this case, the investors profited from having the security responsibility remain with the state. The government can then claim that airline security is a "core" acvitity which must remain state responsibility, while air travel is merely a "peripheral" service which may be safely privatized.

Amir Paz-Fuchs has argued that the state's willingness to take on the costs of security is a complementary aspect of security privatization. Privatization in the financial sector was coupled with deregulation, thereby separating profits from the risk. When the production of security is defined as "risk," investors have an incentive to separate the security aspects from the asset in which they invest. Paz-Fuchs argued that while the security operations are privatized, the risk is nationalized, and private companies are not expected to bear the consequences of security failures.[9] Risks are by their very nature unpredictable and in the case of security could involve loss of life. Israeli law therefore protects insurance companies from losses arising from Israel's image as a state in conflict. The state takes upon itself the responsibility to offer (limited) restitution to people and companies who lose property as a result of a war situation, and insurance companies are exempt from offering such restitution (Israeli Ministry of Finance, 2013b).

As the El-Al company, Israel's first airline, was privatized in 2003 through a stock-issue, the government sold most of its shares in the company, but kept a "golden stock" guaranteeing essential interests such as aerial transport services during emergencies (Hasson, 2006:13–14). El-Al's marketing strategy relies not only on prices, comfort, etc. but also on the company's reputation for offering extra security against the possibility of terrorist attacks. El-Al's special security services include strict control of passengers, beyond the security requirements of the airports in which the company operates, the employment of under-cover security guards who travel in the planes disguised as passengers and Israeli security guards posted in airports around the world to check passengers on their way to Israel. They also include the use of shoulder-missile counter-measures during take-off and landing, even when no missiles have been detected (Naor, 2011).

These measures might boost sales to passengers who are worried about their security, yet their costs are mostly shouldered by the Israeli government. The Israeli airline companies signed an agreement with the Israeli Ministry of Finance in 2011 to gradually increase the state's participation in security costs, which was 60 percent until 2010, up to 80 percent over the process of a few years (Gil, 2011). A 2012 reform began the process of replacing the ISA security guards who travel under-cover in the flights with younger officers. El-Al pilots resisted the reform, explaining that the guards themselves are forbidden to form a union to protect their jobs because they are state security employees (Blumenkranz, 2012a). Even after its privatization, El-Al retains interests in the state-owned security aspects of its operations. The El-Al corporation was able to avoid taking part in the labor dispute, because flight security is the responsibility of the government, although the company benefits from state security subsidies which are not offered to its non-Israeli competitors.

In 2013 the Israeli Antitrust Authority declared El-Al to be a monopoly in the field of airline security, because no other company offers such intensive security services. The company appealed the decision, claiming that it is obligated by the state to implement the security measures, and that its security services are not commercial (as they are paid for by the state, although the company is private). The significance of the Antitrust Authority decision is that El-Al would be forced to share its security services with its competitors, Arkia and IsraAir (Blumenkranz & Coren, 2013). In December 2013, the state increased its subsidy for security by 12.5 percent to all airlines (Blumenkranz, 2013). Thus El-Al was able to simultaneously enjoy the benefits of the state-funded security services while acting as a commercial business.

3.2 CULTURE OF SECURITY

The decades-long centrality of security in the Israeli economy has also affected the Israeli political culture, and given considerable legitimacy and impact to security considerations in everyday matters. In 2009, Israel's Deputy Minister of Defense Matan Vilnai was interviewed by all the large Israeli newspapers regarding an exercise to prepare the "home front" in Israel. He said that "the purpose is to prepare people for the culture of emergency, as if tomorrow morning a war will break out" (Shadmi, 2012a:46). His statement, and indeed the exercise itself, are part of a process to embed the "culture of emergency" in Israeli public discourse and in everyday activities. Yoram Peri considers Israel to be a "political-military culture," and defines the culture of security as a culture of distrust which promotes the use of force as the preferred policy to bring about security, as opposed to a "culture of diplomacy" (Peri, 2006:216–17). Much has been written on the infiltration of military and security thinking into Israeli civilian life. Eyal Weizman writes that "political 'militarism' [is] a culture which sees violence as permanent as a rule of history and thus military contingencies as the principal alternative available to politicians. Israeli militarism has accordingly always sought military solutions to political problems" (Weizman, 2007:253).

3.2.1 Case study: the culture of security in the natural-gas debate

Despite the privatization process, the Israeli government continues to wield the military and security apparatus as a tool to promote state power in areas which are not directly related to security. The culture of security comes into play when security reasoning applies to what would otherwise be a purely civilian debate. In the case of the offshore natural-gas rigs along Israel's coasts the culture of security serves as a clear factor in the debate over privatization of security. Although the taxation of the natural-gas companies is inherently an economic issue, security-based arguments, and Israeli military and strategic interests were evoked by the government and by the natural-gas companies to justify incentivizing the gas companies to accelerate extraction through lower taxes (Hever, 2011b:21–2). Due to public protests over the low taxes, the government set up a fund for the allocation of the gas revenue for "socioeconomic purposes," but defined those purposes under only two categories: education and preparation for emergencies. Emergencies were defined as wars, natural disasters and economic crises. Defense expenditure was therefore included as a "socioeconomic purpose" (Gutman, 2012). On top of that expenditure, a government decision from January 23, 2011 determines that the state will pay half of the internal security costs of the natural-gas rigs, as long as at least 25 percent of the gas is destined to be marketed in Israel, thereby using the security costs involved with the gas extraction as a mechanism for subsidizing the private companies (Israeli Prime Minister's Office, 2011).

Governments normally do not provide security inside company facilities. Security guards in privately owned factories, mines, etc. are paid by a company who owns the facility. Yet in the case of the gas rigs, they are provided by the state. The preference of public security was presented in the framework of the core vs. periphery framework, in which the natural gas is conceptualized as a strategic interest of Israel's security and therefore must be protected by the state. The Israeli navy claimed that a terror attack against them would be considered a "strategic attack" against Israel (Greenberg, 2011; UPI, 2013b; Cohen, 2014a).[10] At the same time, however, the argument serves to divert public funds to private companies.

Case Box 1:	Security of the Natural-Gas Rigs
Type:	Outsourcing of operations
Key interests:	Natural-gas extraction companies
Opposition:	The navy, the social movement for the allocation of the natural-gas profits
Success:	No (security remained state-operated)
Period:	2011–
Similar cases:	Privatized security services for private sector facilities

3.3 CHANGES IN THE OCCUPATION OF THE OPT

The occupation of the Palestinian Territory has been a major force shaping and driving the privatization of security in Israel, as I will show in Chapter 5. These changes dramatically altered the Israeli approach to security. Warfare has changed in the course of the second half of the twentieth century. The Israeli military conventional engagements (in 1956, 1967 and 1973) were abruptly replaced by asymmetrical military operations in civilian spaces against non-regular resistance (known in military jargon as "low-intensity conflict"). The asymmetric nature of conflicts implies that they attempt to impose the asymmetric core vs. periphery demarcation either between states or more commonly inside states, leading to an unjust allocation of resources and of political rights (Harders, 2015:38). The importance of superior firepower has declined, and the importance of repressive techniques applied against a hostile civilian population has increased. Starting with the 1982 invasion of Lebanon, and especially after the outbreak of the first Intifada in 1987, the main activity of the Israeli security forces was to repress Palestinian resistance to the occupation (Table 3.1). Therefore, privatization of any aspect of Israel's control apparatus in the OPT is a privatization of one of the core activities of the Israeli army.

The vast number of troops deployed in controlling and securing the OPT testifies to the importance of the occupation to Israel's security policies. Charles Tilly offered a comparison between the number of troops stationed outside state borders in 1987. Tilly omitted Israel from his list, yet he did include Cuba, France and the UK, which deployed smaller numbers of troops outside their borders (Tilly, 1990:208). Here Israeli troops in the OPT during the first Intifada in 1987 are added to Tilly's data, based on estimates by Arnove and by Shahak, as well as the population of each country, in order to demonstrate the relative impact of foreign deployment of troops on the economy and society of the respective aggressors. The result demonstrates the significance of the occupation as a project undertaken by the Israeli military and society. In 1987 Israel had the fourth largest occupation force in the world. It had the largest ratio of its population deployed as soldiers in occupied territory.

Table 3.1   Troop Deployment Outside State Borders, 1987

Country	Troops Deployed Abroad (thousands)	Population (thousands)	Percentage of its Population as Troops in a Foreign Occupation (%)
USSR	730	282 709	0.26
US	493	242 289	0.20
Vietnam	190	61 750	0.31
Israel	150–75	4 369	3.43–4.01
UK	90	56 802	0.16
France	84	57 483	0.15
Cuba	29	10 396	0.28

Source: Tilly (1990:208), Shahak (1991), Arnove (2012), Faostat (2014), World Bank (2014).

In the 1980s the authority over the OPT was divided between four bodies: the military, the Civil Administration,[11] the ISA and the police force. The Israeli police force set up a special branch in 1994 for administrating the West Bank. The Palestinian Authority (PA) was established in 1994 and became a fifth body. The Civil Administration's size was reduced to about a tenth of its previous number of employees after the establishment of the PA (Berda, 2012:46–7). The existence of five bodies who wield authority over the OPT created large amounts of confusion. The blurred distinctions between them have also seeped inside Israel's borders. After the outbreak of the second Intifada, the focus of operations of the Israeli police force shifted more to "fighting terrorism," partially as an attempt by the police to repair its image in the public eye. The encroachment of the police into areas usually covered by the military and the intelligence services has further diffused the borders between Israel's security institutions (Shadmi, 2012a:17).

After the outbreak of the second Intifada in 2000, the Israeli government attempted to centralize the authority and streamline the decision-making processes. These centralization policies include the construction of the Separation Wall (Amir, 2010:48–9),[12] the withdrawal from the Gaza Strip in 2005 (ibid.:41), but also a comprehensive restructuring of the bureaucratic tools of the occupation. The Israeli government created a unified biometric database for the Palestinian population (especially in the West Bank, but partially in the Gaza Strip as well). A computer program called "Rolling Stone" was installed and implemented in such a way that soldiers can use their palm computers to synchronize with the database and bring up information on any Palestinian who they have detained. Hundreds of thousands of Palestinians have been defined as "prevented for security reasons," so that if a soldier or police officer checks their documents, their status becomes immediately apparent and they will be prevented from crossing a checkpoint, or if caught on the wrong side of the checkpoint they will be immediately arrested (ibid.:72–3).

The biometric digital database is a tool which allows policy to be determined and implemented from a central location. Although the database was conceived as an act of reinforcing the state's sovereignty, concentrating its power and bolstering its core security capabilities, the biometric database was established by the private company HP, thereby increasing the influence of this corporation over government policy (Section 6.5).

The occupation forced Israeli security institutions to expand and add new departments. This expansion was an incentive for privatization.

Rather than breaking up existing departments, the addition of a new function or service through outsourcing to a private company is both politically more acceptable and organizationally simpler than to build a new public institution (or a new branch for an existing institution), and to train its staff with a new set of skills. New policies were formulated in an ever-shifting political situation and reflected economic perspectives of the 1990s with a strong tendency to favor the private sector. Such policies included heightened supervision on Palestinian workers employed by Israeli employers but reduced supervision over Palestinian teachers, journalists, etc. Some of the older policies formulated in the 1970s, such as forcing Palestinian workers to pay membership dues to the Israeli federation of labor unions, the Histadrut (Zohar & Hever, 2010:11), and the prevention of private investments in the OPT to reduce competition with the Israeli market have gradually been abandoned, as such policies reflected a time in which government direct intervention in the economy was more politically acceptable.

3.4 DECLINE IN CONSCRIPTION TO THE ISRAELI ARMY

Among the reasons for privatization is the shortage in soldiers. The privatization of the checkpoints in the West Bank and around the Gaza Strip is the best example of this (Section 5.5), as guarding the checkpoints was a task which required large numbers of soldiers, and a task which many soldiers found undesirable. Ariella Azoulay and Adi Ophir argue that the Israeli regime is organized on a principle of ethnic-national mobilization. As opposed to the social contract envisioned by the scholars of the Enlightenment centering on the civil habitus, in which the citizens agree on a political system in order to safeguard their rights and interests, the ethnic-national mobilization principle envisions a state in which the citizens are mobilized to promote a common agenda, and the state functions as a political organization in order to achieve this goal (Azoulay & Ophir, 2013:167–81). Military service is both the symbolic and the practical means by which the population participates in the national mobilization. Through inclusion in the military service, Israeli Jews are signified as the "true" citizens of Israel, and those excluded (or those who choose to exclude themselves) from military service are considered peripheral, second-rate citizens or even enemies from within. A nation-wide campaign funded by the government under the slogan "A true Israeli does not shirk [military service]" demonstrates how military service is consciously and openly promoted by the government as a prerequisite for full citizenship (Ya'acobi-Keller, 2008). Extended military service was not just a duty but also a mark of honor which distinguished the Ashkenazi[13] elite (Levy, 2003:222).

Socioeconomic conditions have changed, and with them the prestige associated with military service. The neoliberal transformation of the Israeli economy eroded the collective mobilization of the population (Shalev, 2004:88–101). Yagil Levy posits that "the rise of individualism came at the expense of dedication to serving one's country and actually contradicted the very values of military service, such as sacrifice and discipline." The unconditional ideological obligation to serve in the army, he argues, was replaced by an individualistic contractual relationship, in which the soldiers (and their parents) can negotiate and express their own expectations from the military service (Levy, 2012:22, 47). The Israeli army website boasts that "Israel also has one of the highest recruitment rates in the world – some 80% of those who receive summons serve" (IDF, 2010), but the military's report to the Knesset reveals that the actual conscription rate was 48 percent as of 2010 (Pfeffer, 2010b). The military chooses to exempt a large part of the population from service.

Evidence demonstrates that conscription rates to the Israeli army are declining rapidly. Conscription rates around 80 percent were commonplace in the 1980s, although a steady decline was already discernible (*The Economist*, 2008). By 2000, willingness to serve in the army dropped by about 20 percent, according to the Research and Information Center at the Knesset (Spiegel, 2001:2–5). The trend has continued in recent years (Shenfeld, 2007). The army's human resources department revealed that only 74.6 percent of Jewish men and 56 percent of Jewish women enlisted in 2009 (Pfeffer, 2009). Further evidence was provided by the Israeli army to the Knesset Committee for Foreign Relations and Security in 2010 that 50 percent of the Jewish population aged 18–40 does not serve in any military capacity. Although conscription rates in the Jewish population in 2010 were above 50 percent, only a minority of the soldiers have continued to perform reserve duty after regular service (Doron, 2010). Regular service normally lasts three years for men and two for women, but many of the soldiers leave the army before the end of the time period, if found socially, physically or mentally unfit to continue their service. The army reported that 16 percent of men and 7.5 percent of women left the military service before the end of the regular draft period in 2013 (Cohen, 2013b). By recalculating the military figures to include non-Jewish citizens, who constitute over a fifth of the citizenry and only rarely serve in the military, one concludes that only 48 percent of Israeli citizens who turn 18 enlist in the army (Pfeffer, 2010b).

Two reasons therefore account for the steep decline in recruitment: (1) the increase in the ratio of candidates for recruitment who are undesirable to the MOD and (2) the choice of the ministry not to forcefully recruit candidates who seek to avoid military service. Decline in conscription thus erodes Israel's republican citizen-soldier model (Levy, 2012:212), creating an opening for a privatized and professional model of soldiering. The largest group that avoids military service are Palestinian citizens of Israel. In 1954 the MOD attempted to conscript Palestinian citizens. Thousands responded to the call, and the MOD decided to exempt Palestinian citizens from service, fearing that Palestinians might not be loyal to the Jewish state, although small numbers of volunteers are accepted for duty (Shapira, 2001:65; Elad, 2012). An exception was made for Adyghes (otherwise known as Circassian) and Druze, who are obligated to serve. These two groups are a small minority among Arabs with Israeli citizenship.[14] A clause in the Israeli law (State of Israel, 1986) allows the Minister of Defense to choose not to recruit certain candidates. Graph 3.2 (based on data from ICBS, various years) demonstrates that the proportion of Jewish citizens in Israel is declining over the years. The increase in the proportion of young Israelis who are not enlisted because of their nationality, however, is only a partial explanation for the trend of decline in the conscription rates.

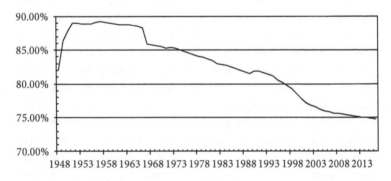

Graph 3.2   Proportion of Jews Among Israeli Citizens

Source: Based on data from the Israeli Central Bureau of Statistics (ICBS) (2008, 2010, 2013, 2015, 2017).

The second largest group with low conscription rates are ultra-Orthodox Jewish yeshiva students. The first Prime Minister of Israel David Ben Gurion reached an agreement with the leaders of the ultra-Orthodox Jews in Israel when the state was founded, to exempt 400 yeshiva students from military service. The number rose to approximately 60,000 by 2010 (Weisman, 2010).[15] In addition to this number, many other ultra-Orthodox Jews avoid military service by being found mentally unfit for service (Channel 2, 2010). Jewish women may be exempt from military service on religious grounds even without being part of this agreement, and as such many women declare themselves religious and thus avoid military service. As a result, nearly one half (44 percent in 2009) of Jewish women do not enlist (Pfeffer, 2009).

The third group of draft-dodgers are from the lower socioeconomic levels of Israeli society. Since soldiers who receive no support from their families are entitled to extra services from the army (Weisblei, 2006:1–2), the army is not keen on recruiting them. Also, Israelis who grew up in poverty rarely have high motivation to serve. Thus, a large number of young Israelis are exempt from service with the official reason that they are "socially unfit for duty." Drug abuse or possession of a criminal record are also grounds for disqualifying candidates. The army does not release data on the number of these exemptions, yet the rapidly growing poverty levels in Israel suggest that the number is rising over the years. This rise in poverty is demonstrated in Graph 3.3 (based on NII, various years), which shows the long-term growth of poverty in Israel (before taxes and transfer payments) between 1979 and 2015. The graph shows that poverty rises at the fastest rate among children, meaning a steady increase in the proportion of people living in poverty among those who reach the conscription age. In the years 2011–15, poverty showed a clear downward turn. As of 2015, 34.7 percent of children in Israel lived under the poverty line before taxes and transfer payments, and 30 percent after taxes and transfer payments (NII, 2013).[16]

The drop in conscription highlights the contradiction between the government's national mobilization policy in matters of security and culture, on the one hand (Azoulay & Ophir, 2013: 167–81), and its neoliberal emphasis on individualism in its economic policies, on the other hand (Ehrlich, 1993:270–1; Shalev, 2004:92–7). The dismantling of the welfare state has eroded the willingness of young Israelis to sacrifice years of their lives in military service for the nation, and many of those who choose to pursue military service do so for employment

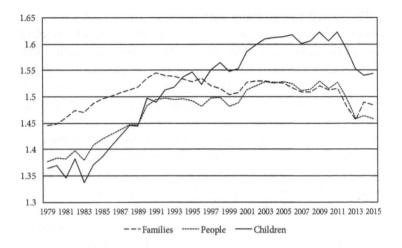

Graph 3.3 Poverty 1979–2015 (logarithmic)

Source: Based on data from the National Insurance Institute (NII) (2010, 2011, 2012, 2013, 2014, 2016).

opportunities or in order to accumulate social status (Levy, 2012:47, 93). The social capital accumulated from military service has declined, and the prestige associated with military service in Israel has fallen, in comparison with the prestige associated with fame and economic success (Cohen, 1995:237–54).

Various benefits are proposed for soldiers to entice young Israelis to enlist. Benefits include discounted studies, discounts when purchasing land, cash grants and more (Azoulay, 2008; Mirovski, 2008). The army has also adopted business-like practices and begun "marketing" itself to the recruits, using every means at its disposal. Colonel Gadi Agmon, in charge of receiving new recruits, said in an interview (my translation):

> In all the processes we emphasize to the candidate that he will receive one of the three choices he made. We allow them to rank their choices and to have a dialogue. If someone cooperates, we make an effort to accommodate. Over 90% of candidates know where they are going thanks to a pre-placement announcement. When we inform him where he is going to be, he has a special internet forum for recruits in his specific unit, and they can chat with their future commanders. They ask if they can get the first Saturday off and how much equipment they should bring with them. The commanders also

visit the homes in advance. They dispel fears of the candidate and the family. We've adopted a conception of service to the customer's house. (Pfeffer, 2010a)

Routine guard duty in the OPT has become unpopular among soldiers, and led to lower motivation to serve (Peri, 2006:194–5). In order to staff the checkpoints, the MOD relies heavily on security guards sourced from private companies (Section 5.5). For the more technologically demanding military roles, the army uses an informal mechanism of reward, through its collaboration with private companies. Although soldiers serving in secretive and high-tech units are not rewarded with more money than other soldiers, they participate in "collaborative public space" which is formed at the nexus between the military and private arms and security companies (Breznitz, 2005:36). Their military experience grants them an advantage in seeking employment with the private companies after their military service, and an entry-ticket to Israel's high-tech sector (Gordon, 2011:156–60).

The declining conscription rates are therefore inseparable from the individualistic neoliberal culture and economic reality which has replaced Israel's previously highly mobilized welfare state. The Israeli military responds with neoliberal methods, using marketing schemes which commodify military service. The idea that military service is a commodity that can be "sold" by private individuals to the state (in exchange for monetary and non-monetary rewards) legitimizes the notion that the state will procure security services from private companies and from NGOs as well.

3.5 CRISIS AND CHANGE IN THE ISRAELI ARMS INDUSTRY

Shimshon Bichler and Jonathan Nitzan analyzed the crisis of Israel's weapon industry in the 1990s not just in terms of a slowdown in sales and profits but as a differential crisis, meaning that other sectors have made quick gains. The Israeli arms manufacturer's capital accumulation fell under the rate of accumulation of other sectors, as part of a trend observed all over the world. It was brought on not only by the end of the Cold War but also by the rise of the global high-tech industry and by the international investments which were attracted to Israel by the Oslo peace negotiations. Arms industries were unable to match the return on capital which was achieved in the high-tech sector. The wave of consolidation through mergers and acquisitions which occurred simultaneously in the global arms sector and in the Israeli arms industry was a private sector response to the decline in differential accumulation in the arms industry. The state-owned arms industry, however, has not been fully financialized and could not take part in the mergers and acquisitions phase (Bichler & Nitzan, 2001:263–4, 306, 345–93, 425–79). It was fully immersed in the crisis, as was evident in the failure of the "Lavi" project, which will be discussed in Section 6.2.3.

Structural changes in the Israeli arms industry in the 1980s and 1990s were perceived as a prolonged crisis in the arms sector by the Israeli media and by the managerial layer in the arms companies, an important part of the Israeli security elite. This crisis was associated with the competition created by the US military aid to Israel. Free arms from the US meant decreased demand of the Israeli MOD for products from Israeli arms companies (Sadeh, 2001:64–77). The end of the Cold War intensified the crisis of the Israeli military industry in the 1990s. It was accompanied by defense budget reductions in important export markets of Israeli companies. The three large Israeli state-owned weapon manufacturers – Israeli Aerospace Industries (IAI), Israeli Military Industries (IMI) and Rafael – all accumulated deficits and losses, prompting the government to provide financial assistance. Despite this assistance, several factories were closed and workers were laid-off. The fact that the three companies were state-owned was perceived as one of the reasons for the crisis. The companies, according to Yaakov Lifshitz (at the time he was the director-general at the Ministry of Finance), expected a government bailout and therefore refrained from adjusting to the lower demand (Lifshitz, 2011:4–5, 15–16). At the height of this crisis, calls were made to privatize IAI (Amit, 2013; Paz-Fuchs & Ben-Simkhon-Peleg, 2014:15).

The armament of the Israeli forces with the aid of the US contributed to greater demand for weapons by other Middle Eastern countries who were threatened by Israel. As the US remains the largest arms provider to the Middle East, this has created a cycle creating greater demand for US arms in the region (Feinstein, 2011:376), partially compensating for the sharp reduction in worldwide military expenditure in the aftermath of the Cold War (Bichler & Nitzan, 2001:19–20). A rapid phase of mergers and acquisitions after the end of the Cold War consolidated the global arms market into a small group of large companies (Lifshitz, 2011:4–5, 15–16). The Israeli corporate media promoted privatization as a solution to the crisis of the arms industry.

3.6 "SOLUTIONS" THROUGH TECHNOLOGY

A major shift in the Israeli security institutions paved the way for privatization. Before the manufacture of security can be handed to the private sector, a reconceptualization of the function of security is needed. Security must be detached from its ideological and political roots tying it to public institutions. The manufacture of security must become a profession, a technical expertise. When the employees and decision-makers in security institutions perceive their roles as experts and professionals, it becomes conceivable that these roles could be filled by employees of private companies which are incentivized by profits. The process in which security is commodified is a key step in the process from state monopoly over the production of security into a private security sector.

Several factors contribute to the change in Israeli security institutions: (1) securitization in the political discourse frames political and social problems as problems of security (Buzan et al., 1998:23–9); (2) soldiers increasingly describe themselves as professionals and less as warriors for a cause (Maman, 1988:64–6); (3) private security companies offer technological capacities and the services of experts with military and police experience which state institutions cannot always match (Singer, 2003:62–3). These changes bring technological solutions to the fore of the security debate. The "a-political" nature of technology is used to create the impression that the state may continue to monopolize security, and that private companies merely provide it with tools, thus dispelling the concern that privatization leads to a decentralization of the government's decision-making monopoly.

Neoliberal ideology, especially in the form of mainstream economic thought, models social relations with a mechanical analogy. It perceives individuals as rational actors who respond to incentives (Brohman, 2010:299–300). Privatization (not just of security) is a direct result of this perspective, as it shifts the government's role from responsibility to provide services to that of "governance" of services provided by private actors which the government incentivizes. The function of the state becomes functionalist and procedural (Harvey, 2005:66; Shadmi, 2012a:63–5). Especially relevant is the rise of neoliberal thinking in the approach to crime and security. The 1970s prevalent "welfarist" approach understood criminality as a product of poverty and inequality, but was replaced in the 1980s with an approach focusing on technologies of crime control through surveillance and spatial control (Abrahamsen & Williams, 2009:4).

An important aspect of the conceptualization of security operations as technology implementation rather than policy is how the security discourse abandons the notion of military victory in favor of the notion of ongoing conflict management. Although the shift from a welfarist to a crime-control approach has occurred in Israel as well (Shadmi, 2012a:82–8), Israel's case is more complex because of the occupation and the prevalence of political violence alongside crime-related violence. After the end of the second Intifada, a discernible change in the discourse of Israeli politicians, high-ranking military officers and economists has taken place. The language of conflict resolution has been replaced with conflict management (Bar-Siman-Tov, 2007:9–41; Ghanem, 2010:21–38). The shift took place in the context of a political shift in Israel from governments promising to pursue a peace treaty with the Palestinians to those arguing that such a treaty is impossible to achieve (Yiftachel, 2005:125–8). Israeli economists and publicists argued that Israel could prosper economically with the Palestinian resistance contained rather than resolved (see for example Sharabi, 2002; Sadan, 2004; Myre, 2006; Landau, 2008:42–6; Dror, 2014). The shift indicates a change in the meaning of the word "solution" in the Israeli political context, from signifying a solution of a durable nature achieved through negotiations, to signifying an ongoing effort to foil Palestinian resistance repeatedly, in order to keep the conflict from getting out of control. The word thus refers to a technical solution rather than a political one.

This technical solution to achieve ongoing conflict management is the "matrix of control" described by Jeff Halper. A complex system of walls, fences, checkpoints, patrols and bureaucratic regulations is a system designed to maximize Israel's control over the territory while minimizing the amount of resources spent to maintain that control (Halper, 2009:31–40). Halper compares Israel's technology of control with that of South Africa under apartheid. Unlike the South African apartheid system, in which the black population had a role as the working class, Palestinians are largely excluded from the Israeli economy and are therefore treated as "surplus" people. Technology is implemented as it would in a prison, ensuring that the Israeli authorities have sufficient advantage in the application of force to prevent the Palestinians from causing a disturbance, using technological mechanisms to keep the Palestinians powerless to resist the occupation (Halper, 2008). The definition of certain areas and populations as peripheral legitimizes the adoption of a technical approach to managing the population rather than a social and political approach (Harders, 2015:42).

Halper's concept of "warehousing" continues this argument of technology taking the place of political process. The result of sharpening social inequalities in the world in the last quarter of the twentieth century has created "surplus" populations, through the increase in poverty and unemployment, which play peripheral roles in the capitalist economic system, and which are treated by local authorities as a threat to social stability. Governments who choose to abandon these populations and seek to minimize spending on public services for them begin to see these populations as a potential threat that must be contained, and seek technological solutions for managing them and preventing them from disrupting the peace. Halper calls these solutions "warehousing" and argues that the Gaza Strip became a paradigmatic example of this phenomenon, in which a large population is contained in a small area, besieged by the Israeli army and disconnected from the global market. Israel's containment of Gaza is not only a manifestation of Israel's local interests but also a means by which Israel strives to play a role in the global warehousing efforts (Halper, 2009:102–6). "Warehousing" is therefore an extreme manifestation of the "matrix of control" and both are ways by which policies are packaged as technologies (Halper, 2015:145, 167). Retired Israeli officers can claim expertise in the applications of these technologies, and thus private Israeli companies can export these technologies to international customers.

It should be stressed, however, that these technologies are presented as solutions, but they have not succeeded in containing the Palestinian resistance and in improving the sense of security for the Israeli society. Security as a commodity already exists, but despite its high cost, this commodity does not fulfill its function.

3.6.1 Labor-saving mechanisms

The sharp decline in the number of available soldiers discussed above, and the growing challenges facing the Israeli police and army help to explain some of Israel's recent military policies and technological investments. Yagil Levy adds a class analysis, and argues that the decline in recruitment (discussed in Section 3.4 above) was mainly among Ashkenazi middle-class recruits. The military implemented technological advances in order to protect the lives of the remaining middle-class recruits while diverting the lower-class recruits (mostly Mizrahim[17]) to less technologically intensive roles in the army (Levy, 2012:28–9, 66–7). Levy sees the reliance on technology as a consequence of casualty aversion, a tendency to shift the focus from "labor-intensive" warfare to "capital-intensive" warfare. "Casualty aversion means that the state upgrades the value of soldiers' lives. This can be done by improving armaments, despite the financial costs involved" (ibid.:29). Moreover, he stipulates that the intensification of reliance on technology is a "balancing strategy" which is used either as complementary or alternative to the strategy of reducing conflict levels (ibid.:26–34). But contrary to Levy's claims, recruitment decreased mainly among lower-class Israelis. Therefore, the examples of labor-saving technologies implemented by the military such as the automated checkpoints (Section 5.5) are better understood through the lens of the core vs. periphery divide, funneling resources and human resources to "core" military activities such as drone operations, intelligence, etc.

Israeli companies are globally renowned for developing unmanned drones, or UAVs (unmanned aerial vehicles, Johnson, 2010; Space War, 2013), unmanned patrol boats (Dagoni, 2006) and unmanned road-patrol robots (Barzilai, 2006). Along with the developments in security cameras, alarm systems and in setting up security periphery zones, these are all developments that allow a small number of soldiers to monitor and control large areas. Drones, especially, allow the Israeli army to monitor the sky over the Gaza Strip, West Bank and Lebanon, without using precious hours by pilots (who require very extensive training, Bamahane, 2007; Bergen, 2012; Dobbing & Cole, 2014:4). These technologies have become the most visible and strongly promoted brands of Israel's largest weapon companies, IAI, Elbit and Rafael.

Elbit Systems refers to their technological solution packages as a "system of systems," a technological array of communications and surveillance which allows a small number of people to control a large area and a large population, giving them the ability to intervene in many locations and deploy a large array of automated systems to address various kinds of threats. IAI has developed a system called "Seeing is Striking" which allows semi-automated weapons systems to be operated remotely, turning the activation of a deadly weapon into an experience similar to playing a video game (Stockmarr, 2014). Rafael's "Iron Dome" system became even more famous, as it was used to intercept homemade rockets fired from the Gaza Strip against Israel. The Iron Dome missiles are much more expensive than the rockets fired by Palestinians, and their rate of interception has been hotly contested. Nevertheless, the system has been covered positively by the Israeli press and was considered a success, because through the use of technology the government could avoid dealing with the question of the reasons that bring Palestinians in Gaza to fire rockets against Israel, and allows the government to avoid a discussion of the diplomatic or social solutions to the problem. South Korea and the US have also expressed interest in the system (Broad, 2012).

The constant need to ease the burden on the soldiers has led the Israeli government to implement new policies as well. Those include building the Separation Wall from 2000 (Cahana, 2003), withdrawing the colonists and the troops from the Gaza Strip in 2005 (Li, 2006:38), privatizing all of the permanent checkpoints in the West Bank and around Gaza (Rapoport, 2007). These are all policies which reduce the number of soldiers that must be deployed, and allow the government to attempt control over the Palestinian Territory and population without using large numbers of soldiers.

The idea that technology can create an impenetrable barrier against terrorism is promoted through extensive media coverage. Idan Landau points out that the Separation Wall, the Iron Dome system and the natural-gas rig security (Section 3.2.1) are cases in which this idea is actively promoted by the government in order to legitimize spending for expensive security technology projects. He adds that the concept of the security envelope is offered as a substitute for social and political policies intended to prevent terrorism (Landau, 2012). Replacement of ground operations with unmanned-drone and surveillance mechanisms has also become a prominent technology of the Israeli occupation (Weizman, 2007:240). Erella Shadmi has further commented that surveillance technology is used to purify public spaces from "undesirables," meaning labor immigrants, minorities, homeless people and people living in poverty. The surveillance cameras can follow the movements of these people and security guards can be dispatched to ask them to leave. Nowhere is this more obvious than in the Old City of East Jerusalem, which is covered with a web of surveillance cameras controlled by a single room (Shadmi, 2012a:50, 76–7). And yet, the existence of this surveillance system did not prevent stabbing attacks in the Old City in 2015–16.

After the end of the Cold War, war has changed, and the willingness of the population in the Western world to support large armies and spend large proportions of the GDP on the military has declined (Nitzan & Bichler, 2006:9, 25). Governments in other countries that are also interested in capital-intensive warfare, labor- and life-saving security technologies, and in sophisticated surveillance and control mechanisms take interest in Israeli technologies in that field (Klein, 2007a). The US military works closely with Israeli arms companies in the development of these technologies and their testing and implementation (Graham, 2011:133–49). A parallel emerges between the use of technology in order to create distance between the soldier and the victim, thereby reducing the burden on the soldier's conscience (Levy, 2012:64), and the use of outsourcing in order to create distance between the government and the operations of the PMSC, thereby reducing the burden of accountability on the government (Minow, 2005:994–5). This parallel shows that reliance on technology and outsourcing of security are linked, especially through the search for legitimacy and for relief from the burden of responsibility.

3.7 CONCLUSION

The privatization of security in Israel has paradoxically emerged in an era of high concentration of security authority in the hands of the state. Neoliberal ideology and policies especially after 1985 have affected Israel's militarism in three ways. (1) The share of state resources dedicated to security has declined compared to the share dedicated to other sectors of the economy. Even if the MOD budget has increased nominally over the years, it has differentially decreased as a share of GDP. (2) The rate of conscription to the Israeli military has steadily declined, increasing the legitimacy for civilian elites with little or no military background, at the expense of the security elite. The decline in conscription is also a direct loss of resources (in this case, person-power) for the military. (3) The prestige of the Israeli security elites has also suffered from the change in roles of the Israeli security institutions. After the 1967 War the security institutions were increasingly tasked with the control of a civilian population under occupation and in asymmetrical warfare. Furthermore, since the 1973 War they have no longer engaged in conventional warfare. These developments lead to the conclusion that the Israeli security elite has entered a state of prolonged crisis, and that this crisis is among the reasons for privatizing of security.

The shift from a highly state-controlled security to privatized security does not occur immediately nor does it proceed without encountering resistance. In order to bridge this gap, security functions which were conceptualized as acts of sovereignty must be reinterpreted as acts of professional skill, and as security technology (Halper, 2015:144–5). When acting and retired officers in the police and the military define themselves less as ideological agents of the state, and more as trained experts of security (Maman, 1988:65–6), their experience and their knowledge and their skills are commodified. The commodification of security is a crucial step in the entry of PMSCs into the Israeli security sector.

4
Processes of Privatization
of Security in Israel

It is not difficult to envisage a military where the role of the soldier is simply to fight or, when not fighting, training to fight, while all non-core military functions are outsourced to contractors. (Kinsey, 2006:109)

In the previous chapter we saw that the very close ties between Israel's political and security elite, and its militarized economy makes the Israeli government reluctant to consider privatization of security. Nevertheless, the decline in conscription to the military, the crisis in the state-owned arms industry, and the reliance on technological solutions for political problems have lent legitimacy to privatization of security. Here four case studies will highlight the way by which privatization altered Israeli security institutions. The purpose of this chapter is to show the different interest groups which promote or oppose privatization of security in order to achieve an advantage over each other, and how these different interest groups are differently aligned along the institutional typology of privatization of security.

Four additional case studies will be discussed in Chapter 5, in the context of privatization of the occupation. The privatizations discussed here (attempted, failed or completed) occurred in the context of the turning point in the 1990s in which PMSCs achieved unprecedented size and influence in the US, Africa and Yugoslavia (Singer, 2003). The privatization in the US is the manifestation of the success of large corporate PMSCs in the country (Nitzan & Bichler, 2006:13, 26). In Israel, the rise of the high-tech industry, fueled by immigration from the former Soviet Union states, raised the communications, high-tech, finance and retail sectors at the expense of the energy and arms sectors (Bichler & Nitzan, 2001:49–72).

4.1 PRIVATIZATION ENTERS THE
MILITARY-SECURITY SECTOR

Privatization, outsourcing and asset-sale of the Israeli MOD is a gradual process, conducted secretly and without public debate (Seidman, 2010:17–19). One of the first examples of outsourcing of security operations was the construction of the Bar-Lev Line in 1968–69. The line of fortification was built along the Suez Canal, on the western edge of the occupied Sinai Peninsula, in order to stop the Egyptian army from invading Sinai and retaking it. The construction was outsourced to private contractors, and its cost was estimated at the very high price of 2 billion Israeli pounds in 1968 prices. The fortification was constructed rapidly, and was considered by the Israeli military to be impenetrable, but the forts fell quickly during the Egyptian attack in 1973 (Leibowitz-Dar, 2009; Shiffer, 2010:215).

This early example notwithstanding, most projects for the MOD in the 1970s and 1980s were conducted by governmental companies or governmental departments. The 1985 Stabilization Plan adopted by the Israeli government weakened labor unions and changed the balance of power between employers and employees. It implemented reforms intended to make the Israeli market more suitable for integration into the global economy. Global integration was accelerated in the 1990s, when the Oslo peace process signaled a possible improvement in Israel's international standing and a collapse of the Arab Boycott against Israel (Ehrlich, 1993:270–1; Shalev, 2004:92–7). The Israeli government also became increasingly exposed to the global neoliberal agenda (and especially the Washington Consensus) which promoted reducing the public sector's ratio of the GDP (Hasson, 2006:4). One of the quickest means to reduce the public sector's size in terms of staff is to transfer activities to private contractors.

The economic discourse supporting privatization has gradually influenced the military industry as well. Privatization of the military industry was prompted by arguments that it is failing and unprofitable (Seidman, 2010:12; Lifshitz, 2011:4–5), and by expectations for a future reduction in military consumption as a result of the peace process (Bichler & Nitzan, 2001:386–93). Even the collapse of the peace process, however, did not change the pro-privatization attitude of the economic media towards the military industries, as by then the belief that private companies were more efficient than government companies was deeply rooted in the public discourse (see for example Korin-Liber, 2010). A parallel process of privatization of military industries in Europe has also served to legitimize the privatization of military industries in Israel (Yaron, 2002:118).

4.1.1 Two committees

A governmental committee headed by Professor Israel Sadan assembled in 1993 to "assist in formulating policy for the defense system in light of the national needs, regarding activities of production, restoration and maintenance by the IDF, as opposed to performing these activities in the civilian industry." It submitted its recommendations in 1994. The committee called for outsourcing storage, distribution, logistical acquisitions, vehicle maintenance, kitchens, dining, laundry, fueling, security of military bases and instruction of troops, thereby defining these functions as "peripheral" to the military "core" functions. The purpose for the outsourcing was to alleviate the burden for these everyday activities from the military. Following the committee's recommendations, the MOD instructed the army to encourage competition between private businesses over the supply of services and equipment to the army (Maoz, 2008). Although the Sadan Committee's recommendations were not released to the public, they were interpreted as a call for privatization of the military industries and for outsourcing of military activities by those who read it (Seidman, 2010:12). The Brodet Committee's report from 2007 (see below) is considered a further continuation of the Sadan Committee's principals (ibid.). The government also decreed in 1994 that military bases must be evacuated from the city centers. The decision was intended to make high-value land available for civilian projects and to create income for the army by selling valuable real-estate assets. To date, only some of the military bases have been evacuated according to this decision, and the military still maintains one of its largest bases in the center of the city of Tel-Aviv (Brodet, 2007:100–1).

These early steps opened the door for the privatizations discourse to enter into the military discourse. By the 2000s, privatization was openly endorsed by the military elite, as the shift in social capital placed the economic elites as a role-model worthy of imitation by the political elite. In a lecture during a conference titled "Security and the National Economy in Israel" in 2001, the Israeli Chief of Staff Moshe Ya'alon announced that the Israeli army was adopting elements of a business, and that decision-making processes and planning processes would be derived from the private sector. His statement was not a direct reference to privatization (because the army remains a public body), but demonstrates the extent to which business logic has penetrated the public sector, and how the border between the public and the private has been blurred (Ya'alon, 2002:94–5).

A third committee convened in 2015, the Locker Committee, and submitted its recommendations the same year. Headed by Major General Yohanan Locker, it was tasked with formulating a reform for the Ministry of Defense's budget, and has gone even further than the first two committees in linking cost-cutting with widespread privatization (Locker, 2015:48–50). The committee recommended a streamlined procedure for transferring functions from the military to the private sector, and made a list of recommended functions to privatize including the maintenance and production of military equipment (especially vehicles), which it considered to be "not at the core of the security task of the IDF." Yagil Levy commented that the committee adopted the privatization discourse to such an extent that it was a stepping-stone towards a shift from a draft-based military to a professional-volunteer military (Levy, 2015).

4.1.2 Privatization of non-military activities of the army

According to core vs. periphery logic (Section 5.1), the non-military functions of the Israeli security organizations would be the first in line for privatization. As the Israeli military is involved in many civilian projects, there are ample possibilities for cutting various functions of the military, and transferring them to external bodies, either through selling them as assets or by procuring services through outsourcing. The military operates, for example, two radio stations which combined had the highest rating compared to all other radio stations in Israel in 2006 (The Second Authority for Television & Radio; Midgam, 2006). In 2014, the head of the Israeli military personpower command, Lieutenant General Moti Almoz, said that "of course if the army would have been established today, we would not have established a military radio station." In 2017 Minister of Defense Avigdor Lieberman decided to move the military stations from the army to the MOD, a step towards privatizing them in the future, but withdrew the decision because of pressure by senior MOD officials (Cohen, 2017a; Toker, 2017).

Further examples include the Nahal (a military infantry division which combines military service with agricultural projects, education projects and social projects operated by soldiers), and the military positions of teacher-soldiers deployed in facilities for new immigrants, in schools, boarding-schools and after-school youth clubs (IDF, 2014). The state-owned IAI company established a UAV training and control center at a school in order to train future air force engineers (Coren, 2012c). The political centrality of the military in the Israeli society acts as a delaying factor in the privatization of security promoted by the Ministry of Finance (Seidman, 2010:6–7).

The "Education Corps" is charged with educating Israeli soldiers, one of the functions which the military defines as "peripheral" and therefore considers privatization in it as legitimate. It has a department for "Israeli-Jewish Identity" (there are no "Israeli-Muslim Identity" or "Israeli-Christian Identity" departments), which was founded as a military unit in 2004 and expanded in 2006 as a counter-weight to the religious influence of the military rabbinical unit (Blau, 2012). The department has a budget for purchasing education services and materials from various organizations through outsourcing, including religious and political organizations. The right-wing Ir David Foundation has been contracted to give tours for officer cadets in East Jerusalem (Harel, 2013b).

Due to the numerous outsourcing contracts of the Israeli MOD, it created a new and large department in 2012 to deal with tenders and outsourcing of MOD activities called the Department of Tenders and Outsourcing. The new department was designed with four sections: a public-private partnership (PPP) unit, a supervision unit, a civilian infrastructure unit and a finance unit. The department has five large projects in addition to the Bahad City (see below) which it was charged with managing, with an estimated budget of no less than NIS 20 billion until 2020. Among the projects slated for the department is a 250,000 square meter enclave operated by three private companies (Minrav Engineering, Electra and RAD-Bynet) which will house and train 11,000 soldiers as part of the Bahad City (Bar-Eli, 2012).

Privatization reduces the load of activities of the Israeli security forces, but creates large contracts for private companies, both for PMSCs and for support and logistic companies. As a result, the Israeli economy does not become de-militarized by the privatization (Havkin, 2014). Because the largest customer for the security contracts is the MOD, the Israeli defense budget continues to show a long-term tendency to increase nominally, but not as a share of total public expenditure.

In 2017, the Israeli air force held a major international air training operation called "Blue Flag." Delegates from seven countries participated in the training, which was managed by a contracted private company for the first time. The air force responded to concerned journalists that outsourcing the logistics would be cheaper, and that the "core" of the training would not be privatized, only the peripheral "administrative" aspects of the training, which includes English communications among the foreign pilots (Cohen, 2017b). In August 2017, the Israeli MOD announced that three gigantic military logistics centers will be established by outsourcing by 2023, and the US arms company Lockheed Martin has already expressed interest in competing in the tender, which is estimated at NIS 3–4 billion. The justification for the large expenditure, for the outsourcing and for foreign companies being allowed to participate in the project is the "cost-cutting" argument, as the logistics centers are designed to make military logistics more efficient (Amit, 2017b).

4.1.3 Case study: Bahad City

One of the largest projects in the history of outsourcing in the Israeli security sector is the establishment of the "Bahad City," a giant military base in the south of Israel. The name "bahad" is an acronym in Hebrew which stands for "instruction bases." Israel's military training bases have been established close to the population centers along the Mediterranean coastline, and the real-estate value of the land upon which they are built is extremely high. The Sadan Committee from 1993 recommended that military bases in Israel's coastal area should be relocated to cheaper lands. The government ratified this recommendation as policy in August 1993 (Brodet, 2007:100–1). In 2002 the Israeli military began to prepare plans for building a military city of training bases (Director, 2011). The Brodet Committee from 2007 reminded the government that the policy needed to be carried out, as the military headquarters remained in the center of Tel-Aviv (Brodet, 2007:100–1).

The Bahad City project serves a political, as well as economic purpose, tied to the resistance against outsourcing. The Bahad City bases were built in a contested area, and two Jewish municipalities agreed in 2014 that municipal taxes paid by Bahad City would be split between them, leaving out the impoverished Bedouin communities in the area (Arlozerov,

2014). Privatization is a policy of redistribution (Nitzan & Bichler, 2009:393), and Bahad City promotes redistribution through the tenders and the private companies, but also through the real-estate redistribution. After the bases began operation in 2015, soldiers complained about crowded quarters, infrequent maintenance schedules and slow training courses. Those are indications of the private companies attempting to increase their profit margin, and are therefore direct results of the privatization (Bukhbut, 2016).

Case Box 2:	Bahad City
Type:	Outsourcing of services to the military
Key interests:	Investors, Negev cities, real-estate investors
Opposition:	Bedouins
Success:	Yes
Period:	2002
Similar cases:	Security companies

The connection between cost-cutting policies and privatization is a recurring theme in the MOD policies (Menahem, 2010).[1] The case of Bahad City is a prime example of relying on private companies based on a cost-cutting rationale. Arid lands of this area are relatively cheap, so the government can reduce the alternative cost by transferring the bases there. Even if the MOD is not able to show a financial income from transferring the bases, opening up the lands in the center of Israel for civilian use would generate income for the Israeli economy as a whole (Brodet, 2007:47; Director, 2011). The expected cost-cutting, however, is explained by the geographic move of the bases, and not by the outsourcing to private construction and maintenance companies. The idea that privatization leads to cost-cutting has become so entrenched in the Israeli political discourse that Minister of Defense Moshe Ya'alon froze the Bahad City project in 2014 in an effort to pressure the Ministry of Finance to allow increased budget for the MOD. Delaying the transfer of the military's main training centers to the south through outsourcing (while continuing to use the existing publicly operated training centers) was considered by both ministries as a costly measure (Steinman, 2014).

The spokesman of the Israeli military published a press release quoting Brigadier-General Maharan Prozenfer, the economic advisor to the chief of staff, that the Bahad City project would create an income of

NIS 6 billion annually to the Israeli economy, as well as a NIS 14 billion one-time benefit by opening up construction options in the center of Israel. The press release emphasized that the project would be managed by Israeli companies, with a preference for employing workers who are reservist soldiers (Director, 2011). The cost of the construction and operation of the project as well as the cost of evacuating the old military bases, however, was estimated by the government at NIS 23 billion (Buso, 2014). The project would be done through outsourcing, using the BOT system (Build-Operate-Transfer), a privatization system in which a private company is paid to build and operate the asset and after a pre-determined timeframe the asset reverts to government ownership. Brigadier-General Prozenfer stressed that "it is a deep cultural change which the IDF is undergoing – because we are privatizing a lot of services which the IDF provides itself, and transferring them to the private sector." The tender process was also supervised by consultants from the McKinsey company, a private company hired to help in the process of privatization (ibid.). A private company was also sought in the tender to develop a marketing plan, to convince military officers to move to the south (Cohen, 2013d).

The tender for building Bahad City was won by a group of companies who banded together to compete in the tender together (increasing their chances and lowering the competition). The group, called Minrav-Electra-Zisapels, combines a holding company specializing in real estate, an engineering-electronics company and two brothers who are high-tech entrepreneurs. Keren Noy ("the Noy Fund"), which is an investment fund of a large bank and an insurance company joined the project in September 2012, investing 12 percent of their total capital in the Bahad City. A consumer club of Israeli soldiers and former soldiers called "Hever" also invested in building the Bahad City, although "Hever" is a non-profit organization (Reich, 2012).

The construction company selected to build the structures of Bahad City continued the process of outsourcing, and signed contracts worth NIS 700 million with subcontractors up to 2013. Many large Israeli companies won contracts to develop parts of the project. The MOD itself was only allowed to participate in the construction if it competed in the tenders as if it was a private company (Director, 2011). An additional NIS 200 million contract was awarded to Dania Cybus, one of Israel's prominent real-estate corporations (Buso, 2013). The Shultz Group has received an exclusive commission to operate the restaurants and cafeterias in Bahad City (Coren, 2014c). Although the Bahad City project was presented as a cost-saving project for the Israeli MOD, the Minrav company reported a rise of 530 percent in its net profit for 2012 after joining the project because of the ability of the company to benefit from the gap between the payment it received from the MOD and the actual costs it had to pay for fulfilling its obligations in the project. The company's high profit after joining the project casts doubt over whether involving private companies in such large-scale projects truly reduces the overall costs (Reich, 2013b).

4.2 PRIVATIZATION OF THE MILITARY INDUSTRY

Israel's military industry was established even before the founding of the state. The purpose of these industries was to arm Zionist para-military groups, and later the Israeli military. Profits from arms sales were a secondary motive (Lifshitz, 2000:372–3; Sadeh, 2001:64–77). The largest factories have been operated first as departments of the Israeli MOD, and gradually been transformed into state-owned companies (Table 4.1). Although the change is mostly bureaucratic, and does not imply a change in the employees or the function of the department/company, it does indicate a redefining of the institution from a section of the government performing a service, to a semi-independent company producing goods.

The change also made it possible to sell parts of the companies to private investors. In 1967, following the occupation of extensive territories, the Israeli government was concerned that the world community would not accept the occupation (Swirski, 2008). France, Israel's largest source of weapon imports in the 1950s and early 1960s, ceased arms sales to Israel after the war, and the government considered the possibility that other countries would follow (Farr, 1999). These concerns were also a business opportunity for investors who wished to fill the void that a military embargo would create. Elbit Systems was founded in 1966 as a joint private-public company, and turned out to be the fastest growing Israeli military company, becoming the second largest military company in Israel (Elbit Systems, 2013). Elisra was founded in 1967 as a private weapon company, and merged into Elbit Systems in 2005 (ibid.).

Discreet and unofficial steps towards privatization of the military industry include the abandonment of intellectual property by the Israeli MOD, allowing arms companies to use technology developed by the MOD and the military, and then to market it as their own. In 2014 the

Israeli State Comptroller exposed that the MOD did not register patents for technologies (both military and those with civilian applications), allowing state-owned companies and private companies to simply take over these technologies and use them to generate revenue. The value of these technologies was estimated in tens of billions of NIS (Coren, 2014a).

Sale of government-owned companies to private investors starts with the sale of sections of these companies. The government also plans the sales of full companies as well (Section 4.3). Israeli Aerospace Industries (IAI) was ranked by Dun & Bradstreet as Israel's largest arms company, and the fifth strongest industrial company in 2010–14. Its sales in 2010 were NIS 11.75 billion (79.8 percent for export), a growth of 9.3 percent compared to 2009, and its net profit was NIS 347.2 million. Sales increased in 2014 to NIS 13.15 billion, 73.4 percent for exports, and net profit fell to NIS 263.6 million (Dun & Bradstreet, 2012, 2015). The manager of Israel's Company Authority Doron Cohen called for an immediate privatization of IAI through the stock exchange in 2010. The Israeli Ministry of Finance stated that as a government-owned company, IAI must obtain a permit for each military deal and this restriction would affect its income adversely. By citing this argument as a reason for privatizing the company, the ministry suggested that as a private company, IAI would be free to conduct military deals without government approval. Together with this reduction of regulation, the Ministry of Finance declared in 2010 its plans to issue stocks to the public as a first step towards privatization. The assumption is that reducing regulation will make the stocks more attractive to investors.

Table 4.1 provides an overview of Israel's largest arms companies.

Out of the four large Israeli weapon companies: IAI, Elbit Systems, Rafael and IMI, three remain under government ownership: Rafael, IAI and IMI. Rafael was separated from the MOD and became a government-owned company (preparing the ground for privatization). Elements from the IAI were privatized and the government and the company's own management expressed plans to privatize the entire company (Neuman, 2012). A special consultant to promote the privatization of IAI was appointed in 2008 and served until 2011 without successfully advancing privatization (Haruti-Sover, 2017). IMI is now in the advanced stages of privatization, and several of its factories have been sold (Section 4.2.2). Rafael is a state-owned company rated the eleventh biggest industrial company in Israel in 2014 (Dun &

Table 4.1   Selected Israeli Military Companies and their Year of Founding

Company	Founding Year	Notes	Source
Elbit Systems	1966	Founded as a private company in cooperation with the Israeli MOD, began a series of acquisitions in the 1990s, purchasing private and state-owned companies.	Elbit Systems, 2013
Elisra	1967	Purchased by Elbit Systems in 2005.	Elbit Systems, 2013
El-Op	1937	Was founded as a private company, purchased by Elbit Systems in 2000.	Elbit Systems, 2013
Israeli Aerospace Industries	1953	Founded as a state-owned company, but sold sections to private investors.	Israeli Aerospace Industries, 2011
Israeli Military Industries	1933	Founded as a supporting department to the MOD and turned into a state-owned company in 1990. The government decided to privatize the company in 2005, the first factory sold is the small-arms factory.	Israeli Military Industries, 2015
Magal Security Systems	1984	Founded as a private company, now traded in the US.	Securities and Exchange Commission, 2010
Rafael Advanced Defense Systems	1958	Was turned into a state-owned company in 2002 (previously was state-owned, but not incorporated).	Rafael Advanced Defense Systems Ltd, 2016
Soltam Systems	1950	Founded by Shlomo Zevlodovitz, the Solel Boneh company and the Finnish Thempla company. Started producing weapons in 1954, and in 1973 was purchased by Koor.* Sold to private investors in 1998 and bought by Elbit Systems in 2010.	Wikipedia, 2017
Tadiran	1962	The merging of two factories ("Tadir" and "Ran") owned jointly by the MOD and Koor. In 1969 the MOD sold 35% to a US company. "Tadiran Kesher" was bought by Elbit Systems in 2007.	Akhikam & Morgenstern, 2009

Note: * Koor Industries Ltd was at the time owned by the Histadrut, the federation of Israeli labor unions. The Histadrut operates in Israel almost as a state body, and Koor at the time should be seen more as part of the public sector than part of the private sector.

Bradstreet, 2015). It paid a dividend of NIS 316.4 million to the state for its 2010 profits (Coren, 2012b). In 2012 a program for a gradual privatization of the company was formulated in a way that was designed to restrict possible enemies of Israel from attempting to purchase the company (Coren, 2010c; Paz-Fuchs & Ben-Simkhon-Peleg, 2013:14). The Israeli government announced in May 2013 its decision to begin the process to issue 20 percent of the stocks of Rafael and IAI to the public (Israeli Government, 2013b).

Rafael co-developed the famous "Iron Dome" system with IAI and with the US company Raytheon. It proceeded to offer the system for sale in India in February 2013, three months after its effectiveness was demonstrated in the conflict with Gaza in November 2012 (Coren, 2013c). The success of Rafael was quickly capitalized by MOD officials to resist the company's privatization and directly oppose the plan of Government Company Authority manager Uri Yogev to privatize Rafael and IAI, exploiting the fact that privatization arguments in the arms industry rely on criticizing inefficiency in government-owned companies (Azoulay, 2014).

Elbit Systems was established as a private company, but has expanded through the acquisition of smaller companies. In 2013 it was ranked the 35th biggest arms company in the world (SIPRI, 2015:455). Among many contracts in which Elbit is the sole provider of services to the MOD is a contract to provide flight training to the Israeli air force, through the "Tor" corporation which was established by Elbit Systems (Paz-Fuchs & Ben-Simkhon-Peleg, 2013:56–7). The Tor project makes the Israel MOD dependent on Elbit for continued supply of the equipment in which its soldiers are trained, as well as on the training needed to use the equipment in its inventory, ensuring that the contract with Elbit will be prolonged. It also allows Elbit to sell both physical equipment as well as provide training in the use of that equipment, thereby taking on the role of both arms company and PMSC.

4.2.1 Privatization in the arms industry: competition or consolidation?

Mergers and acquisitions are a strategy (among several) undertaken by corporations to increase their command over the rate of capitalization. Mergers create larger companies with monopolistic power and greater political influence (Nitzan, 2001:226–74). Two parallel and seemingly incompatible trends emerge from the public debate in Israel regarding the military industries. Both of these voices emerge mainly from the system itself – by senior officials in the (state-owned) military industries or in the MOD, as owners and managers of the private security companies rarely express opinions about these matters openly. One opinion promoted by the Israeli Ministry of Finance calls for privatization of military industries in order to make them more efficient and therefore more profitable, arguing that state ownership promotes a faulty management culture in these companies (Sadeh, 2001:64–77). The other opinion calls for the merging of Israel's military industries into one large company, in order to avoid competition between the different companies over the same contracts and to solidify the technical knowledge of the companies (Coren, 2012d). The argument is frequently made that when competing for a contract with a foreign country, all the Israeli military industries should be on the same side, rather than lowering their prices and profit margins in an attempt to outbid the other companies (Lifshitz, 2000:391–3). This argument was made, for example, by Ya'akov Goldman, vice president of operations, acquisitions and logistics in IAI (Coren, 2012a). In a 2013 interview, new IAI CEO Joseph Weiss reiterated his support for "any form of privatization" of the company (Opall-Rome, 2013).

The two arguments are seemingly contradictory because conventional economic theory argues that privatization is effective only in conjunction with competition, and that monopolies are special cases in which government ownership is preferable to the overall welfare of society. Creating a privately owned monopoly through a combination of a merger and privatization defies the economic theory which is used to justify privatization. While the argument that Israeli military companies should not compete with each other in international tenders sounds like a patriotic or nationalistic argument at face value, the fact that the Israeli MOD is a major customer of the military industries paints this argument in a different light. A private monopoly would be in a position to profit more in international tenders, but could also increase the costs of security to the Israeli government. The fact that the two arguments are raised simultaneously demonstrates the conflicting interests within Israel's security elites, who consider the policies pertaining to the structure of Israel's security institutions relevant to their private fortunes.

Israel's publicly owned arms companies have not been merged yet, but the private company Elbit Systems has set on its own path of acquisitions since 1996, buying smaller companies or divisions from larger companies until it became the world's 37th biggest defense company in 2010 (Hever, 2011a:148). A similar tension is observed in Europe. While mergers and acquisitions accelerated after the end of the Cold War (Lifshitz, 2011:17–19), there are also governments that try to slow the process of mergers in order to keep profits of arms companies domestic and to keep the companies under control. In a recent example, an attempt by two large European weapon companies to merge – EADS and BAE Systems – was blocked by Britain, France and Germany (Michaels et al., 2012).

4.2.2 Case study: Israeli Military Industries (IMI)

Israel's oldest arms company, IMI (Israeli Military Industries) was the first company the government decided to sell as a whole. It produces a variety of combat systems, with an emphasis on ammunition, electronic systems and military bridges. It also offers a variety of homeland security products. Although it remains state-owned, it has been undergoing a constant process of privatization demonstrating the privatization forces active in the Israeli government.

Case Box 3:	Israeli Military Industries (IMI)
Type:	Sale of a state-owned arms company
Key interests:	Investors, neoliberal forces in the Israeli government, competing Israeli arms companies
Opposition:	Union of IMI workers
Success:	No
Period:	2005–
Similar cases:	Israel Weapon Industries (IWI), parts of Rafael

In 1996, the US arms company Lockheed-Martin attempted to purchase IMI, but was refused by the Israeli government (Sadeh, 2001:64–77). The Israeli government considered the company to be of strategic importance, and insisted on keeping it in public ownership. In contrast, in that same year the Israeli government approved the sale of Bank Hapoalim, Israel's largest bank, to the Arison-Dankner consortium (Hasson, 2006:6–9). IMI was therefore seen as more than an economic asset. The fact that the company provides the Israeli soldiers with rifles imbued it with a symbolic value and protected it from privatization. Over the next 15 years, the Israeli government reversed its decision on the company, indicating the progression of the privatization ideology. The government decided to privatize IMI in 2005.

After the initial refusal in 1996, the pressure by private sector investors to see the company privatized did not relent. As typically happens with companies marked for privatization, the company's high profits turned to losses and deficits starting in 2000 (Marom, 2001). In 2005 the CEO Udi Ganani retired, after expressing pessimism about the company's future in an interview, and was replaced by a temporary CEO Avi Feldar (Goldstein, 2005). The media commenced to refer to the company as inefficient.

The first step was the sale of one of the factories, "Magen" to the businessman Sami Katzav for $1.5 million, although its value was estimated at $25 million. This sale provoked criticism in the State Comptroller's report and in the Knesset Committee for State Comptroller Matters, and can be seen as part of a process in which IMI was emptied of its value towards privatization. An additional argument was raised in the committee that a private investor would be free to close any non-profitable factories of the company after the privatization, which would lead to loss of jobs and of technologies available to the Israeli military (Knesset Committee for State Comptroller Matters, 2008; Paz-Fuchs & Ben-Simkhon-Peleg, 2014:16).

Doron Cohen, who in 2010 was the manager of the Government Company Authority (and therefore in charge of managing all the state-owned companies), claimed that the company was poorly managed, suffered from heavy debts and from a deficit in its cash flow. He argued that the company could not issue stocks in the stock exchange because it was in such bad shape, and therefore rejected the idea that the company's management should be reformed. Instead, he acted to sell the company as a whole (Coren, 2010a). It is notable that Cohen, in his capacity as manager of the Government Company Authority, damaged the reputation of the company under his responsibility, thereby driving down its value in direct contradiction to the government's interest.

Despite these comments, Elbit Systems saw IMI as a worthwhile investment and expressed interest in purchasing it. The situation in which the owners of the company (the state) express open contempt towards the company, and the official in charge of selling it describes it as a failing company, improves the chances for Elbit Systems to purchase the company for a low price. Furthermore, because it is a military company, only a handful of companies (and only Israeli companies) would be allowed to compete with Elbit in purchasing IMI (Coren, 2010a, 2010b).

The IMI company's financial reports for 2006–14 are partial and skip some years, but reveal the company's subsidiaries, including 100 percent ownership in Eurotaas, IMI Services, IMI Trading, International Technologies and Systems, Palindent, SIMI PTE, 85 percent ownership in Ashot Ashkelon Industries, 75 percent in IMI Security and Anti-Terrorism College and 11.68 percent in SDT (those stocks were sold before the end of 2010). IMI acquired through Ashot Ashkelon 100 percent ownership over a gear-producing US company, Reliance Gear (Government Company Authority, 2015:161c). As the entire financial reports are written with an emphasis on the company's weakness and the urgent need for privatization, the acquisition of new assets is marginalized in the reports to the very minimum description required by law. IMI also owns factories which specialize in different kinds of production but are not registered as separate companies. Of these subsidiaries and factories, some are profitable and some are losing money. Losing factories are kept open because IMI is state-owned and must meet the MOD demands for components even when the transaction is not profitable (Government Company Authority, 2012, 2014, 2015). Overall, the company held NIS 1.723 billion in assets in 2006, which increased to NIS 2.003 billion in 2010, NIS 2.3 billion in 2013 and NIS 3.93 billion in 2014. The company's liabilities, however, have increased at an even faster rate, and the company's liabilities (such as commitments to customers and suppliers) remain higher than its total asset value (ibid.).

The media presented the worker's union in IMI as the company's biggest burden. The workers were opposed to the privatization unless they were compensated, and saw the privatization as a means to enable mass layoffs and undermine their rights (Coren, 2010a). The resistance of the worker's union to the privatization made the government consider merging the company with Israeli Aerospace Industries (IAI) or with Rafael (Coren, 2010d), but the private arms company Palsan Sasa objected to this plan, and asked to purchase only the Salbin factory of IMI which produces armor for armored personnel carriers (APCs). The CEO of Palsan Sasa, Danny Ziv, argued that merging IMI with a state-owned company would lead to layoffs, thereby trying to mobilize the IMI workers to support his bid to purchase the Salbin factory (Gabizon, 2011).

Unlike in many sectors of the Israeli labor market, workers in the military industry enjoy higher prestige, and therefore wield more negotiating power during labor disputes. The union successfully prevented the privatization of the company in 2011, and in October 2012 the Knesset's Finance Committee approved a NIS 35 million capital injection to keep the company afloat despite its financial difficulties while privatization negotiations continued. This decision was taken when the media released news that a "breakthrough" had been achieved in the privatization negotiations, thereby legitimizing the continued bailout of the company (Azoulay, 2012). A total of NIS 1.4 billion in further loans were approved in the years 2011–14, adding to the discourse on the company as a burden on the government (Government Company Authority, 2015:154c).

Both the Ministry of Finance and the media presented the privatization as an urgent necessity to save the company and stop its losses, but privatization was not possible given the contradictory restrictions of ensuring competition but restricting the sale to Israeli inveostors. The Ministry of Finance accused the MOD of delaying the privatization (Coren, 2013e). Hurrying through the privatization process improved the negotiating power of the potential buyers (private investors in the arms industry), and weakened the negotiating power of the government. Due to the effort to expedite the privatization, Ashot Ashkelon Industries was added in 2013 to the privatization deal, a profitable subsidiary of IMI, producing armor components for land and air vehicles. The government decided to sell IMI along with Ashot Ashkelon Industries in order to make IMI more appealing to buyers (Coren, 2013f). In July 2013, a new chairman was appointed to IMI, Major General Udi Adam, in order to hasten its privatization (Coren, 2013g). The final agreement with the workers and the company was signed on April 9, 2014. The press reported the agreement in a very positive way, and only criticized the fact that it was not signed earlier (Coren, 2014b).

In the case of a privatization of an arms company, the government's commitment to privatize opens up opportunities for certain bidders to exert influence, which would not exist in other forms of privatization. Restrictions were placed on foreign companies from bidding for the company, forcing them to make their bid in conjunction with Israeli investors in order to ensure that the company remains Israeli and serves the strategic interests of the MOD (Coren, 2013j). Although the government announced its commitment to ensure competition in the arms industry after privatization, by restricting foreign companies it has effectively given a great advantage to Elbit Systems, already the largest privately owned military company in Israel. The MOD also committed to purchase goods and services worth at least NIS 2.8 billion from IMI after the privatization for five years, in order to increase the incentive of investors to buy the company (Coren, 2013k). A series of quick reforms were approved for IMI's structure, including: (1) a partial debt-forgiveness; (2) compensations to laid-off employees; (3) a promise of 3 percent of the privatization's revenue to the workers; (4) a separation of two IMI departments from the company in order to exclude them from the privatization – the confidential "Givon" department and the "Slavin" tanks and armored vehicles factory; and (5) renaming the company "New IMI" (Azoulay, 2013; Coren, 2013h, 2013k). These reforms caused concern that they would become a precedent for future privatizations, in which debts of government companies would be forgiven prior to privatization (Arlozerov, 2013b).

By January 2016, all contenders apart from Elbit Systems withdrew their bid to buy IMI, leaving Elbit as the sole contender for the tender. The Ministry of Finance delayed the privatization in an effort to attract competition into the tender (Coren, 2016a). The costly incentives to encourage investors did not counterbalance the restrictions placed on the sale of the company. In March 2016 it was revealed that the company Prometheus, which was outsourced by the Government Company Authority to evaluate IMI, had been employed by Elbit Systems, the main contender for the privatization of IMI, creating a conflict of interests. The Ministry of Finance froze the privatization process. Ironically, the reliance of the Ministry of Finance on a private company to help with the privatization of IMI has resulted in delaying the privatization (Coren, 2016b).

Minister of Defense Avigdor Lieberman was originally opposed to the privatization of IMI, but was pressured by the Ministry of Finance to restart the efforts. In June 2017 he gave his approval to resume negotiations with Elbit Systems, the only company interested in IMI and that meets the criteria (Amit, 2017a).

4.2.3 Loss of policy options due to privatization

One of the results of privatization is the restriction of the government's independence in making security-related decisions. As the 2012 example of Elbit System's lawsuit against the Israeli government shows, private companies have different considerations than states, and the two can come into conflict. After the killing of nine Turkish citizens by Israeli forces on board the ship *Mavi Marmara* in May 2010 there was a deterioration in relations between Israel and Turkey. The Israeli MOD revoked Elbit System's license to sell UAVs to Turkey. The company responded with a lawsuit, demanding $73 million in damages. Such a lawsuit would not have been possible if the UAV exports had been undertaken by a state-owned company (Opall-Rome, 2012). Even while diplomatic relations between Israel and Turkey remained sour, the Israeli MOD approved an arms deal for Elta, a subsidiary of the state-owned IAI, to supply Turkey with electronic warfare systems for aircraft (UPI, 2013a). The seeming contradiction between the diplomatic channels and the arms trade also indicates the extensive influence wielded by the arms companies (in this case a state-owned company) over government policy.

Elbit System remained an indispensable supplier to the Israeli army. The Israeli State Comptroller criticized the army in 2012 for becoming dependent on the company's services. Elbit installed a digital monitoring system to serve the needs of the land units of the Israeli army, but the military made no effort to learn how to operate the system independently. Instead, it relied on Elbit engineers to maintain the system, resulting in the contract with Elbit being renewed indefinitely, and the government not risking direct confrontation with the company (Cohen, 2012b).

Another example is the dependency of the MOD on the company Sanmina. Sanmina is a global company which produces electronic equipment. Its factory in the city of Lod in Israel produces smart cards for Israeli arms companies. These cards are used for building the "Iron Dome" system (Sections 3.6.1 and 4.2). Although the Iron Dome system is produced by the state-owned Rafael company, when Sanmina announced its intention to close its factory in Lod, the MOD appealed to the company to keep the factory open in order to ensure access to the smart cards in the future, promising to increase orders (Coren, 2013a).

In 2013 the Knesset invited Udi Shani, CEO of the MOD, to talk about the project to produce the Merkava tank, a project in which about 8000 Israeli workers are employed. Shani explained that the ministry distributes cuts to its budget among various projects, and attempts to keep the factories in peripheral areas of Israel (where unemployment is high), while laying off workers in the center of Israel. He admitted in the debate that pure security considerations, such as which parts of the tank are in greater demand, or how many tanks are to be produced, are of secondary importance to the primary goal of keeping Israeli factories open and providing contracts to the local military industry (Knesset Committee for Labor, Welfare and Health, 2013). This Knesset discussion demonstrates the resistance to privatization, and the fact that Israeli decision-makers consider security institutions as a tool not just for promoting security policies but also for social policy goals.

4.3 PRIVATIZATION OF INTERNAL SECURITY OPERATIONS

4.3.1 Privatization by default

Unofficial norms in the state vs. private security relations in Israel legitimize and even urge private citizens to participate in the manufacturing of security. This falls under the controversial "privatization by default" as the state encourages the undertaking of security responsibilities by private groups and individuals only indirectly. Such private security activities blur the boundary between the state and the private sphere, and open up the opportunity for private companies to hire civilians without any special authority to act as security guards. Among the first acts of bringing private citizens into the production of security was the establishment of the Civil Guard in 1974 (Section 3.1.4). The "readiness units" of the colonists in the West Bank are armed para-military units, working in close cooperation with the military in defending Israeli colonies in the West Bank (Harel, 2003), and serve as a strong example of the blurry line.

The occupation of the OPT created additional opportunities for mobilizing civilians to the production of security. Employers of Palestinian workers from the OPT in Israel were required to supervise the workers and keep track of their whereabouts, a policy which was implemented through the establishment of the Department of Payments in 1970 (Zohar & Hever, 2010:6–7). The Israeli ministries announced that in cases where Palestinian employees are involved in illegal activities, the Israeli employer will be investigated (Berda, 2012:96–8). Ariel University, a controversial academic institution established in a West Bank colony, has received different forms of government support in an attempt to establish it as a stable university, and thereby strengthen Israel's control over the West Bank. The MOD (along with the Ministry of Education) has used outsourcing as part of these efforts, and used the university as a human resources company. The university provided the

MOD with guides for MOD museums, although these guides remained officially employees of Ariel University (Hasson, 2012). Businesses, institutions and civil society organizations are also required to provide security at their own expense. The Small Business Registration law of 1968 requires small businesses to obtain police approval, giving the police the authority to demand the placement of security guards as a responsibility of the business itself. This regulation is not uniformly enforced, but was widely invoked during the second Intifada, and placed tens of thousands of security guards without the need to increase police patrols (Skhayek, 2003:2–3).

The mobilization of the civilian population in the production of security is an act of privatization by default. Among its early manifestations even before the State of Israel was founded was the intentional establishment of communities (especially agricultural communities) in frontier areas, in order to entrench control over the land. Civilian residents in such communities are expected to be vigilant and report suspicious activities, such as Palestinian refugees who attempt to sneak through the border to return to their lands (Newman, 1989:218–22). A similar policy was implemented in the 1990s to create a string of "lone farms" in southern Israel in order to prevent Bedouins from retaking land which was expropriated from them by settling Jewish farmers in highly subsidized farms spread over a large area. These farms were built without a legal permit, but legislation was enacted retroactively to legalize them (Roded & Tzfadia, 2012:85). The "lone farms" are an attempt to adapt the policy of frontier communities to a neoliberal era of high individualism. Rather than mobilizing the patriotism of "pioneers," the "lone farms" mobilize individual farmers to bear arms in order to secure their private property, which was granted to them in order to promote a strategic demographic plan.

Private citizens' participation in the production of security in the public space in Israel is more extensive than the obligatory military service. The general population is also educated to be alert and assist the security forces by identifying threats themselves (Ochs, 2011:81–6). Private ownership of firearms is common, and in many cases citizens have used these firearms to respond to terror attacks, or what they perceived to be terror attacks, rather than waiting for the police or the army to intervene. A study conducted by Shlomo Shapiro found that armed Israeli civilians have intervened in 70 percent of the terror attacks against Israel (Shapiro, 2011). In 2010, there were approximately 190,000 permits held by private citizens for carrying firearms, in addition to about 140,000 permits for organizations and businesses. By 2013 these numbers had declined somewhat, to 147,000 private permits and 130,000 permits for organizations (Mizrahi, 2010; Shadmi, 2012a:73; Cohen et al., 2013). As of 2010, 94 percent of all permits to private citizens to own and carry firearms were given to Jews (Mizrahi, 2010:6–7).

A seminal and highly publicized court case from 2007 reveals that the intersection of public mobilization, private firearms ownership, education to security and demographic policies through individual land ownership result in a layer of security which has been privatized by default. Shai Dromi, a Jewish Israeli and owner of one of the "lone farms" in the Negev, opened fire on two Bedouin burglars who broke into his farm. He killed one of them and injured the other. Dromi was charged with manslaughter and assault, but was acquitted by the court, and convicted only of carrying a weapon without a permit (Koriel, 2009). The Knesset passed a law in 2008, nicknamed the "Dromi Law," which stipulates that use of force against intruders to a home or place of business will not be considered a criminal offense. The Knesset was swayed by the fact that the "lone farms" serve a double role as private property as well as fortification constructed for national purposes. The precedent allowing the use of lethal force in the protection of property (and not just in self-defense) was only possible because the private citizen is perceived by the government as an agent of state security (Maranda, 2008). The court case and the following legislation were intensively discussed in Israel, and used as an example of decentralization of the application of force to private citizens (Shadmi, 2012a:60–3).

4.3.2 Security goods

Physical goods and not just services can serve as security products. Physical security goods are private by default. The state is not expected to provide civilians with weapons, armor, cameras or other security equipment, except in extreme cases. A notable exception in Israel is the center for the production and distribution of kits against chemical warfare, which were distributed to the public at the state's expense, at a cost of NIS 1.3 billion in production costs in addition to NIS 300 million annually in maintenance and distribution costs. Distribution began in 1991 during the Gulf War in Iraq because of concerns that Israel might be attacked by chemical weapons, and was continued irregularly until

2014, when it was eliminated due to the cabinet's assessment that Syria's chemical weaponry had been dismantled (Ravid & Cohen, 2014).

An increased demand for private security goods is an indication of privatization of security by default. When the demand for security is no longer satisfied by the state institutions and individuals are compelled to outfit themselves with security equipment to fill the gap, it indicates a decline in the state's monopoly over the production and distribution of security. This is demonstrated by the example of the fortified shelters inside private apartments, called *mamad* in Hebrew (an acronym for "protected space"). Construction companies are incentivized by the government to include them in newly built apartments. The cost of building these fortified rooms, which have a negative impact on the quality of life in the apartments because of thick walls, heavy doors and small windows, falls on the shoulders of the private citizens. Citizens are expected to participate in the effort of creating security by paying for such security rooms in their apartments (Zandberg, 2013). Nehama Bogin's real-estate appraising firm estimated in 2012 that the presence of a *mamad* can increase an apartment's cost by up to 20 percent, and that residents' fear of living in an apartment without a *mamad* has caused a reduction of 5 percent in the value of apartments without it in the center of Israel (Pauzner, 2012).

4.3.3 Consultancy: privatization of thought

Rivka Rozner coined the term "privatization of thought" in reference to the tendency of Israeli government bodies, and especially the military and the MOD, to turn to private consultancy firms to assist in formulating policies (Rozner, 2011:31). Lieutenant Colonel Eli Weiss noted that the standard procedure in the Israeli military for obtaining expert advice used to be by calling experts into reserve service, but this procedure has been phased out, and replaced with budgets with which private consultancy firms can be hired at much greater cost. Among the companies which have been recently hired by the army are Bplanned for assistance with the privatization of a civilian rehabilitation center and replacing transport trucks; Dor Technologies for consultation on communications and data systems; Aviv for consultation on construction project management; CEO for Bahad City planning (see above); and El-Tal for consulting the Home Front Command. Many of the employees of these companies are former military officers, who were trained by the

Israeli military but then sell their expertise back to the army. Military units also commission consultancy reports in order to affirm pre-made decisions with the stamp of approval of a high-prestige consultancy company. Vadik Rosenblit from the El-Tal consultation company argued that consultation firms have the advantages of using their experience to compare between different situations (as opposed to internal experts) and not being dependent on the system which commissions their consultation (ibid.).

Case Box 4:	Consultancy in Security Planning
Type:	Outsourcing of planning of government ministries
Key interests:	Outsourcing companies, civil servants
Opposition:	Academics
Success:	Yes
Period:	2007–
Similar cases:	Consultancy report for the police

The most famous case of a consultancy contract was the contract of the MOD with the McKinsey company to formulate an efficiency plan for the Israeli military in line with the Brodet Committee recommendations. The project was called "Time to Gather." The contract served the MOD as a trump card to demonstrate it took the committee's recommendations seriously. Alex Fishman, military analyst for the *Yedioth Ahronot* journal, called the McKinsey Report a "fig leaf" for the MOD, because it was used to distract from the fact that the defense budget is not efficient (Una, 2011:34).

The Brodet Committee itself has received a budget to hire private consultations, proving the prestige of such companies and how embedded is the respect for external consultancy in the Israeli government, but chose not to use it. In contrast, CEO Pinkhas Bukharis of the MOD chose to increase its reliance on private consultation firms and hired McKinsey to help in the implementation of the committee's recommendations. The army announced in 2009 that it had finished locating opportunities for efficiency in 40 percent of the defense budget, which would create expected savings of NIS 1.6 billion, out of a total NIS 30 billion savings demanded by the Brodet Committee. The remaining 60 percent would be covered in the McKinsey Report, which was supposed to be published in 2011 (Rozner, 2011:26). The second part of the efficiency plan was never published, but in May 2016 another contract was awarded to McKinsey, exempt from tender, to advise on merging the military's land command with the logistics command (Amsterdamsky, 2016).

The contract which McKinsey won awarded the company NIS 22 million for its services, but in 2011 it was exposed that the company had received about five times the amount specified in the contract, despite the fact that the company did not finish the second part of its work (Sikolar, 2011). McKinsey operated under strict confidentiality, and published no updates. The MOD reported no regulation of the company's operations. Brigadier-General Maharan Prozenfer, the economic advisor to the chief of staff, admitted that he did not even know (as of 2011) if McKinsey was still working with the MOD. In June 2016, however, the Israeli MOD approved a further contract with the McKinsey consulting company for NIS 20 million and without a tender (Bassok, 2016).

The lack of proper procedure in the management of the contract suggests that the MOD is more interested in the prestige of having McKinsey as a consultant and of unburdening itself of the responsibility for budgetary cuts than in the actual results of the McKinsey work. It appears that McKinsey itself has identified this tendency in the Israeli MOD and exploits it.

4.3.4 Van Leer annual report

The Van Leer Institute in Jerusalem started in 2012 to publish an annual report on privatizations in Israel, contributing to the public debate in Israel on privatization. The reports have been covered in the media (Bassok, 2013), and in 2015 their format was changed to a website categorized by theme, rather than chronologically. Among the themes covered by the reports are: (1) health services in the army;[2] (2) contracts between the MOD and the army with civilian companies; (3) privatizing security for Israeli delegations abroad; (4) the expanded authority of private security guards; (5) financing of security purchases through private companies; (6) privatization efforts of IAI, Rafael and IMI; (7) the outsourcing of the biometric database of the Israeli population; (8) outsourcing of consultation in the Ministry of Public Security; (9); expanded authority of municipal inspectors; (10) outsourcing of the establishment of Bahad City; (11) absorbing subcontractors as public employees; (12) privatization of policing; (13) outsourcing the estab-lishment of the national police training center; and (14) outsourcing the electronic tracking of prisoners (Paz-Fuchs & Leshem, 2012; Paz-Fuchs & Ben-Simkhon-Peleg, 2013, 2014; Van Leer, 2017).

A recurring argument in the Van Leer reports is that privatization creates a dependency of the public sector on private companies, beyond the scope of the contract signed between the state and the companies. This emerges from four examples of private companies who won contracts to provide services to the Israeli MOD in 2011. (1) The first was Elbit System, whose NIS 1 billion contract for maintenance and upgrade of various devices was severely criticized by the State Comptroller for faulty practices, sabotaging the possibility of the MOD to switch to another company (Paz-Fuchs & Leshem, 2012:54). (2) The State Comptroller also criticized a contract between the Israeli Air Force (IAF) and an unnamed software company, which received information about budgets, human resources and cost estimates from the air force (against regulations), allowing the company to tailor its offer to the IAF accordingly and win the tender. According to the Comptroller, it received excessive sums for the contract and without due supervision. (3) The decision of the army to obtain vehicles through leasing companies from 2001 – although several studies have shown that the costs of using leasing companies' vehicles exceed by far the costs of maintaining the vehicles directly by the army – resulting in losses of over NIS 560 million. The leasing contracts were renewed in 2011 (Paz-Fuchs & Leshem, 2012:53–60). (4) In 2011 the ISA stopped providing security for Israeli delegations abroad (especially sports teams), requiring public institutions to outsource security to PMSCs instead (ibid.).

4.3.5 Case study: private prison

The attempt to outsource the construction and operation of criminal prisons to a private company is the most well-known case in which the Israeli government failed to privatize state security operations. Prison privatization has taken place in other countries since the 1990s, especially in the US, UK, Australia and New Zealand (Gal, 2004:14–22; Trivedi, 2013), although in August 2016 the US Department of Justice announced its intention to phase out private prisons and eventually end them entirely (Yates, 2016). In 2006, the Israeli government signed a contract with two companies: Africa Israel and Minrav, to establish a privately owned prison (Ynet, 2006).

In the Israeli case, the High Court considered incarceration to be a key function of the state and a mark of its sovereignty, part of the "core" security functions which may not be privatized. Although the demarcation between core and periphery of security operations exists both in the US and in Israel in the privatization of security discourse, the private prison case demonstrates that different institutions occupy different positions on this demarcation in different contexts.

Case Box 5:	Private Prison
Type:	Outsourcing of prison operations
Key interests:	Investors: Africa Israel and Minrav
Opposition:	Human-rights organizations
Success:	No
Period:	2006–09
Similar cases:	G4S

Resistance to the private prison project began during its early stages. A group of lawyers from the Academic Center for Justice and Business formed a team and appealed against the privatization in the Israeli High Court of Justice. The court ruled that the prisoners have the right that their punishment will be carried out by state employees who represent the state in the act of punishing the prisoners (Israeli High Court of Justice, 2009:2–9; Otsari et al., 2009:1–4). The decision stressed that the proposed privatization of prisons would be an essential change in Israel's regime, as it would not only privatize government activities but also award responsibilities to a private company, which should be restricted to public institutions of a sovereign state (Israeli High Court of Justice, 2009:96). The court's decision highlights the standard approach to privatization in Israel, separating core from peripheral activities.

The contract with the private companies was cancelled by the court's order. As per the contract's "step-in"[3] contingency, the companies received a large sum of money. This was a problem which was anticipated by activists against the privatization, in light of similar examples in the US (Gal, 2004:53). Minrav demanded tax-free compensations worth NIS 1.6 billion for the cancellation of the project (Tal-Sapiro, 2009). The step-in clause loads the dice in favor of privatization. It allows the company to ensure its profits even if the contract is overruled, while the government must pay the cancellation fee without receiving anything in return. The clause also served a secondary purpose, as it applies pressure on the High Court to allow the privatization to go through, knowing that it would cause heavy losses to the government if the project was not allowed (Gutman, 2009).

Peripheral privatizations in Israel's prison system have already begun, despite the court's decision to outlaw full prison privatization. These include two major aspects: the outsourcing of prison canteens and the outsourcing of surveillance inside the prisons. Because these two elements have been considered "technical" rather than matters of policy, they have been allowed to pass to private companies. Although the distinction is far from clear-cut, the argumentation remains anchored in the distinction of core vs. periphery.

Canteens are of extreme importance in regulating the lives of prisoners, especially the thousands of Palestinian political prisoners in Israeli jails, who make up about a third of the prisoner population (IPS, 2015). Prisoners have an account at the canteen which serves as their bank account, and this account allows them to purchase food, hygiene products, clothes and other personal items. Palestinian prisoners receive support from the PA's Ministry of Prisoners and from their families directly to their canteen accounts, which are regulated by the Israeli Prison Service (IPS). Fines imposed on prisoners are taken directly from their canteen accounts (Addameer, 2011:55). Despite their central role, the canteens were privatized in a contract with the Dadash company from August 2009, although IPS documents show that Dadash operated prison canteens as early as 2005, before the contract was signed (IPS, 2006, 2009).

The tender in which Dadash won required a large turnover throughout 2007–08 (either $36.3 million annually, out of which 70 percent from a list of specified items, or $54.63 million annually, out of which $23.41 million from a list of specified items). This requirement limited the competition in the tender, and disqualified small companies (ibid.). Dadash accumulates profits from selling products to the prisoners, and pays royalties to the IPS. According to the IPS, the royalties are used to buy products for the prisoners such as fans, refrigerators, freezers, televisions and candy. Therefore, the royalties enable the IPS to avoid paying out of its own budget for certain necessities for the prisoners, for example, refrigerators which are necessary because prisoners can only purchase foods on certain days, and perishable foods do not last long in the arid conditions such as in the Negev, where the prisoners live in tents. The prisoners are not allowed to choose how the royalties from the canteens will be spent (Zansh, 2011). Privatization of the canteens helps to conceal the fact that the prisoners are required to indirectly pay for their own incarceration.

The outsourcing of surveillance on prisoners has taken two forms, and only the first of which was successfully implemented. In 2005 Hashmira company won an important tender with the Ministry of Public Security to operate a system of electronic bracelets to keep prisoners and people under house arrest under surveillance. The contract was renewed repeatedly. A new tender was issued in 2013, but only G4S, through its subsidiary Hashmira (see Section 6.4) met the requirements. The Ministry of Public Security has paid NIS 2.5 million every month since 2005 for operating the system (Van Leer, 2017).

In 2013 the IPS introduced a system based on voice-recognition that tracks and records telephone conversations of prisoners, and enables IPS personnel to eavesdrop on conversations held by prisoners without a warrant. The tender for this project was published in November 2010 under the title of "upgrading phone lines" – and therefore did not attract media attention. The tender allows the company winning the tender to charge a fee for its service from the prisoners, who will finance the surveillance by paying for their phone conversations. The tender was won by the Binat company. An appeal to the Israeli High Court has been filed by the Justice and Business Academic Center against the violation of the prisoner's right to privacy (Hoval, 2013). The appeal succeeded in convincing the Israeli government to halt the privatization project pending legislation to specify which surveillance activities may be privatized (Israeli High Court of Justice, 2015:1–2).

4.3.6 Privatization of police operations

Deputy legal advisor to the police Commander Ayelet Elishar acknowledged in 2012 that regulation of privatization of police operation is lacking, but that a special branch to regulate private security guards was established that year.[4] According to Haim Rivlin, an Israeli journalist and former police correspondent, Israel's most-watched television channel, "Channel 2," has never broadcast a single story about the privatization of the police. This is despite the fact that large capital owners in Israel form their (small) private police forces.[5]

Private investigators (many of them are retired police officers) and bodyguards (frequently former combat soldiers) are providers of private security who have existed since the founding of the state, but their prevalence has increased over the years. In 1972 the Israeli parliament passed the Private Investigators Law, which defined the authorities and rights of private investigators. In 2009 the Department for Licensing Private Investigators listed 1648 licensed private investigators with a valid license and 11 corporations licensed to conduct private investigations (Shadmi, 2012a:62–3, 160–2, 214–15). Even state security organizations hire private investigators. The MOD, for example, pays NIS 2.8 million every year to private investigators in order to check the validity of claims made by draft-age women about their religion and social situation, which could grant them exemption from service or special benefits (Cohen, 2013a).

Just as McKinsey signed a contract to develop an outline for improving efficiency through privatization in the Israeli military (Section 4.3.3), the RAND Corporation was contracted in 2013 to write an assessment about the Israeli police force, for which the corporation received NIS 1.6 million (Arlozerov, 2013a). The report came out that same year. It recommended that the Israeli police rely more on procedural justice, as opposed to racial profiling or emphasis on different police behavior regarding different social groups (RAND, 2013:20). The report mentioned the need for a review of Israel's police force (implying that RAND's report itself was sorely needed): "Despite having crime rates in most categories lower than those for similar crimes elsewhere, the Israeli public perceives an increasing threat to personal security" (ibid.:33). The RAND Corporation has therefore stressed the importance of the "perception of security," which private companies are better positioned to produce than public security institutions. It did not articulate a direct recommendation to outsource police operations, however. The Ministry of Public Security followed immediately in the same year with a tender for further consultation services for the ministry, this time for a prolonged duration rather than for a single report (Paz-Fuchs & Ben-Simkhon-Peleg, 2014:58).

The training of Israeli police officers is also undergoing privatization. In 1995 the Ministry of Public Security decided that the police force needed a national training center. After comparing between Britain, Canada, the Netherlands and the US, the ministry found that only in the US was the training partially outsourced to private companies. Nevertheless, a committee formed in 2006 to formulate a plan for a national training center in cooperation with the private sector. The committee was authorized to choose between three models, in all of which the center was to be built and maintained by a private company (through a private finance initiative or PFI).[6] The committee had to choose, however, what degree of the training would be outsourced to private companies. It recommended involving private companies alongside public workers in teaching the law, in combat training, in driving instructions and in other fields (Israeli Ministry of Public Security, 2006). The timeline of the project specified that the national training center's construction would commence in September 2008 (Inter-Departmental Tender Committee, 2006).

The tender results were published only in 2010, revealing that just four groups competed for creating the training center. All four were private companies with a history of tenders with the Israeli government: Shafir Training Inc., Policity (a combined group of the Shikun Ubinui company and G4S), Minrav Electra Training Inc. and the National Policing Campus (a combined group of Africa Israel and Elbit Systems). The tender was won by Shikun Ubinui and G4S through Policity. The companies signed a PPP contract with the government for a period of 25 years (Israeli Ministry of Public Security, 2010). The center became operational in April 2015, and despite costing NIS 3 billion (the Policity group won the tender with a much lower offer, but negotiated an increase in payment after the tender was over, Van Leer, 2017), the privatization element was cited by the police as a cost-saving measure (Bar-Eli & Arlozerov, 2015). Furthermore, in 2015 stage B of the project was agreed to include a second compound of over 50,000 square meters for the training of the IPS and Border Police personnel, in which the Policity group is expected to be awarded the contract with a tender exemption (ibid.).

Israeli police Chief of Staff Assaf Hefetz during 1994–97 was one of the main promoters of privatization in the police force. His policies included cooperative projects between the police and private companies, especially with insurance companies. The "Etgar" ("challenge") unit was founded even before Hefetz's tenure in the late 1980s as a police unit, but one which operates in close cooperation with insurance companies in efforts to locate stolen vehicles. Hefetz expanded such cooperations. Civil society organizations, such as the Or Yarok ("green light") organization to reduce traffic accidents, have also been able to provide the police with assistance and resources since the 1990s, and thus gained influence over police policies.[7] Traffic tickets (specifying fines as well as demerits) are issued by volunteers who wear police uniform (Laor, 2014). Security guards accompany police officers in police cars on patrols, and their presence during police activities as well as the presence of police officers during routine municipal enforcement activity blurs the distinction between the private security firms and public police. Shadmi adds that almost any kind of service that one receives from the police can be augmented by spending money to hire lawyers, private investigators, security companies, SOPs (special operations police officers), etc. (Shadmi, 2012a:56–61, 231–2).

The model of the municipal police was also implemented in the 1990s. Municipal policing is commonplace around the world and does not in itself indicate privatization, but merely decentralization. In Israel, however, it includes elements of private police, and wealthier municipalities use a well-paid and well-equipped police force to keep labor immigrants or homeless people away, such as by driving them to municipalities that cannot afford a large police force. In 2009, the Israeli High Court ruled that municipalities may not deploy privately funded police patrols for purposes other than to prevent terrorist attacks, but in 2011 the Knesset approved an order to overrule the High Court's decision and allow wealthier municipalities to collect a special tax in order to finance police patrols (Van Leer, 2017). In 2017 Israeli municipalities were awarded the operation of security cameras and the right to issue fines to drivers on public transportation lanes, away from the police (Dori, 2017).

The "City Without Violence" project was included in the municipal police program in the 2000s, as a channel allowing private donors to contribute to police operations. The project's policy of "zero tolerance" means immediate and harsh responses to any activity which does not comply with the law. It was developed in conjuncture with NGOs who provide resources and labor to the project, but also create a dependency. If the NGOs withdraw from the project, the police will have gaps in its operations (Shadmi, 2012a:54–6, 146–7). The project also relies heavily on multiple security cameras installed and operated by private companies (Hattem, 2014).

A 2007 addendum to the Police Law specifyed the conditions under which private individuals, companies or bodies may hire police officers to provide police services in a private function or a private location, and pay the police for their service (Government Bills Register, 2007). A complaint by the Association for Civil Rights in Israel (ACRI) has convinced the Knesset to soften the bill, but the addendum still allows individuals with means to employ police forces to serve their needs, creating unequal access to police services by the population. The police trains SOPs: fully uniformed police officers operating with full police authority, receiving payment from private individuals and companies (Shadmi, 2012a:50–1, 211–13). In 2011 a total of 7400 police officers were rented for NIS 67 million, and in 2012 the number was 8400 police officers, rented for NIS 94 million (Van Leer, 2017).

According to regulations set by the Ministry of Police in the 1970s, private security guards only had the authority to prevent terror attacks. A series of legislations gradually expanded their authority. In 1999 the government ordered that security of sporting events will be the responsibility of the organizers rather than of the police. In 2005 the Knesset expanded the authority of security guards to "protect against violence" and "use reasonable force" (State of Israel, 2005:1–4; Maoz, 2008). This vague instruction allows security guards to wield force to serve the needs of private companies which hire them. In 2008 Knesset legislation authorized private security companies to detain civilians and use reasonable force while securing sporting events (Guata, 2014; Van Leer, 2017).

The law authorizes security guards to operate within their undefined "close surroundings."[8] In 2012 municipal inspectors (equivalent to parking enforcers) were documented using racial profiling in the beaches of Tel-Aviv, demanding identification papers from Arab-looking bathers. The Tel-Aviv municipality commented in response that it cooperates with the police with the purpose of preventing terrorist attacks (Chiki-Arad, 2012). In 2014 the Israeli Ministry of Transportation launched a campaign to train bus drivers as security guards and authorized them to conduct searches on suspicious passengers, detain them and confiscate dangerous-looking items (Schmil, 2014). As some of the bus companies in Israel are privately owned, this policy clearly demonstrates how decentralization of enforcement leads to privatization of security. Private security guards of Avidar Group providing security at Tel-Aviv's central bus station reported that their instructions were to use racial profiling and demand identification from people with an "Arab look," while "Jewish-looking" people were not checked at all (Lior, 2017).

Human-rights lawyer Anne Sucio added that the legislation process expanding the authority of private security guards progressed in 2012, with almost no media coverage, which "revolutionized" the authority of private security companies. That year Tel-Aviv passed a municipal by-law (further elaborated in 2014) allowing it to collect a special security fee from the city residents in order to operate a privately owned and managed security patrol. While mechanisms exist to lodge complaints against the police and for supervision and regulation of police officers, security companies can operate anonymously and without proper regulation.[9]

In that year (2012) legislation clarifying the authority of security guards was voted through. Resistance to the legislation was overcome after a compromise was reached to exclude security guards in education facilities, but municipal inspectors were included in the bill (Paz-Fuchs & Ben-Simkhon-Peleg, 2013:54–5). The Knesset allowed security guards of private companies to wield authority which was hitherto restricted to police officers alone, including the authority to force civilians to identify themselves, to prevent people from entering certain locations or to remove them from locations, to detain people until the police arrives and to employ "reasonable force." The legislation dramatically shifted the allocation of responsibility between the police and the private security companies (Hoval, 2012). The law has been applied gradually, in 17 municipalities as of 2013 (Paz-Fuchs & Ben-Simkhon-Peleg, 2014:61). A further major step in the privatization of police operations was taken in March 2016, as the Knesset Committee for Domestic Affairs expanded the authority of volunteers in the police force to conduct arrests, even through the use of force, and to search homes. The police opposed the move but failed to stop it. During the committee deliberations it was revealed that volunteers outnumber the official members of the police (Kobowitz & Idelman, 2016).

Private security guards cost money but give their customers, organizations and individuals greater control over security than public security workers. In July 2012, as Israeli social activists erected a protest outpost near Kibbutz Yakum in the Sharon area, the kibbutz hired a private security company to forcefully remove the activists at 4 a.m., choosing not to use the police (Gabai, 2012). That same year, Tel-Aviv University also preferred the Bnei Tal private security company to the police in removing protest tents erected by students on October 24 on campus grounds. The security guards refused to give their company name to the students, claiming that they could not speak Hebrew. Their discretion demonstrates that by paying for private security, the university could buy minimal accountability for the use of force. Other academic institutions – Ben-Gurion University, Ramat-Gan College and the Weizmann Institute – have all resorted to using private security companies in order to suppress student protests, and in order to avoid calling police forces into the campus area, an act which would have violated the tradition of keeping the police off the campus (Shadmi, 2012a:116–17, 2012b).

The allocation of police-like authority to non-police enforcers erodes the uniqueness of the police institution, and what Bourdieu refers to as the "mystery of ministry" (Bourdieu, 1985:740). Although the authority of low-level enforcers to enforce laws prepares the ground for large-scale privatization of the police, it was actually the Israeli police's own policy of requiring private business to hire security guards which has led to the prevalence of private security guards in Israel's public space (Skhayek, 2003:2–3). Resistance to the use of force by private security guards eventually forced the Israeli police in July 2012 to absorb 650 contractors into the police force (Van Leer, 2017), but there remain subcontractors of the police who continue to outnumber the official police force (Kobowitz & Idelman, 2016).

4.4 CONCLUSION

The case studies presented in this chapter are defined by the clear interests of private sector actors in either advancing or delaying privatization. Although the decision to privatize or not to privatize has varied among the case studies, the role of the Israeli security institutions – the MOD, the Ministry of Public Security, the military, the police, the ISA and the Government Company Authority – in managing state-owned arms companies has been almost constant in all of these cases and across all of the institutions: playing a passive role.

The privatization of arms manufacturing companies, the establishment of the Bahad City military base cluster and the reliance on private consultation companies for Israel's security ministries are all cases in which privatization was advanced according to the schedule dictated by private companies and in a manner which guarantees the differential accumulation advantage of investors who are simultaneously members of the Israeli security elite. The two cases in which privatization was rejected for the security aspect of the project but not for the project itself were discussed in Chapter 3: the security of Israeli airlines and the offshore natural-gas rigs. These are interesting because the main investors were not members of the Israeli security elites, and yet this fact was not to their disadvantage, as the security in those projects was perceived (by the investors and by the media) as a burden. The government agreed to undertake that burden and therefore reduced the risk to the private companies.

In the case of the private prison, investors were not disadvantaged despite the narrative of a "failure" following the High Court's decision to disallow the project, because of the compensations which were paid to them. Only the government, and specifically the Israeli security elite inside the government, was disadvantaged, as it was required to maintain the public prisons while also compensating the private companies. The case studies did not end in the same outcome, but were all representative of struggles between competing private actors, while the state assumed a passive role. Nitzan and Bichler described this role as that of a "night watchman." The state holds on to assets only until private actors deem the moment ripe for privatization (Nitzan & Bichler, 2002:85–8).

Privatization in the case studies described in Chapters 3–4 have been discussed within the parameters of the "core vs. periphery" framework which I will address at the beginning of the next chapter. Successful privatizations were promoted in functions which were acknowledged by the government as peripheral to the state. Functions which were perceived as "core functions," such as the operation of prisons and the security of natural resources and of airlines, remained under state operation. This distinction contributes to the descriptive utility of the "core vs. periphery" dichotomy. The next chapter, however, will focus on the cases in which this dichotomy breaks apart.

5
Outsourcing the Occupation

The transfer of quasi-military powers to an ideological group, some of whom do not recognize the State of Israel and some of whose leaders have called for the elimination of the democratic regime, can only be seen as the waiver by the army of its authority to exercise power. Or in other words – privatization. (Gurvitz, 2014)

Chapters 3–4 discussed how outsourcing and privatization were introduced to the Israeli military and security sectors. Nowhere has the privatization of Israeli security been more significant, extensive and revolutionary, however, than in the framework of the 1967 occupation. The introduction of non-state actors to undertake security operations for the Israeli government in the areas conquered in 1967, and to a lesser extent in the areas conquered in 1982, has been the policy which brought the term "privatization of security" into the Israeli political discourse. The reluctance of the Israeli security elites to view themselves as a form of colonial police made it easier for them to outsource key functions of control and the production of security in the OPT, while arguing that no privatization has taken place.

Five stages of the outsourcing of the occupation will be analyzed. First, the Israeli government relied on a foreign armed group which was trained and equipped by the Israeli military (since 1979) to control the 1982 occupied South Lebanon until the year 2000. Second, the formation of the Palestinian Authority to manage security operations in Area A of the OPT (1994–). Third, the rise of security companies and the homeland security sector, which were private companies capable of offering services to the Israeli government. These companies have expanded in number and scope during the second Intifada (2000–04), and continued to increase their sales afterwards. Fourth, the Israeli government privatized yet another layer of the occupation by outsourcing the largest checkpoints in the West Bank and around the Gaza Strip (2005–). Finally, a recent court case will reveal that the authority to wield deadly force in order to enforce the occupation has become diffused.

5.1 THE CORE VS. PERIPHERY DEMARCATION

The 1967 occupation changed the nature of the Israeli military, and the nature of the conflicts in which it engages. During the first 19 years of Israel's existence, it engaged in three conventional wars: in 1948, 1956 and 1967. The 1967 occupation created a new task for the Israeli military: controlling a large civilian population in the OPT. Afterwards, the Israeli army fought only one additional conventional war in 1973, and arguably an additional war in 1982. It engaged, however, in a series of military operations which have not been officially defined as wars, and which were directly or indirectly connected to the 1967 occupation. Counterinsurgency has become the central activity of Israel's security forces (Khalili, 2010). These military operations have almost never achieved their strategic objectives, and demonstrated the limits of the Israeli military power. Privatization in various forms has been proposed to meet the challenges posed by these conflicts.[1]

The core vs. periphery demarcation is a spatial analogy, envisioning the "core," those activities which are most associated with the main function of the state, as occupying the center, while other functions are considered to be distant from the center. The geographic conceptualization of core vs. periphery was studied by Cilja Harders, which in a political economy sense differentiates the economically powerful "global North" which occupies the core of the global capitalistic system and the "global South" which is at its periphery. Harder argues that the relationality analysis made possible with the core vs. periphery demarcation is a useful analogy for non-spatial demarcations as well (Harders, 2015:37). She shows that neoliberal reform is more prevalent in the periphery, as resistance to neoliberal reform is easier to overcome there (ibid.:38). This analysis adds to the descriptive power of the core-periphery demarcation made by Israeli policymakers in privatization of security decisions. The analogy is not only useful for analyzing the discourse of privatization but also for viewing the US-Israeli relations as a case of core vs. periphery (see the quote by Shimon Peres in Section 6.2.4 below). The privatization of security can replicate this model in the local level, simultaneously positioning Israel in a "core" function within the Middle East while relegating unwanted and controversial functions of Israeli security institutions (the occupation of the OPT) to a "peripheral" status.

Amir Paz-Fuchs reported that all state ministers are guarded by private security guards, and only eleven "state symbols" (the prime minister, the president, etc.) are guarded by security guards in the public service.[2] The distinction between "state symbols" and other high-ranking officials is a manifestation of the core vs. periphery divide, in which public security services are reserved only for those functions that are defined as "core functions." The choice to exclude state ministers from the "core functions" of security indicates that the "core" is in a state of retreat, as even central state institutions become "peripheral" in their importance.

The tension regarding demarcation between center and periphery in the function of security and military institutions emerges from the unacknowledged colonial nature of Israel's occupation of the OPT. The essential difference between the 1967 occupation and previous and subsequent occupations is the large civilian population that came under Israeli control without being considered citizens of the state. The central activity of the Israeli military became the control of this population. The Israeli military, police and the ISA were tasked with establishing a regime of classification to differentiate between different kinds of Israeli citizens and different kinds of Palestinian subjects (Berda, 2012:62–87). The distinction between military and police becomes diffuse in colonial situations.

The main strategy employed by the Israeli forces to repress the Palestinian uprising has been the control and redistribution of space (Halper, 2009:47–56), as in other colonial regimes such as Egypt under British rule (Mitchell, 2002:9, 90–1). By restricting movement and dissecting the OPT into small and fenced regions, the checkpoints became the main tool for the Israeli military (Halper, 2009:47–56), and therefore the outsourcing of the checkpoints demonstrates that privatization has penetrated the very heart of the occupation. To a lesser extent, the Israeli occupation of South Lebanon in 1982–2000 followed similar patterns (Human Rights Watch, 1996:2–9). The scale (in terms of human resources) of the importance of the occupation to the Israeli military operations is demonstrated in Table 3.1, which shows that during the first Palestinian Intifada in 1987, no other state in the world had a larger percentage of its population serving as troops in foreign lands than Israel. The Israeli security elite, however, does not consider itself to be a colonial force and considers the control over the Palestinian population to be a secondary function.

5.1.1 Security elites adapting to the loss of prestige

The transformation of the main role of the Israeli military in enforcing the occupation has created a crisis for the Israeli security elite, which at the time was fully embedded in state institutions. The crisis takes a double form. One is reduced differential access to material resources (a smaller share of public spending on security, Section 3.1.3), and the second is a simultaneous loss of symbolic capital, or prestige. The repression of protesting civilians did not generate the glorious military victories necessary for maintaining the status of the Israeli security elites, nor did it motivate the public to accept the same levels of allocation of public resources to security as was the norm until 1979 (Sadan, 2004). Levy comments that "These crises have led to a dilution of the army's resources, a reduction in its political support, a decline in its symbols, and even its gradual abandonment by social elites" (Yagil Levy, 2008:117).

It is no wonder, then, that the Israeli security elite considers the occupation as a secondary task, and longs for the heroic victories achieved in conventional wars. Outsourcing becomes a desirable policy, because it relieves the security state institutions from their responsibilities towards the maintenance of the occupation.

Paradoxically, the same military and police officers and MOD officials who retire from their positions frequently find themselves engaged in similar counterinsurgency operations in the OPT. They move from state institutions into PMSCs, in a process that alters the relation of the state institutions with the occupation, but keeps the security elite comprised of the same people. For the individuals who make the move from state institutions into PMSCs, the loss of prestige is mitigated with the increase in monetary income which they receive in the private sector (see Krahmann, 2010:216–19).

The outsourcings of security to the SLA and to the PA (see below) are exceptions, because these organizations are comprised of individuals who did not originate from the Israeli elites (and were of different nationality). The members of these institutions did not enjoy the monetary nor the social capital rewards of the members of Israeli security institutions (whether state-owned or not).

Despite being one of the most decisive factors in the development of Israel's society, economy and international relations, Israeli officials treat the occupation of the OPT as a temporary phenomenon (Azoulay & Ophir, 2013:7, 14–16, 24). Due to the ambivalent position of the

Israeli authority on the occupation, it did not develop a comprehensive terminology to categorize it, and the act of privatization of security has been implemented with very little public debate, and without the term "privatization of security" itself being invoked. Policymakers who promoted the outsourcing have borrowed terminology from other fields, such as "civilianizing the checkpoints," "compromise with" and "autonomy for" the Palestinians, "alliance with" or "cooperation with" local forces in Lebanon, etc. Despite the lack of an official debate on the issue, these policies affect the top category in the institutional typology of privatization of security. Privatization itself is concealed, as occupation policies are secretive and contradictory (Berda, 2012:19), which allowed it to occur with minimal resistance.

5.1.2 Origins of the core vs. periphery discourse

Senior Israeli policymakers have sketched a framework for privatization and outsourcing of security, differentiating between "core" and "peripheral" functions. This demarcation appears as a guiding principle in interviews and speeches of senior officials, in which they seek to explain the guiding principles behind Israel's security policies both to the general Israeli public and the functionaries who are charged with implementing those very policies (Ben-Israel, 2002:1639–40; Halutz, 2002:53–4; Brodet, 2007:37; Sikolar & Amsterdamsky, 2009; Tzur, 2011).

The Israeli demarcation mirrors the US official line on privatization of military functions (see Section 6.2 on the US influence over Israeli security policies). The US DOD published a document in March 1996 entitled "Improving the Combat Edge Through Outsourcing" (DOD, 1996). This document clearly articulates the view according to which outsourcing in military and security operations is generally desirable (to the DOD), except when one of these three conditions apply: (1) when it does not lead to an improvement in either costs or performance; (2) when there is no competitive market from which to draw companies; and most importantly (3) the "DoD will not consider outsourcing activities which constitute our core capabilities" (ibid.). One can argue whether the US authorities have indeed followed these criteria, but on the declarative level, the analogy to the statements of Israeli officials is striking.

The analogous discourse indicates that the desirable limit to privatization of security in Israeli government institutions has developed in parallel to the discourse in the US. In 1993, a governmental committee headed by Professor Israel Sadan was assembled to "assist in formulating policy for the defense system in light of the national needs, regarding activities of production, restoration and maintenance by the IDF, as opposed to performing these activities in the civilian industry." The committee submitted its recommendations in 1994, but those were never published to the general public. Officials referring to the recommendations, however, stressed that they encourage the privatization of military industries and the outsourcing of military functions (Seidman, 2010:12–13). The Brodet Committee of 2007 has published its recommendations, and called for selling military assets and restructuring the military budget (Brodet, 2007). These committees' recommendations have also been interpreted as a call for outsourcing according to the demarcation between the military's "core activities" which must remain within the military and its peripheral functions which can and should be outsourced. The term "core activities," however, was not clearly defined and was a source of tension regarding outsourcing policies in the decades following the Sadan Committee.

Statements of senior officials corroborate that the demarcation between core and periphery has been internalized as a policy guideline regarding privatization of security. Lieutenant General Ehud Barak, as the commander in chief of the Israeli army between 1991 and 1995, said that "everything which doesn't shoot or directly helps to shoot – will be cut" (Tzur, 2011). "Cut" in this sentence should be understood as "outsourced," as the practicalities of the security policies demonstrated (Menahem, 2010). For example, food services to the soldiers which were prepared and distributed by soldiers have been outsourced to a private company (Shekem), but the soldiers continued to receive food. So the service was not "cut," but outsourced (Ben-Israel, 2002:1639–40). This policy outright declared with the "Commander in Chief 2000 Plan" to deal with budget cuts, stating that certain core strategic functions of the military will be considered peripheral, so that they may be put up for outsourcing (Korin-Liber, 1999).

Israeli soldiers returning from the 2006 war in Lebanon reported that workers of private catering companies have refused to go into harm's way in order to keep the troops supplied (Hasson, 2006:14; Rozner, 2011:30). Soldiers resorted to looting grocery stores in Lebanon, an act which hindered both the military effectiveness of the Israeli forces and their public image. Limor Pumranz-Zurin has written extensively on the failure of logistics in the 2006 Lebanon war, but has not mentioned privatization. Her article appeared in the military's own magazine, *Ma'arakhot*, but nevertheless expressed critical views on the failure of logistics. The choice of the institutional publication not to discuss the outsourcing of the logistics services as part of the reason for this failure prevents a critical discussion in the merits and drawbacks of the outsourcing policy itself. Pumranz-Zurin uncritically stressed the consensus in the Israeli military command which sees the fighting as the core activity of the military, while logistics are considered peripheral, as she writes: "As a generalization, non-fighting activities in the army are marginal activities. The fighting is the core activity of the army, and everyone who are not warfighters, who are called 'fighting-supporters,' are there to serve it" (Pumranz-Zurin, 2014:41). The assertion of the demarcation narrative in an official publication demonstrates the strength of this narrative, especially when discussing an instance in which the policy based on the demarcation has led to disaster.

Lieutenant General Dan Halutz, Israel's chief of staff between 2005 and 2007, who holds a degree in economics from Tel-Aviv University and a business degree from Harvard University, studied in departments dominated by neoliberal teaching. He was the commander of the air force in 2002 when he said that "the principle guiding the air force is, that every theme which is not directly related to the security missions of the air force can be managed by another body," thereby demonstrating how pro-privatization neoliberal ideology has seeped into the military command. Halutz also boasted that the army uses PFI and BOT systems in introducing private companies to military activities (Halutz, 2002:53–4).[3] In a 2009 interview, military economist colonel Eyal Hans said that "Part of the processes of efficiency is the outsourcing to civil companies." Colonel Meir Ben Tzuk, head of the planning division and economics of the navy, qualified that "it is important to stress that we source out when it brings us money, not everywhere and certainly not when outsourcing is more expensive" (Sikolar & Amsterdamsky, 2009).

Of special importance to the argument is a statement of Yitzhak Rabin who was Israel's prime minister as the Palestinian Authority (PA) was founded. A former commander of the army and minister of the defense, Rabin was concerned about the effect which policing an occupied civilian population is having on the Israeli military readiness for conventional war. Rabin told his cabinet that the PA will keep the Palestinian population under control "without the High Court and without B'tselem"[4] (Gordon, 2008:171, 189). Rabin paved the way for the largest privatization in the history of the Israeli security forces, the establishment of the Palestinian Authority (Section 5.3 below). He did not stress the core/periphery demarcation explicitly. However, his goal to preserve the army's fighting readiness while shifting the responsibility for the policing of the Palestinian population to an external organization guided the actions of his successors. Although Rabin's efforts did not return the Israeli military to its former structure as the military continued to be embroiled in the occupation, his policies broke the monopoly of the Israeli military on the application of violence in the OPT.

5.2 THE SOUTH LEBANESE ARMY
AS A CASE OF OUTSOURCING

The South Lebanese Army (SLA), nicknamed "Uwat Lahad" (after Antoine Lahad, its commander), was founded in 1979 after the Israeli invasion of Lebanon of 1978 (Human Rights Watch, 1996:13; Alakhbar, 2012). It collapsed in 2000. It was armed, trained and funded by the Israeli authorities in order to control the Israeli-occupied southern Lebanon strip. The formation of the SLA is pertinent to understanding the experience which Israeli decision-makers employed in the formation of the PA as part of the Oslo negotiations.

Case Box 6:	South Lebanese Army (SLA)
Type:	Outsourcing of military units
Key interests:	South Lebanon Christians, Israeli interests in Lebanon
Opposition:	Amal, Hezbollah, Palestinian Liberation Organization (PLO)
Success:	No (temporary success)
Period:	1979–2000
Similar cases:	Palestinian Authority

5.2.1 The nature of the SLA

The SLA was not a clear case of privatization of security, but a proxy force equipped, funded and trained by Israel to promote its interests in Lebanon. Nevertheless, Neve Gordon considered the SLA to be a case of outsourcing within the context of the efforts of the Israeli government to distance itself from human-rights violations by having the SLA perform the "dirty work" for the Israeli military (Gordon, 2002:324).

Nevertheless, the SLA is relevant because it prepared the ground for the outsourcing of security in the OPT to the PA. The relations between Israel and the SLA have changed over its 21 years of existence, such that as it collapsed it was no longer considered a proxy or allied force, but an arm of the Israeli security forces. It can be said that although the SLA did not start as a case of privatization of security, it transformed into such a case as the practices of privatization of security became more acceptable in the 1990s.

Israel invaded Lebanon in order to target the operation of the Palestinian Liberation Organization (PLO) in the refugee camps in Lebanon. The Army of Free Lebanon, under the command of Major Saad Haddad, was a faction that broke away from the Lebanese army in 1976, and which was identified by the Israeli government as a possible ally. Israeli agents helped to transform this faction into the SLA. The SLA was trained and equipped by the Israeli army, and has fought the PLO, the Amal Movement and the Hezbollah (Human Rights Watch, 1996:13). SLA troops were trained inside Israel's territory, and relied heavily on Israeli weapons, ammunition and vehicles (Ravid-Ravitz, 2013:95–100). Israel spent roughly $30 million annually on the SLA (Wehrey, 2002:63–4). Yagil Levy confirmed that "The SLA was funded, trained, politically backed, and monitored by the IDF," and called it a "satellite army" (Levy, 2012:63).

The formation of the SLA is an outsourcing of military operations (see the typology in Section 2.8), and therefore a privatization at the core of the Israeli security sector. Although the SLA was referred to in the literature and the media as a "militia," most lower-ranking SLA troops were motivated by the employment opportunity rather than by ideology (Wehrey, 2002:63), and acted as employees of a PMSC. The SLA was not officially a PMSC, because its financial structural components (such as its funding and payment and procurement procedures) were concealed within the Israeli secret forces.

5.2.2 Outsourcing as a mechanism to avoid responsibility

The SLA not only undertook the tasks of holding the South Lebanon territory for Israel and of engaging the Hezbollah forces, but has also conducted activities which the Israeli government wanted to wash its hands of. During the Israeli invasion of 1982, the SLA's operations were coordinated by Israel, and in the Sabra and Shatila massacre of September 16, 1982 there were SLA troops among the Phalangists who committed the massacre, while the Israeli army provided lighting and prevented the escape of the Palestinian refugees from the area, although the SLA did not officially participate in the massacre (Alakhbar, 2012).

A more direct SLA involvement was the establishment of the Khiam Detention Center. It was founded in 1985, a year in which the Israeli military implemented a partial withdrawal from Lebanese occupied territory (Amnesty International, 1992; Human Rights Watch, 1996:14). This prison became notorious for torture and other human-rights violations, and was severely criticized by human-rights groups (Human Rights Watch, 1996:14; Alakhbar, 2012). The outsourcing has therefore served not only to relieve Israeli soldiers from the risks of war but also to relieve the Israeli government from responsibility for torture (Gordon, 2002:324–5).

The Israeli government chose to augment its control by using a local Lebanese faction as a contractor, and to outsource responsibilities to this faction. The SLA troops have advanced Israeli interests in Lebanon (mainly by fighting the PLO, the Amal Movement and the Hezbollah), but they did not receive the full benefits and subsidies which Israeli soldiers receive, they took risks which Israeli soldiers could therefore avoid. The Khiam Detection Center facilitated the punishment, intimidation and interrogation of Lebanese citizens outside of Israel's territory. Although the Israeli army could use the intelligence gathered from the detention center (Human Rights Watch, 1996:14), it was not directly accused of committing torture.

In 1999, two Israeli human-rights organizations challenged the policy of disavowing responsibility by the Israeli government through the SLA, by appealing to the Israeli High Court, demanding the release of four Lebanese prisoners from the Khiam Detention Center. The Israeli military responded that the detention center is under the responsibility of the SLA, and that therefore Israel has no responsibility over it. The Israeli response to the court demonstrates one of the purposes of the outsourcing occupation to a subcontractor. Israeli intelligence officers were present in the prison and actively participated in interrogations, but the Israeli military was not held accountable by the Israeli court for the human-rights violations which took place there (Israeli High Court of Justice, 1999; Gordon, 2002:325).

5.2.3 The failure of the SLA

The SLA has been ultimately unsuccessful in maintaining Israeli control over South Lebanon. It suffered from rapid attrition and collapsed as soon as the Israeli military withdrew from its fortification line in July 2000 (Human Rights Watch, 1996:15–38; Norton, 2000). Very few sources in Hebrew or English discuss the aftermath of the SLA collapse. Although the Israeli government sought to use the SLA as a buffer and minimize the political and economic burden stemming from injuries and casualties among Israeli troops, it was forced to assume responsibility towards the defeated SLA troops. About 6000 members (and former members) of the SLA and their families have fled to Israel and were given asylum there. The majority of them, however, have gone back to Lebanon or to other countries. By 2010, only 2541 people remained in Israel of those who fled in July 2000. The majority of those who chose to stay received Israeli citizenship. The Israeli government allocated special budgets in order to facilitate the absorption of the former SLA members into the Israeli economy and society, including assistance with rent, employment projects, education projects and special stipends. Those who chose to leave Israel and return to Lebanon received a one-time grant. Altogether, the Israeli government spent NIS 35.93 million between 2003 and 2010 on former SLA members and their families (Phares, 2001:61–70; Agmon, 2010).

Despite the large amounts of money and equipment that were invested, the Israeli authorities did not succeed in creating a military force with the ability to hold its own ground when faced with a direct assault by the Hezbollah. Furthermore, the Israeli government found itself forced to take responsibility for the soldiers and family members of the SLA inside Israel's borders and to grant them citizenship. It should be noted that granting citizenship to non-Jews is a policy undertaken only rarely and with extreme reluctance by the Israeli Ministry of the Interior. The attempt to outsource the military operations has not succeeded in transferring the risks involved to the contractor, and the objectives of the Israeli government – control over South Lebanon, a buffer between Israeli soldiers and the risks of combat and a buffer between the Israeli government and responsibility towards policies in Lebanon – were not achieved.

5.2.4 The Amal Movement and the PA as counter-examples

The Amal Movement stands out as a counter-example to the SLA in the same context of the Israeli occupation in Lebanon. Amal was a Shi'a movement founded in the early 1970s in southern Lebanon. It fought against the PLO in the refugee camps of South Lebanon, and later against both the Hezbollah (although the Hezbollah itself is a Shi'a party and was founded by former Amal members) and the SLA (Norton, 2000:23–4). There was a tacit alliance between Israel and Amal, despite the armed clashes between Amal and SLA, when their interests coincided. Augustus Richard Norton argues that "No Amal leader of stature could accept an overt relationship with Israel, or with its puppet Saad Haddad. Nonetheless, there was no lack of understanding of the benefits of a tacit alliance." He continues: "Clumsy efforts to co-opt Amal during June and July 1982 failed. While the southern leadership of Amal did not eschew a quiet dialogue with Israeli personnel, they were both unwilling and unable to allow themselves to follow the Haddad prototype of open clientship" (ibid.:85, 109). The Amal Movement therefore highlights the difference between an alliance and the outsourcing of security.

5.3 THE PALESTINIAN AUTHORITY
AS A CASE OF OUTSOURCING

Many similarities exist between the cases of the SLA and the PA. In both cases, the Israeli authorities have enlisted a local group to perform security operations in an occupied territory, in which Israeli troops are simultaneously deployed, with the purpose (among others) to relieve the burden from the Israeli soldiers. However, there are also differences between the two cases. One of the striking differences is that the SLA troops were trained inside Israel and armed directly by Israel. Their reliance on Israeli assistance could not be concealed, which eroded their legitimacy inside Lebanon, and branded them as foreign agents (Wehrey, 2002:63). The PA, however, received training and arms from other sources (mainly the US), which allowed it to claim greater autonomy and establish itself as a representative of the local population. Experience accumulated by senior Israeli policymakers with the SLA informed their policies in establishing the PA. This experience is not unique to the case of Israel, and is part of a process of a shift from "externally imposed" to "locally owned" security reform in an attempt to create more stable security institutions (Schroeder et al., 2013:382).

The idea that the formation of the Palestinian National Authority, as part of the reformulation of the Israeli occupation of the OPT, was an act of privatization was advanced by Neve Gordon in his book *Israel's Occupation*. Gordon classifies the establishment of the PA as an act of outsourcing of security (Gordon, 2008:169–96). Although the PA was dressed as an autonomous, partially sovereign institution, sovereignty remained in Israeli hands. Several functions of the Israeli military and police in the OPT have been outsourced to the PA, however, for reasons which will be discussed below. In terms of scale, the formation of the PA is the largest privatization of security in Israel's history.

Case Box 7:	Palestinian Authority (PA)
Type:	Outsourcing of military and police units
Key interests:	Israeli government, PLO, foreign donors (mainly US)
Opposition:	Israeli military, right-wing opposition in Israel, parts of the Palestinian public
Success:	Yes
Period:	1994– (until 2007 in the Gaza Strip)
Similar cases:	South Lebanese Army

5.3.1 Is the PA a sovereign body?

The complexity of the topic of the PA's founding, its political and economic aspects, enable varying perspectives on the PA's nature. From the point of view of the Palestinian public in the OPT (especially in the early years of the PA), the PA was seen as a proto-state establishment, established in the interim period before evolving into the state apparatus of a future Palestinian state. For the purposes of the discussion here, however, the PA will be examined only from the point of view of the Israeli authorities. The Israeli authorities (at their top) have consistently treated the PA as a subcontractor, facilitating the occupation and performing activities which previously were under the responsibility of the Israeli military.

Although the PA uses trappings of a sovereign state (titles, flags, a national anthem, political institutions), it has the organizational and financial structure of a civil society organization. The PA is dependent on external donations and funding forwarded by the Israeli government.[5] Similar to civil society organizations, it must submit reports to its donors and allow outside scrutiny of its operations. Only a third of the PA's budget is generated through its own activities, making the PA dependent on its donors. This (1) dependency on donors and on (2) Israel's willingness to allow the PA to operate, the fact that (3) the result of the January 2006 elections for the PA's Legislative Council were overturned by external pressure, and the fact that (4) Israel disabled the Palestinian Legislative Council after 2006 by preventing the council members from assembling and arresting some of them (AMAN, 2013:50) demonstrate that the PA is not subject to the Palestinian public, and is not a sovereign body. Although the PA has a limited capacity to collect taxes and can employ violence, it is subjected to Israeli sovereignty.

5.3.2 The Oslo Agreements

The Oslo Agreements have defined the roles and responsibilities of the Palestinian Authority. The OPT was divided into different regions (Areas "A," "B," "C," "H1," "H2" and East Jerusalem) in which the PA received different degrees of authority. The PA received security responsibility over Areas A and H1, and civilian responsibility extending to Area B as well. Mechanisms for coordination of security and civilian responsibilities were established between the Israeli government, the Israeli military and the PA (Berda, 2012:50-2). The media covered the treaty as if it was a result of a negotiation between governments (Azoulay & Ophir, 2013:65-7, 74-6), but the agreement is equivalent to an outsourcing contract which governments sign with PMSCs, and as such it is at the center of the relations between the state and the PA. The frequent allusion to "violations" or "obligations" stemming from the agreement (MFA, 2000) indicate that the contract is the framework which both sides refer to in defining their relations.

The nature of the Oslo Agreements (signed over a period of several years) as a contract for the outsourcing of security becomes apparent from its content. It includes elements in which the agreements specify the security responsibilities of the PA, even at the resolution of force deployment, but not those of Israel. These clauses indicate that the PA is not permitted to develop its own security policy:

> The Palestinian Police will act systematically against all expressions of violence and terror. (Interim Agreement, Appendix I, Clause 2b, MFA, 1995b)

The Council will issue permits in order to legalize the possession and carrying of arms by civilians. Any illegal arms will be confiscated by the Palestinian Police. (Interim Agreement, Appendix I, Clause 2c, MFA, 1995b)

[in Area B] The Palestinian Police shall establish 25 police stations and posts in towns, villages, and other places listed in Appendix 2 to Annex I and as delineated on map No. 3. The West Bank RSC may agree on the establishment of additional police stations and posts, if required. (Interim Agreement, Article XIII, Clause b1, MFA, 1995a)

The agreements specify the distribution of well-defined areas of responsibility over security to the PA, while leaving the Israeli forces sovereign. These clauses indicate that the agreements do not distribute sovereignty, but rather delineate a restricted sphere in which the PA would undertake responsibilities previously borne by the Israeli authorities:

Nothing in this Agreement shall affect the continued authority of the military government and its Civil Administration to exercise their powers and responsibilities with regard to security and public order, as well as with regard to other spheres not transferred. (Agreement on Preparatory Transfer of Power and Responsibilities, Article VI, Clause 5, MFA, 1994)

Israel shall transfer powers and responsibilities as specified in this Agreement from the Israeli military government and its Civil Administration to the Council in accordance with this Agreement. Israel shall continue to exercise powers and responsibilities not so transferred. (Interim Agreement, Article I, Clause 1, MFA 1995a)

Additional clauses have been added to the agreements in order to ensure the transfer of certain risks from Israel to the PA. The undertaking of these risks is among the chief reasons for the creation of the PA from the Israeli perspective, as an act of outsourcing:

The transfer of powers and responsibilities from the Israeli military government and its civil administration to the Council, as detailed in Annex III, includes all related rights, liabilities and obligations arising with regard to acts or omissions which occurred prior to such transfer. Israel will cease to bear any financial responsibility regarding

such acts or omissions and the Council will bear all financial responsibility for these and for its own functioning. (Interim Agreement,
Article XX, Clause 1a, MFA 1995a)

In the event that an award is made against Israel by any court or
tribunal in respect of such a claim, the Council shall immediately
reimburse Israel the full amount of the award. (Interim Agreement,
Article XX, Clause 1e, MFA 1995a)

The unequal power distribution between Israel and the PA is
concealed by mechanisms of negotiations and coordination, such as the
Israeli-Palestinian Joint Water Committee. Jan Selby demonstrated that
the committee is in fact a tool which enforces Israeli decisions regarding
water on the Palestinian population through the PA (Selby, 2013:1–4).
The Israeli Ministry of Foreign Affairs has referred to the committee
as a testament that Israel cooperates with the PA (MFA, 2009:26), but
Selby demonstrates that the "cooperation" is merely a convenient (for
Israel) facade under which an unequal power structure operates, and
in which the Israeli government is dominant (Selby, 2013:4). Therefore,
international law defines the PA as an "agent" of the Israeli government
in the OPT:

the Palestinian Authority and the Palestinian Police have been
considered "agents" of Israel under Article 29 of the Fourth Geneva
Convention (GC IV), which obliges Israel as Occupying Power to
be responsible for the treatment of protected persons (civilians in
occupied territory) by its agents "irrespective of any individual responsibility which may be incurred. (Program on Humanitarian Policy and
Conflict Research, 2008:10)

5.3.3 Privatization of colonial practices and of risks

During the 25 years of occupation prior to the establishment of the PA,
a complex array of control mechanisms was established including the
issue of permits, arrests, investigations and interrogations, repression of
demonstrations, security for VIPs (very important persons), institutions
and facilities, among others. Many of these activities have been transferred
to the PA (while undergoing changes), whereas the sovereignty and the
ability to determine the overall policies of the security operations in the

OPT remain Israeli. For example, the PA submits a weekly report with an update to the population registry to the Israeli authorities. The Israeli authorities therefore maintain the official record of the Palestinian population in the OPT, which serves as a base to issuing travel permits (Berda, 2012:81).

In November 2013, the Palestinian Police was invited to perform an enforcement operation in the A-Ram neighborhood of Jerusalem. The neighborhood is in Area C (and therefore under official Israeli security control), but lies outside of the Separation Wall and therefore has been neglected by the Israeli police. The neighborhood became a haven for criminals. Although many residents of the neighborhood carry Israeli residency cards, the Israeli authorities prefer not to send in the police. The PA was called to perform a service for the Israeli authorities, and has agreed to do so because of the opportunity to extend its authority into a part of Area C (Hasson & Khoury, 2013).

The Israeli authorities outsourced to the PA responsibilities as well as the risks stemming from mechanism of colonial control. The PA's prison facilities came under criticism for violating the civil rights of Palestinians, and for torture (Al-Haq, 2008). As with the Khiam Detention Center operated by the SLA, the outsourcing of security relieves the Israeli army from responsibilities arising from activities which could be criticized by the Israeli High Court and by human-rights groups. There are also differences between the two cases: the PA enjoys higher levels of legitimacy among the Palestinian population than the SLA received in Lebanon, and is accused of fewer human-rights violations. The coordination between the PA and the Israeli army and the sharing of intelligence is less overt.[6] Nevertheless, the cases of certain Palestinian prisoners who were released from Israeli jails only to be rein-carcerated by the PA in Palestinian prisons have caused uproar among the Palestinian public, as the PA was seen to offer incarceration services to the occupying Israeli government (Alsaafin, 2012).

5.3.4 Scale of the outsourcing

The size of the PA's security forces varied wildly over the years, impacted by budget constraints, by Israel's security needs and by the PA's political needs to ensure its own stability. In 1994, the PA counted about 10,000 in its various security forces, which increased to 16,800 by 1995 and jumped to 42,000 in 1997 (Lia, 2006:310). Before the January 2006 elections in the PA, which were followed by a split between the West Bank and the Gaza Strip, the PA commanded a force of 70,000 police and other security forces, organized in one battalion (Institute for National Security Studies, 2010). This can be compared to Israel's standing army of 176,500 soldiers in that year (ibid.), and 19,996 police officers (ICBS, 2006). Without including private security guards, the PA provided 26 percent of the military and police forces in the area controlled by Israel in 2005. After the split, the Hamas-led government in the Gaza Strip exhibited less dependency on donors and less cooperation with the Israeli government. The discussion of the PA as a form of outsourcing of the occupation is therefore restricted to the OPT in the years 1994–2006, and only to the West Bank in the years following 2007. The size of the PA forces after the split have declined to 60,000 in 2007, 40,000 in 2008, 30,000 in 2009–10 and increased again to 35,000 in 2011. By 2011, the PA forces were organized in eight battalions (Institute for National Security Studies, 2011). The Israeli army has not seen a similar reduction in size, and therefore the PA comprises a smaller percentage of the forces deployed in Israel/Palestine. From the Israeli point of view, the 2006 elections and the Hamas takeover of the Gaza Strip in 2007 was a failure of the PA in maintaining control and public support, and the result was a weakening of Israeli control over the Gaza Strip (Abunimah, 2007).

In delegating authority to the PA, the Israeli government pursued outsourcing for various reasons. Cost-cutting played an important role, as foreign donors shouldered security expenses which were previously paid by the Israeli MOD. The PA was also seen as capable of delivering security more efficiently because the security forces are drawn from the local population, and are not subject to the same legal and media scrutiny to which the Israeli military is subjected. The transfer of risks and responsibilities also serves a political purpose for the Israeli government, especially in its foreign relations efforts.

5.3.5 Funding structure of the PA

The unique structure of the PA's funding sheds light on the interests which shaped the outsourcing of security to the PA. Unlike most cases of outsourcing, the Israeli government does not directly purchase services from the PA. Between 1994 and 1997, the US and EU funded and trained eight different security forces belonging to the PA,[7] all deployed in the OPT to keep the public peace and to prevent terrorism against Israel.

Unlike the concealed structure of the SLA, the transparent civil society organization structure of the PA helped to establish the PA's legitimacy as well as to draw international resources to fund its operations. The outsourcing of security to the PA was a process fraught with conflict within the Israeli as well as the Palestinian publics.

The training and reforming of security forces in transitionary states (such as in Iraq, Afghanistan, Liberia, Kosovo, Bosnia, etc.) has been considered "peripheral" security tasks and often delegated to PMSCs (Krahmann, 2007:103–4). The PA case seems similar, and indeed the view that the colonial control of the OPT is a "peripheral" task of the Israeli military has been a crucial prerequisite for outsourcing. In the case of the occupation of the OPT, rather than relying on a private company, the PA itself took the role of a subcontractor, and suffers from a similar dilemma described by Krahmann regarding PMSCs in transitionary states, of divided loyalty between the interests of the donors and those of the local population (ibid.:103).

Neoliberal ideology played a central role also in the shaping and management of the PA. Its economic policies were heavily influenced by the World Bank and the International Monetary Fund, especially after the death of Yasser Arafat in 2004. In 2006 Salam Fayyad, a former International Monetary Fund representative to the OPT, was appointed prime minister of the PA. Subsequently the PA issued a series of publications articulating its plans for economic and policy reform, with an emphasis on good governance. "Good governance," a term associated with the neoliberal idea of restricting the role of government to routine management (Krahmann, 2010:41) has been presented by the PA documents as a requirement for Palestinian statehood and independence. The documents focused on the role of the PA in promoting the private sector in the OPT, creating a link between the private sector and Palestinian independence.[8] The PA's security policy history was divided by Alaa Tartir into three stages: (1) Yasser Arafat's stage in which the PA attempted to co-opt the armed resistance groups; (2) the crisis stage in which the PA's security capacities were largely destroyed by the Israeli military; and (3) the neoliberal stage directed at first by PM Salam Fayyad (but continued after his resignation) in which the PA's forces fully aligned themselves with Israel's interests in repressing the armed resistance groups, while simultaneously adopting a neoliberal policy package (Tartir, 2015:1–14).

5.3.6 Resistance to outsourcing

The outsourcing of security to the PA has not gone smoothly. It encountered stiff resistance within the Israeli political sphere. The opposition vocally objected to the Oslo Agreements, right-wing groups demonstrated against the Agreements, culminating in the assassination of Prime Minister Rabin in 1995 (Zertal & Eldar, 2009:126–8). The military and ISA objected that their role in the negotiations was not more central (Seliktar, 2009:48). The Palestinian public itself was divided on the issue, and Chairman Yasser Arafat used oppressive measures to quell protests within the OPT (Rubin, 1998:162).

In a seeming contradiction to the argument that the PA is a case of outsourcing of security by Israel, open armed conflict broke out between the Israeli military and the PA's forces in 1996, and again in 2000–03 during the second Intifada. The fighting between the Israeli army and the PA has never escalated into all-out war. According to the 2003 "Road Map," the PA committed to make visible efforts to prevent attacks on Israelis (Amrov & Tartir, 2014). There is no doubt regarding the ability of the Israeli army to dismantle the PA and re-establish the previous system of military administration in the OPT. Instead, the fighting took the shape of short rounds of violence, restricted in time and place, focusing on symbolic targets (for example PA police stations and the assassinations of senior officers and politicians, Allen, 2008:453). The PA armed forces have never attempted to organize a concentrated effort to end the occupation by force of arms. Furthermore, the Israeli army did not use the fighting as an opportunity to expand its civilian authority or its territorial deployment at the expense of the PA, allowing the PA to re-establish checkpoints, prisons and patrols as before.

Between these armed conflicts, the PA continued its cooperation with the Israeli military after the fighting, serving as a channel by which Palestinians can apply for permits from Israel (Berda, 2012:50–61), arresting, investigating and punishing Palestinians and maintaining checkpoints within the OPT (Arouri, 2012; Collard, 2012; Amnesty International, 2013:1–22). A member of the PA's Preventive Security force admitted that they receive lists of names from the Israeli authorities and collect the individuals to be delivered to the Israeli authorities for arrest and interrogation (Amrov & Tartir, 2014). The Palestinian Investment Conference in Bethlehem in 2008 was a PA-organized event out of several in which only holders of Israeli-issued permits could attend. The

PA forces provided security for Israeli delegates in the event (Alternative Information Center, 2008).

The armed clashes should not be seen, however, just as interruptions in the privatization process. They served a purpose both for the PA and for the Israeli authorities. For the PA they helped in establishing its legitimacy and differentiating itself from the Israeli occupation forces (this has been only partially successful, see Ghanem, 2010:90). The Israeli authorities used lethal force in these clashes to exercise regulatory control over the PA. There were opportunities to encourage certain elements in the PA and repress others. The siege on President Yasser Arafat's government compound during the second Intifada, for example, was accompanied by a statement by then Israeli Prime Minister Ariel Sharon that "Arafat is irrelevant" (FMEP, 2002:1). Following Arafat's death, Mahmoud Abbas, considered by the Israeli government as more agreeable to Israeli interests (Cook, 2013), became the president of the PA.[9] On the command level of the Israeli army, Israel's public security apparatus, the armed conflict with the PA served an additional purpose. Yagil Levy argues that the Israeli military leadership weakened the PA's ability to prevent Palestinian attacks against Israeli citizens, which enabled the military leadership to claim increasing amounts of resources for the army in order to provide more security for the Israeli population. The attacks on Israeli citizens also increased the legitimacy of the military leadership in the public (Levy, 2012:157).

The fact that members of the Israeli government and the military use belligerent language towards the PA and portray it as an enemy of Israel can create the impression that the PA is more of an independent actor than an agent of the Israeli authorities. The view that the PA is an "enemy" of Israel came not from the political leadership of Israel but from the military (Michael, 2010:57). The army, threatened by the concept of outsourcing some of its key activities to an external body, has used its professional authority and its ability to generate intelligence reports in order to attack the legitimacy of the PA in the eyes of the Israeli government, and pressured the Israeli government to authorize the use of lethal force against PA forces. While the Israeli government welcomed the outsourcing of risks to the PA, the Israeli military acted in this respect as a public institution threatened by competition arising from privatization.

In light of the opposing forces acting within the Israeli government for and against the outsourcing of security to the PA, the policies undertaken by the Israeli authorities were complex and sometimes contradictory. In the spring of 2011 Israeli Prime Minister Netanyahu accused the PA of incitement to violence against Israel (Ravid et al., 2011), but in the summer of 2012 he acted in support of the PA. As a wave of demonstrations in the West Bank against the PA threatened its stability, the Israeli government responded by giving the PA an advance on tax money it was scheduled to transfer, and authorized several alleviations in its economic restrictions on the PA, in order to save the PA from collapse (Harel & Issacharoff, 2012). The Israeli reaction (among many other similar actions) demonstrates that the Israeli government considers the PA's existence as an Israeli interest.

Furthermore, the decision to form the PA was not taken by the Israeli government in a vacuum, but was strongly influenced by outside pressure. Just as the privatization of Israeli arms companies was strongly influenced by the Israel-US relations (Section 6.2), the decision to outsource security responsibilities to the PA has been taken in an environment of international pressure. The Israeli government was hard-pressed to formulate a policy regarding the occupation after the end of the Cold War. The Israeli official position was that the occupation was temporary, but it has been prolonged without a timeline for ending it. Israeli officials considered the options of withdrawal from the OPT or annexation of the OPT into Israel. The annexation would bring the risks of international ire and demands by the Palestinian population in the annexed territory for equal citizenship. Withdrawal was resisted by the commitment of the Israeli political elite to the occupation project (Doron & Maoz, 2013:252–9). The Oslo Agreements, the division of the OPT into areas and the establishment of the PA as a proxy were a compromise between withdrawal and annexation. At the cost of partial autonomy to the PA, Israeli control over the OPT in the long run was ensured (Gordon, 2008:171, 189).

In addition to the Israeli government, other institutions have participated in the decision to establish the PA. The PLO and the Fatah party supported and actively pursued the establishment of the PA (Ghanem, 2010:82), and large proportions of the Palestinian public supported the founding of the PA as a step towards actual Palestinian sovereignty (Dabdoub, 1995:60–3). Indeed, the PA's agency is not completely subjugated to Israeli interests and the PA did pursue policies which conflicted directly with Israeli interests, such as the boycott of products from the Israeli colonies in the West Bank in 2009

(Prusher, 2010) and the unilateral appeal to the United Nations (UN) for a non-member observer state status in November 2012 (UN, 2012). Clearly, the Palestinian public did not want to facilitate or streamline the Israeli occupation of the OPT (Amrov & Tartir, 2014).

Foreign donors, mainly European and US state actors, have also considered Palestinian autonomy to be consistent with their own political interests. Large investments of the international community enabled the PA and shaped its structure. The European Union is the biggest donor to the PA (European Commission, 2010), followed by the US, which places a larger proportion of its funding on equipping and training the PA's armed forces (Arouri, 2012). The way in which the PA made the occupation easier for Israel to maintain was an unintended result of the aid efforts (Le More, 2005:983, 987).

The US support to the armed forces of the PA is especially relevant to the question of privatization of security. The US sent senior US military officers to help with the training of the PA forces. General Keith Dayton, for example, trained a special PA unit in Jordan (Elmer, 2009). The US has also increased support for the PA's Presidential Guard during the split between Fatah and Hamas following the 2006 elections to the PA's Legislative Council. While the Presidential Guard was fighting Hamas militants in the Gaza Strip (and supporting the Fatah party), US Secretary of State Condoleezza Rice moved to increase the size of the Presidential Guard from 3500 to 6000, and offered a special $20 million budget for this purpose (Associated Press, 2006). Gabriele Mombelli found that the US was set to increase its funding for PA security by orders of magnitude, in a plan which was not implemented due to the Hamas takeover in Gaza in 2007 (Mombelli, 2014:16–17). After the appointment of Prime Minister Salam Fayyad, the US approved an additional security budget of $86 million to support the PA's forces in 2007, and an additional $75 million in 2008 (Dayton, 2009). The US claims that every form of support to the PA is approved first by Israel, further demonstrating where the sovereignty truly lies (ibid.). This form of the implementation of force by proxy can be considered an outsourcing of US military power through the PA, in a similar way to the outsourcing exercised by Israel. Unlike most donors to the PA, the US takes a greater interest in using its funding to dictate the PA's agenda, to the point of restricting members of certain political parties from being employed in their aid projects (Lazzarini, 2009:3).

Despite the opinion expressed by Rabin on the role of the PA (see Section 5.1 above), the idea being that the PA is a contractor of the Israeli security system, is not widely accepted in Israel's political and economic discourse. Seeing the occupation as a temporary fixture, or an accident of history, diverts the public (and even academic) discourse away from the nature of the regime which is developing in the region (Azoulay & Ophir, 2013:67–9, 103). Sovereignty is the opposite of privatization. Therefore, until the PA will come to be a sovereign state, one can conclude that the establishment of the PA is the largest act of privatization of security in the history of Israel. The largest Israeli security institution, the military, has outsourced its most active operation.

5.4 PRIVATIZATION THROUGH SECURITY COMPANIES

After the outbreak of the second Intifada in 2000, privatization of security in Israel was accelerated. The second Intifada profoundly affected the everyday life of Israelis. Although the death toll and devastation on the Palestinian side was far greater than on the Israeli side, daily life was disrupted for Israelis as well. The violent conflict and the many civilian casualties have deterred many civilians from visiting public spaces (Gronau, 2002:20–2, 31). Although the security of the population is a government responsibility and a public good, the atmosphere of fear during the Intifada created a sense of urgency in which the state monopoly over application of security was de-prioritized (ibid.:17–22), facilitating the transfer of responsibility for guarding the public space to the hands of private security companies. Security guards were placed in visible locations in order to create an immediate and localized sense of security. The Israeli government (through the police force) encouraged the creation of a sense of security through private companies, a policy which amounted to privatization by default of activities which previously fell under the responsibility of the police force.

Case Box 8:	Private Security Companies in the Public Sphere
Type:	Privatization by default of police operations
Key interests:	PMSCs, Israeli police force
Opposition:	Israeli public, human-rights and worker rights organizations
Success:	Yes
Period:	2000–
Similar cases:[10]	Airport security, G4S

5.4.1 Privatization by default: PMSCs fill the void

Although at no point did the Israeli government officially withdraw from its obligation to protect the public, it allowed security to become commodified, a service which can be bought and therefore which is not available to everyone in the same quantities (Section 2.5.2). This is essentially privatization by default. Security companies also began to offer services which were traditionally the sole purview of the police force, such as securing public institutions, securing demonstrations and commercial centers, locating missing persons and stolen vehicles and even tracking and capturing criminals (Shadmi, 2010). PMSCs also provide security for international dignitaries visiting the OPT (Ghantous, 2012:24). With the outbreak of the second Intifada in late 2000, the Israeli police began to extensively implement an already existing (but rarely enforced) clause of the Law for Business Registration to force private businesses open to the public (restaurants, coffee shops, shopping malls, supermarkets, banks, etc.) to hire security guards to guard the area. Even businesses which were exempt from the law due to their small size were advised by the police to hire guards (Skhayek, 2003:2–3). The security guards were deployed to prevent terror attacks in these public areas, and would search customers for weapons upon entering the premises. This created a rapid increase in the number of security guards employed by private security firms. This sector of the Israeli economy has effectively been charged with a responsibility for preventing terror attacks which previously belonged to the military and the police (Shadmi, 2012a:146–7).

During the second Intifada the number of workers in security companies rose rapidly (Handels, 2003:3–4). In 2004 (the last year of the second Intifada), the Dun & Bradstreet website listed about 3000 security companies. By 2013 the number dropped to 2112. By 2017 the number dropped to 723.[11] Two factors can explain the fall in the number of companies. One is the end of the second Intifada, which brought about a reduction in the demand for security guards. The other is mergers among security companies. The volume of operations of the branch according to Dun & Bradstreet for 2012 was estimated at NIS 4 billion (Shadmi, 2012a:164). Because the Israeli Central Bureau of Statistics aggregates the security sector with the cleaning sector (ibid.:164–6), an updated data series on the number of security guards employed by private companies is not available. Between 1995 and 2003 the number of security guards in Israel has increased by 91 percent, to 46,500 in 2003 (Handels, 2003:3–4). Unofficial sources estimated that the number approached 100,000 in 2004, but after the end of the second Intifada it has declined, and by 2008 there were 27,900 private security guards in Israel (Shadmi, 2012a:162–3).

A regulation by the Israeli Ministry of Public Security, which came into effect in September 2012, helped to reveal the number of guns owned by private security companies. The ministry began to collect an administrative fee whenever security companies change the person responsible for company weapons. While announcing the new regulation, the Ministry of Public Security revealed that according to its records, there were 130,000 weapons belonging to institutions, organizations and private companies who hire private security guards (Cohen, 2012a). This indicates that the rise in the number of private security guards did not halt with the end of the second Intifada, and that the decrease in the number of companies indicates capital concentration rather than a decrease in the size of the sector.

5.4.2 Crossovers between the civilian and the security sectors

The results of the rise of private security companies are two-fold. On the one hand, it creates a militarization in the civilian market, because private companies are more likely to be engaged in military and security activities. On the other hand, it brings considerations which are normally restricted to the civilian sector into the security sector. For example, while police officers and soldiers (in Israel) are not allowed to form unions and to strike, security guards in a large security firm Modi'in Ezrakhi ("civilian intelligence" in Hebrew) formed a union (Weisberg, 2012). The largest labor union federation in Israel, the "Histadrut," claimed in court that security firms operating in occupied East Jerusalem are in fact serving as mercenaries, engaged in police and fighting activities which should be reserved only to the police and the army, and should not be privatized (Biur, 2012). Human-rights lawyer Anne Sucio revealed that approximately 350 private security guards were stationed in certain areas of East Jerusalem (especially in Silwan), guarding a handful of Jewish Israeli colonists. Private security guards were stationed in East Jerusalem from 1987, when they were tasked with guarding a house bought by Ariel Sharon, who was then the Israeli Minister of Housing. Only in 2010, following an appeal by the Israeli NGO "Peace Now," did the Ministry of Justice give the security guards authority to operate in the area.[12]

The Histadrut leveraged this case to reach a deal with the government, to allow 650 security contractors to become state employees and part of the police in 2012, but this deal had little effect on the ratio of private to public security forces overall (Rimon, 2012).

Private security firms have also won contracts to secure the industrial zones in the illegal Israeli colonies in the West Bank. The State Comptroller of Israel published a report criticizing the neglect and lack of enforcement in the security of the industrial zones. His report revealed a practice in which private companies (especially in the OPT) can designate a private citizen as "security trustee," as long as that individual has sufficient experience in the army or a security organization. The Comptroller argued that insufficient security measures are implemented in these colonies, pointing out that private security companies have been deployed in areas in which military presence would have been expected. The army responded to the allegations by arguing that it lacks the budget to secure these areas (State Comptroller, 2012:1667–80, 1685–7). The Comptroller has also pointed out that in certain documented cases, the military allowed colonists to use areas which were confiscated from their private owners for security purposes for industry and agriculture (in violation of the regulations for confiscating land). The Comptroller has thereby exposed a system in which outsourcing of key military functions operates in the service of private businesses (ibid.).

Of special interest is the prevalence of Civilian Security Coordinators (CSCs) as a case of outsourcing of security in the Israeli colonies in the West Bank. CSCs are either individuals or employees of PMSCs who receive payment from the MOD in order to coordinate security operations around the colonies. Although CSCs have been deployed since the early years of the occupation (before the deployment of "security trustees" which were mentioned above), very little is known about them and the policies pertaining to their use. The organization Yesh Din published a report in 2014 which is currently the main source of information about CSCs. The report found that CSCs wield a great deal of responsibility and often occupy de facto command positions over regular troops. Their loyalties are split between the MOD and the local municipality of the colonies, and numerous cases were recorded in which they used their authority to promote municipal policies (such as driving Palestinians from nearby agricultural lands invoking security reasons). The MOD employs almost no regulation on CSCs, and almost no mechanism exists to punish CSCs who abuse their power. CSCs therefore constitute one of the elements of the privatization of the occupation which is the least transparent (Hareuveni, 2014:8–49).

The prevalence of private security companies has far-reaching social implications. Companies, individuals and organizations who can afford to hire security companies can impose their will directly and without waiting for police intervention, while those who cannot afford such services remain dependent on the increasingly weakened police force. (See Section 4.3.6 above for a discussion of the police functions which are undertaken by PMSCs.)

The growing reliance on both security and homeland security companies results in a collection of outsourcing policies intended to achieve a myriad of results. Cost-cutting can be achieved if and when private companies finance the fixed costs required for the development of their capacities and technologies through contracts with multiple customers. The Israeli MOD, or the Ministry of Public Security, may save on costs because they are not required to develop these capacities at their own expense. In this, they shift the burden of funding the security of public space from the government budget to the private sector. The reliance on private security guards also reduces costs because of the reduced employment benefits awarded to employees of private companies. Other reasons for outsourcing (efficiency, transfer of responsibility) are of smaller relevance to this type of privatization by default, because privatization by default indicates a withdrawal of the state's interest in the field, rather than an effort to model it for a specific purpose.

5.5 PRIVATIZATION OF THE CHECKPOINTS

After private security firms established a foothold in the Israeli economy and accumulated legitimacy, economic capacity and connections with the political elite, the Israeli MOD launched a program to involve these companies in the most prominent aspect of the Israeli occupation of the OPT: the checkpoints. Checkpoints are a form of security operation in which sovereignty is at its most visible. The decision whether a person is allowed through the checkpoint is an essential function of the sovereign. Although the checkpoint itself is established in a certain location and crewed by a small staff, the policies of the entire bureaucratic apparatus of the state manifest themselves in the checkpoint (Berda, 2012:23,

32–4). The checkpoints are also a location in which a military mission defines a military unit, thereby driving the privatization into the heart of the Israeli military institution. Oded Na'aman, a former soldier stationed in checkpoints in the West Bank, testified that the checkpoint's main function is to radiate a presence, to be a visible symbol of control (Na'aman, 2012).

Case Box 9:	Privatization of the Checkpoints
Type:	Outsourcing of military units
Key interests:	Israeli MOD, PMSCs
Opposition:	Palestinian public, human-rights organization
Success:	Yes
Period:	2005–
Similar cases:	HP, airport security

5.5.1 What are the checkpoints

There are three types of checkpoints currently in use and that are relevant to the discussion on privatization:

1. The permanent border-passes of Israel, in the Ben Gurion Airport, in the seaports and the land passages with Jordan and Egypt. These border-passes have employed private security guards for many years operating alongside the police. The process of selecting the private security companies and the contracts with them remain confidential.
2. Temporary checkpoints, or "flying checkpoints," can take many forms. Within Israel these are police checkpoints, set up on roads or pedestrian walkways when the police want to restrict a certain area (for example when there is a bomb threat or during a demonstration). Inside Jerusalem (both in West and East Jerusalem), the Border Police operates these checkpoints. The Jerusalem checkpoints are used not only for security purposes but also as a means to collect debts for public bodies from East Jerusalem residents (ACRI, 2008). In the West Bank, these checkpoints are set up by the military. Some of them are merely physical obstacles and are not staffed. The UN recorded a total of 543 obstacles and checkpoints in the West Bank. Minus the 48 checkpoints under category 3 below, leaving 497 "flying checkpoints" at the end of 2015 (OCHA, 2016). By May 2017 "flying

checkpoints" were down to 160, leaving the privatized checkpoints a much larger role in regulating the movement of Palestinians in the West Bank (OCHA, 2017).

3. The terminals on the "seam-zone" in the OPT, built inside the OPT, adjacent to large colonies or to the Green Line. In the case of the Gaza Strip, the terminals are built just outside of the Gaza Strip, inside Israel. These terminals are new (they have been constructed since 2000), and are part of the Israeli new policy towards the OPT. Most of these checkpoints have been privatized, and therefore will be discussed more extensively below. They are referred to as "passages" by the Israeli MOD.

During the construction of the Separation Wall in the West Bank, over 30 new checkpoints were constructed, which the army called "last checkpoint before entering Israel." In truth, many of the checkpoints were not placed on the Green Line, but inside the occupied West Bank. However, they create a distinction between the temporary checkpoints (the second type) and the permanent "terminals" (the third type). Those new checkpoints represent a different strategy. The process in the checkpoint became more organized and centralized, with a greater emphasis on procedure and regulation, and a lower emphasis on the considerations of the soldiers or guards at the checkpoint itself. Soldiers and guards were no longer encouraged to use their own judgment in making decisions about whether individuals should be allowed through the checkpoints or not. Nevertheless, the training courses for checkpoint security guards were open only to graduates of Israeli military combat units (Ghantous, 2012:25). The checkpoints, nicknamed "terminals," are built to resemble border passages. In the past, the Israeli government was reluctant to create a semblance of border, because it could be perceived as a willingness of the Israeli government to withdraw from some of the OPT (Berda, 2012:77–8).

The tender for the operation of the checkpoints was published in 2005, and five companies were selected to operate the checkpoints: Modi'in Ezrakhi ("civil intelligence"), Sheleg Lavan ("white snow"), Mikud ("focus"), Shmira Ubitakhon ("guarding and security") and Ari Avtakha (Ari security). Due to capital concentration only two companies remained by 2014 and took over the operation of all the privatized checkpoints: Modi'in Ezrakhi and Sheleg Lavan (Havkin, 2014). In 2006 the Israeli government set up the Defense Ministry's Crossing Administration, and designated 48 checkpoints to be "civilianized"[13] – meaning that they will become terminals with the semblance of a border crossing.[14] In its budget proposal for 2013–14, the MOD published a list of 13 checkpoints which have already been privatized, and five additional passes which are yet to be privatized (Israeli Ministry of Finance, 2013a:72). This list does not include the checkpoints surrounding Jerusalem, nor adjacent checkpoints which have been merged into larger terminals. Because the security guards in the checkpoints dress like soldiers, carry similar weapons and operate alongside soldiers (Ghantous, 2012:31), it is not always apparent which checkpoints have been privatized.

5.5.2 Reasons for privatizing the checkpoints

In the 2013–14 budget proposal, the MOD mentioned two goals that the outsourcing of the checkpoints was intended to achieve: improving the security produced by the checkpoints and improving the services to the population by use of specially trained employees (a goal aimed at the Israeli population); and reducing friction between the soldiers with a civilian population (a goal aimed at the Palestinian population, Israeli Ministry of Finance, 2013a:71–2). However, five reasons may be identified which are reflected in the privatization policy, and partially acknowledged by Israeli officials.

The MOD's official main reason for privatizing the checkpoints was to save on costs (Rapoport, 2007). This argument is surprising. Cost-cutting through low wages and minimal employment benefits to private security guards is impossible, considering that regular troops that were staffing the checkpoints before the privatization were not paid a salary, and the cost of deploying regular troops during compulsory service was calculated by the military economists as a combination of alternative costs to their deployment elsewhere and through logistic costs which remain relevant for private security guards. Private security guards, in contrast, must be paid a full salary. The seeming contradiction can be explained only if the military economists have written in their recommendation that they expect the private companies to be significantly more efficient than the army itself in managing the resources allocated to the checkpoints. A second reason is the shortage of regular troops to staff the checkpoints. This reason was not acknowledged by the MOD. The drop in conscription (Section 3.4) is not discussed openly by the MOD. A third reason for the privatization is to address concerns of the MOD that activities in the checkpoint are harmful to the military and to Israel's public image. Violations of human rights and excessive cruelty in the checkpoints have been made public in the international media and made the occupation visible to the outside world. The MOD argued that private companies will be better-equipped and their employees better-trained in handling a civilian population (who are referred to as "customers"), in following regulations more strictly (and offering a "service"), and therefore in avoiding embarrassing incidents for the army[15] (Zwobener, 2005:3). A fourth reason is to consolidate the checkpoint policy by placing the MOD as a governance body, rather than the operator of the checkpoints. The unified policy is intended to prevent economic damage to the Israeli and the Gaza economies due to the unpredictable delays in shipments of goods and the passage of workers (Zwobener, 2005:7). The distancing of the MOD from running the checkpoints serves an additional purpose, which is not officially acknowledged, of allowing the ministry to disavow accountability to crimes committed in the checkpoints, because the security guards are not official representatives of the state (Ghantous, 2012:33).

Military officers in charge of regulating the privatized checkpoints referred to a "service consciousness" of the security guards in the checkpoint, a term taken directly from the business sector (Maoz, 2008), but which stands in contradiction with the fact that the actual customer of the private security companies is the Israeli MOD. In 2004, a Palestinian passing through the checkpoint in Beit Iba was forced by the soldiers at the checkpoint to play a violin he was carrying. This incident was covered extensively in the Israeli press, because it evoked memories of similar incidents in which German soldiers forced European Jews to play for them during the Second World War (Daniel Levy, 2008). This incident was quoted by Baruch Spiegel. He argued that regular troops are too young and inexperienced to understand the damage caused by violent and humiliating behavior in the checkpoints, and that private security guards will be properly trained to preserve the image of the checkpoints by being "considerate" to the needs of the Palestinian population.[16] Despite these claims, however, lawyer Neta Patrick found that private security guards do not receive instructions over regulations for opening fire as normal soldiers do, and could therefore be more dangerous to Palestinian lives than regular soldiers (Johnston, 2009). Guards also do not receive instructions in international humanitarian law (Ghantous, 2012:36).

5.5.3 Consequences of the privatization of the checkpoints

The tension between the core and the periphery in the privatization of security reaches a peak with the privatization of the checkpoints. On the one hand, the checkpoints are considered an undesirable mission for soldiers and one which soldiers are not properly trained for, but, on the other hand, the checkpoints are the key element in Israel's military policy in the OPT. Betzalel Tyber, the first head of the Crossing Administration from the MOD, explained to Knesset members that the checkpoints will employ private guards alongside state employees, because certain functions of the checkpoints must not be given over to private companies (Knesset Committee for Domestic and Environmental Affairs, 2005). The MOD, however, noted in the budget proposal for 2013–14 that "Taking the soldiers out of the various checkpoints is in line with the recommendations of the Brodet Committee, that the IDF will only focus on its core themes and not in areas which are not its responsibility or function," thereby indicating that the MOD considers the checkpoints to be a non-core theme of military operations (Brodet, 2007:37; Ministry of Finance, 2013a). This MOD text runs in direct contradiction to a text published by the State Comptroller of Israel in 2010:

> The civilianizing of the passages between Israel and Judea and Samaria [the West Bank] is a national project, which entails significant political, security and economic implications, and which has an essential influence on the way of life and on the security of the residents of Israel, including the residents of East Jerusalem, and of the Palestinian population. (State Comptroller, 2010:13)

The State Comptroller wholly embraces the logic of privatization for the checkpoints, but considers the checkpoints to be an essential function of the state, at the very core of its activity. This exposes the inherent contradiction which privatization of elements of the occupation pose to the core/periphery approach of the Israeli authorities.

The unpredictability and arbitrariness of the occupation's policies are intentional and central elements of Israel's policy in the OPT, designed to increase Israel's control through an old colonial tradition of keeping the authority's policies opaque and mysterious (Berda 2012:160–3). The permanent checkpoints, therefore, are a weak point in Israel's strategy of control because their location and their procedures are steady and predictable.

While "flying checkpoints" could be added as punishment or removed as a gesture of goodwill during negotiations, the permanent checkpoints are less flexible. The "flying checkpoints," therefore, remain under the direct control of the government and serve as a tool for instantaneous implementation of policy (ibid.:71–7), while the permanent checkpoints have been privatized (Maoz, 2008). The service centers in which Palestinians can apply for permits have been transferred to the responsibility of the PA, a different form of outsourcing (Berda, 2012:48–9). The distinction between what is privatized and what remains under direct governmental management reflects a distinction of importance in the eyes of the Israeli government. The distinction follows the structure that elements closer to the decision-making remain public, while elements of implementation of the decisions are privatized.

Very little published data exists to allow a comparison between privately operated and military-operated checkpoints in terms of ease of passage, human-rights violations and the levels of security. What can already be observed in the private checkpoints, however, is the high level of automation and reliance on technology (Section 3.6). The privatized checkpoints contain complex systems designed to reduce to a minimum the interaction between the passengers through the checkpoint and the staff. Palestinians crossing the checkpoints receive instructions from speakers in the walls (from guards they cannot see), are separated from each other by metal turnstiles, and are told to place their belongings in scanning machines, so that the belongings are inspected outside of their line of sight (Weizman, 2007:150–2). By using magnetic cards containing their biometric information, the decision whether a person has permission to pass or not is taken further away, removed from the checkpoint itself. The automated and impersonal treatment of people who attempt to cross the checkpoints has reduced the opportunities for soldiers or security guards to torment and humiliate Palestinians, but also prevents Palestinians from negotiating and asking to be let through on special occasions and in cases which do not fall into the pre-determined regulations (Havkin, 2014:3). The journalist Meron Rapoport found that in order to reduce the costs of operating the checkpoints, companies keep the people in small rooms in conditions of incarceration, with minimal supervision to prevent suffocation (Rapoport, 2007).

The role of the checkpoint is reduced to enforcing the decision taken by a distant bureaucrat, to ensure that the person's biometric characteristics match their biometric card, and to ensure that they are not carrying forbidden items on their bodies. The companies operating the checkpoints attempt to automate these three functions as much as possible, so that the checkpoint can be operated with a minimal staff (and therefore at minimal cost) and with minimum chance for human error (State Comptroller, 2010:14, 30). The technological "modernization" of the checkpoints also contributes to the image promoted by the Israeli government that it attempts to facilitate the passage through the checkpoints and invest in the more humane treatment of Palestinians (Zureik, 2011:31).

This is in contrast with the previous decentralized mode of control which reigned in the Israeli checkpoints up to their privatization, allowing local officers a great deal of leeway. For example, the decision to allow Palestinians to keep trading with Jordan after 1967 (although Israel only established diplomatic relations with Jordan officially in 1994) was taken by a local sergeant guarding the border between the West Bank and Jordan (Segev, 2005:470). Soldiers at the checkpoints or on patrol could also make up their own punishments for Palestinians (Na'aman, 2012). In the case of the privatized checkpoints, privatization served a function of centralization of the occupation, because the decision-making power has been more clearly contained within the authorities with access to a single computer program, "Rolling Stone" (Berda, 2012:76). The Israeli MOD, the Israeli Ministry of Trade, Industry and Labor, the ISA and the police have loosened their direct control over the operation of the checkpoints, but gained the power to monopolize the decision about which Palestinian is denied the right to pass through the checkpoints. Before the privatization of the checkpoints, an officer or a soldier could decide on the spot to disregard the rules and allow a Palestinian to pass because of a "humanitarian consideration" or to deny entry based on their own judgment.

Among the consequences of the privatization of the checkpoints, the most significant one for the argument here is the resistance it generated. Policies regarding the operation of the checkpoints are taken independently by nine different organizations: the Israeli military, the Defense Ministry's Crossing Administration, the Border Police, the police, the National Security Council (affiliated with the Office of the Prime Minister), the Central Command of the army, the Ministry for

Public Security, Coordinator of Government Activities in the Territories (COGAT) and the private companies who won the tender. The multiple foci of decision-making create ambiguity regarding the identity of who bears responsibility for the checkpoint's operations and whom the staffs of the checkpoints are expected to obey (Levinson, 2010). Although the centralization of authority over the checkpoints has been one of the reasons for the privatization, none of the nine organizations mentioned above are willing to relinquish their influence over the checkpoints, because they continue to be of key importance to formulating and enforcing policies on the OPT.

5.6 THE AZARIA TRIAL AND KILLING BY DEFAULT

The series of violent outbreaks which started in October 2015 was nicknamed the "Individuals *Intifada*" by the Israeli media, framing the violence as uncoordinated and unprovoked, and ignoring the cause of the anger and frustration: the occupation and the collapse of the peace process (Pfeffer, 2016; Swift, 2016). Security technology and training failed to suppress the uprising. The panopticon-like surveillance network in the Old City of Jerusalem (Shadmi, 2012:50, 76–7) has proven of little use, as the Old City became one of the areas considered the most insecure, and largely abandoned by Jewish-Israeli shoppers (Rosenberg, 2016).

The Israeli government attempted to mobilize the public to use individualized violence to answer for these individual attacks. In October 2015, the Mayor of Jerusalem Nir Barkat as well as Minister of Defense Moshe Ya'alon called the general public to arm themselves, and carry guns as a "force multiplier" to help the security institutions in quelling the Palestinian uprising (Eli, 2015; Galatz, 2015). Barkat gave a personal example by patrolling the Palestinian neighborhood of Beit Hanina while holding a gun (Hasson, 2015). He thereby identified the Palestinians of East Jerusalem (his own constituents) as dangerous enemies, and at the same time suggested that private civilians can and should arm themselves and act as self-appointed enforcers. Barkat proudly announced that (Jewish) Jerusalemites do not wait for the police to protect them, but rather charge terrorists on their own (Binyamin, 2016).

The Ministry of Public Security reversed its decision to regulate the weapons of security guards outside of working hours in order to encourage security guards employed by private companies to also carry guns when not on duty, and relaxed requirements for individual firearm permits (Kobowich, 2015; Efraim et al., 2016). Meanwhile, senior Israeli politicians including ministers and the chief Mizrahi rabbi have uttered a series of statements calling on the security forces, which may or may not include armed civilians, to make sure that Arab terrorists will not survive after being stopped, that they will be killed rather than detained (Human Rights Watch, 2017).

These statements create a tension with security operations, because they contradict Israeli law. Rather than being interpreted in the light of the "nation in uniform" militaristic nature of Israel in its early years, the prospects of civilians carrying firearms in public spaces and being encouraged to use them at their own discretion take on a different meaning in a highly individualistic neoliberal society: one of decentralized security production (Ha'aretz, 2015). Specifically, statements in the passive tense that "terrorists should not be allowed to live" encourage the privatization by default of the killings. This tension has reached a boiling point with the trial of Elor Azaria.

Case Box 10:	Killing by Default
Type:	Privatization by default
Key interests:	The Israeli government
Opposition:	The established Israeli security elite
Success:	No
Period:	2015–17
Similar cases:	The Civil Guard, vigilance education

On March 24, 2016, an Israeli soldier in Hebron by the name of Elor Azaria shot and killed Abdel Fattah al-Sharif, a Palestinian who was previously shot by Israeli soldiers and was lying injured on the ground (Mackey, 2016). The event was captured on camera by a human-rights activist from the B'tselem organization, and the video was made public. The fact that charges were pressed against Azaria caused immediate uproar in Israel, and provoked a large wave of support for the Israeli soldier, including by the prime minister himself (Ravid, 2016), and a demonstration calling for his release (Hartman, 2016). Azaria was eventually convicted of "manslaughter" and "inappropriate behaviour" (Zitun, 2016), and sentenced to 18 months in prison after his appeal failed.

While Azaria was charged under the military court system, a similar case in which private security guards opened fire and killed two

Palestinian siblings at the Kalandia checkpoint causes difficulties for the Israeli legal system. This is because private security guards are not protected under the military court system and could therefore be tried in a criminal court, a reality which was called a "legal vacuum" by the OHCHR Working Group on the Use of Mercenaries (Gómez del Prado, 2010; Brown, 2016).

The controversy sparked by the Azaria trial was not focused on the execution of Abdel Fattah al-Sharif, but on the question of whether a soldier may act in violation of procedure due to his own judgment. The argument made in favor of Azaria was that individual soldiers, and especially low-ranking ones, should be supported by the public and by the government in acting according to their own judgment, a call to decentralize the military hierarchy. It was pointed out that Azaria is a Mizrahi Jew, and that higher-class soldiers (mostly Ashkenazi) are almost never held accountable for killing Palestinians. It was also pointed out that Azaria was caught on camera, while hundreds of Israeli soldiers and police killed Palestinians off-camera and no charges were pressed against them. The argument calling for his arrest and trial was that the military should operate in a hierarchical fashion, and that individual freedom of low-ranking soldiers can lead to a loss of control over the military.

This argument was made by Minister of Defense Ya'alon, former chief of staff of the army and a member of Israel's security elite, who warned against the military becoming "beastly" (Kam, 2016), and also indirectly by the deputy chief of staff of the Israeli military General Yair Golan, who on the eve of the Holocauast Remembrance Day gave a speech in which he warned of the military becoming "beastly" (thus alluding to the previous comment by Ya'alon), and expressed concern that the Israeli society might be displaying similar signs to those observed in Europe in the 1930s and 1940s (Jpost.com Staff, 2016). Golan's speech split the government in a similar way to that of the Azaria case. While Ya'alon supported Golan and the speech, other ministers, including Prime Minister Netanyahu, criticized him fiercely, and forced him to apologize (Beaumont, 2016). In the aftermath of this scandal, Netanyahu forced Ya'alon to resign from the MOD and appointed Avigdor Lieberman in his stead (Glanz & Pazner Garshowitz, 2016). While Lieberman is considered to be further to the right than Ya'alon, he is also much less connected to the Israeli security elite, and his aggressive populism masks the fact that his appointment is a blow to the Israeli military brass (Harel, 2016; Kershner, 2016).

Itamar Mann pointed out that beyond the Mizrahi-Ashkenazi divide, and beyond the issue of Azaria being caught on camera for doing what many other Israeli soldiers have done with impunity, the greater issue at the heart of the trial is that it exposes the confusion in the Israeli society about the legitimacy over the application of violence. In light of statements by senior Israeli officials condoning and encouraging violence against Palestinians by civilians and by security personnel acting outside of their official instructions and outside of the law, Azaria's murder of Fattah al-Sharif was not perceived as a murder, but as part of a norm. When he was brought to trial, the outrage from right-wing Israeli activists was that the security elite attempted to re-establish legal limitations on violence after those limitations were lifted by the same security elite (Mann, 2017).

5.7 CONCLUSION

Chapter 4 discussed the empirical evidence of privatization of security in Israel, but it is the four cases presented in this chapter – the SLA, the PA, the private security companies in the public space and the privatization of the checkpoints – which strike at the heart of the main policy of the Israeli military and security institutions: military occupation. The policy of outsourcing has been formulated within a discourse which denies the centrality of the occupation, by developing the core vs. periphery discourse and by referring to the tasks required to maintain a military occupation as peripheral. Nevertheless, the resistance to the outsourcing of the occupation activity from within Israeli institutions and from the occupied populations indicates that the occupation is anything but peripheral. Frustrated with their inability to crush this resistance, members of Israel's security elites have started to move in large numbers from state security organizations into private security companies. Although those companies did not have better success rates at repressing resistance, the monetary rewards for the members of the security elites have increased and motivated additional outsourcing. Even though the initial results of outsourcing of security, through the SLA, have been a failure (from the Israeli point of view), the scale of the subsequent acts of outsourcing, in terms of human resources, have been even larger.

The four cases presented in this chapter are cases of privatization of military and police units, and therefore occupy the top position of the institutional privatization of security typology presented in Section 2.8.

They are also larger in terms of human resources allocations than all the privatization cases presented before. Yet these cases differ from the cases presented in Chapter 4 not only in scale and institutional importance but also in their justification. While most of the cases presented in Chapter 4 were motivated according to official statements by cost-cutting (and an underlying purpose of redistribution of public resources towards the private sector), the outsourcing of security to the SLA, to the PA and to private security companies is driven more by the motivation to release the Israeli government from direct responsibility to violent acts committed in the name of security. In these cases, outsourcing created an intermediary agent to absorb political and legal consequences for the benefit of the government, even if relief from accountability for the government has not always been achieved.

It is still premature to estimate the long-term effects of privatization of security in relation to the occupation. Only the SLA was an outsourcing whose end-result can be observed. There are conflicting opinions about whether the PA will end in a similar fashion, or whether it will eventually succeed in achieving independence and sovereignty. The fate of the PA will also have long-reaching implications on the function of the private security companies in public spaces and in the checkpoints. In this chapter I argue, however, that outsourcing of core functions of the Israeli security institutions has been promoted despite the core vs. periphery demarcation due to the crisis of the Israeli security elites which was brought about by military occupation.

The individualization of violence goes hand in hand with the privatization of violence, and weakens the ability of the Israeli security elites to distinguish themselves from the angry mob. The security elite then seeks to distinguish itself from the application of amateurish violence by defining itself as a group of "security experts" (Gordon, 2009:3). The crisis of the security elite unfolds due to the fact that the experience which establishes the elite's expertise is the application of violence against Palestinians, and yet this experience is not exclusive to the security elite but gradually becomes available to untrained civilians, such as Shai Dromi (Section 4.3.1), to Mizrahi low-ranking soldiers such as Elor Azaria, and even to civilians (with no more than a very basic military experience) elevated to positions of authority over the military such as Avigdor Lieberman.

6
Global Dimensions of Security Privatization in Israel

What Israel has been exporting is the logic of the oppressor, the way of seeing the world that is tied to successful domination. What is exported is not just technology, armaments, and experience, not just expertise, but a certain frame of mind, a feeling that the Third World can be controlled and dominated, that radical movements in the Third World can be stopped, that modern crusaders still have a future. (Beit-Hallahmi, 1987: 248)

The previous three chapters focused on the history of privatization of security in Israel, and now in this chapter I want to move on to the international dimension of this privatization. An international comparison will help position Israel in the context of the global trend towards privatization of security. The developments in Israel's arms export and the shift to homeland security follow the story of Israel's security elite in becoming increasingly globalized. Israeli security policies have become tethered to US security policies by the military aid which the US provides to Israel. This chapter will introduce two final case studies, demonstrating the role of international security companies in Israeli decisions to privatize security.

Privatization through sale and by default has given rise to the Israeli private arms manufacturing sector, which warrants a discussion of the arms trade. Israeli companies, however, specialize in security products and services which do not necessarily fall into the category of weapons. This specialization derives from the needs of Israeli PMSCs to control a resisting civilian population, rather than marching armies. Therefore, adopting broader global perspective in which Israel's industry is seen as a part of a greater whole necessarily shifts the focus of the discussion more in the direction of the arms trade. No other country in the world specializes in homeland security products, such as surveillance equipment and riot gear, more than Israel. In comparison, the US,

European and Russian military and security sector remains dominated by conventional arms[1] (Gordon, 2009:24, 31–5, 42).

Privatization, not just in the field of security, has been increasingly embraced as a policy worldwide during the 1980s and 1990s (Megginson & Netter, 2001:2–8). Privatization of state-owned enterprises has been recommended by economists from the Chicago School (Harvey, 2005:8, 16–17), by privately owned media, by politicians connected in the private sector and by economists working for the Bretton Woods organizations, the World Bank, International Monetary Fund and World Trade Organization (Stiglitz, 2002:54). In Western countries, privatization was pushed in order to provide investment and profit opportunities for capital owners and in order to weaken the bargaining power of labor unions (Harvey, 2005:60–1). In developing countries, privatization of state-owned enterprises has been even more intensive (Megginson & Netter, 2001:8), as it was frequently demanded as a prerequisite for receiving much-needed loans from the IMF (Stiglitz, 2002:54). In the former Soviet bloc countries, privatization was seen as part of the process of dismantling communism and adopting a market economy (ibid.:157–9). The US used its influence to promote privatization of state assets and services, especially in countries which were major aid recipients such as Egypt (Mitchell, 2002:227–9).

Israel does not fit neatly into any of the first three groups of countries, but fits strongly with the fourth, as no other country receives more US aid than Israel (Section 6.2 below). Israel's voluntarily embraced "Stabilization Plan" of 1985 resembled the IMF-imposed "Structural Adjustment Programs" in countries which applied for loans. The Israeli "Stabilization Plan" included massive budget cuts, commitment to a low deficit, disallowing printing money, ensuring the independence of the Central Bank of Israel, a wage freeze in the public sector, etc. The plan therefore symbolized the adoption of the Washington Consensus by the Israeli government (Brodet, 2005:10). The acceleration of privatization was not merely an economic phenomenon, but a result of an economic ideology which has achieved hegemony and affected decision-makers around the world, and also in Israel. Simha Ehrlich, Israel's Minister of Finance during 1977–79, boasted that he has read all of Milton Friedman's works and spoke with him on the phone, claiming that Friedman is his "economic consultant" (Bichler & Nitzan, 2001:280). Like many other Israeli decision-makers, Ehrlich adopted the Chicago School's ideology as a source for legitimacy. Privatization as a policy has been extensively adopted by the Israeli government after 1985, especially in the 1990s (Hasson, 2006:10). Privatization, however, is a global phenomenon. Its adoption in Israel in the 1990s was not unique, but must be understood within the global neoliberal shift of the four decades since the 1970s.

6.1 THE PRIVATIZATION CONSENSUS REACHES THE SECURITY INDUSTRY

The magazine *Defense News* reported on the pressure to privatize the French state-owned arms company Nexter. The article quoted Christian Mons, representing the Conseil des Industries de Défense Françaises (Board of French Defense Industries, a trade association) that "As long as Nexter remains a 100 percent state-owned company, without being privatized, this evolution will continue to be slow, even weak." Mons also lamented that no cooperation is possible with German weapon companies which are privately owned (referring mainly to Rheinmetall and Krauss-Maffei). He argued that private companies refuse to cooperate with state-owned companies, because their subjection to political whim makes them unreliable. Mons and the *Defense News* magazine warned the French government to follow the trend of privatization or have the company lose value (Tran, 2012). If privately owned companies avoid cooperation with state-owned companies, while at the same time state-owned companies do not avoid cooperating with private companies, this creates a dynamic in which the pressure to privatize increases with each consecutive privatization, as state-owned companies become increasingly isolated.

The manufacture of weapons is not normally considered a core function of state security, and some weapon production companies were founded as privately owned companies in the US from the nineteenth century, and even earlier in Europe. US military operations, however, were conducted mainly by public employees. Prisons were also state-operated, until the first private prison was established in the US by the Corrections Corporation of America on January 1, 1984 (Wade, 2013). Privatization of security in the US gained momentum in the 1990s (Markusen, 2003:471). In 1991, Defense Secretary Richard Cheney commissioned the company Brown & Root Services to produce a study on the ways in which private military companies could provide support for US soldiers in combat zones. Brown & Root Services, a subsidiary of Halliburton, was paid nearly $9 million to produce the study. Thus, the study which informed US policy formulation regarding the role of the private sector in military operations was itself written by a private company. It is not surprising that its recommendations were favorable for increased privatization. Cheney later became CEO of Halliburton, and the company was awarded at least $2.5 billion in contracts with the US army even before the company was hired to support the US invasion of Iraq when Cheney was the vice president of the US (Yeoman, 2003). This development was one of the major turning points in privatization of security in the US.

Private security companies have grown through their contracts with governments, and especially with the US government. Approximately 80 percent of all registered PMSCs are registered in the US and in the UK (Gómez del Prado, 2009:438). The growth of homeland security was also accompanied by large-scale privatization of the military regular forces. The fall of the Soviet Union and the subsequent fall of Apartheid in South Africa created an influx of unemployed former soldiers who were ready to offer their services to these PMSCs (Singer, 2003:12, 53; Alexandra, 2008:89–91).

6.2 US MILITARY AID TO ISRAEL

US aid to Israel is a key factor in the process of privatization of Israel's military industry. The US has provided military aid to Israel (Foreign Military Financing, or FMF) since 1949, but the amounts were rather small until 1973 (approximately $120 million per year). During the 1973 War, the US increased FMF to Israel by an order of magnitude. The increased aid flows reached an average of $3 billion annually between 1973 and 2010 (Sharp, 2010). US aid had a profound effect on Israel's policies, encouraging Israeli institutions to imitate the US model of purely private ownership of arms production and high levels of privatization of the military and security (Singer, 2003:14) have had a dramatic effect on Israel's policies, through aid.

6.2.1 History of the US military aid to Israel

In its early years, aid was divided approximately into $1.2 billion in annual civilian aid (40 percent) and $1.8 billion in annual military aid (60 percent). Starting from 1996, civilian aid has declined while military aid has increased; by 2006 civilian aid remained at only 9.5 percent of

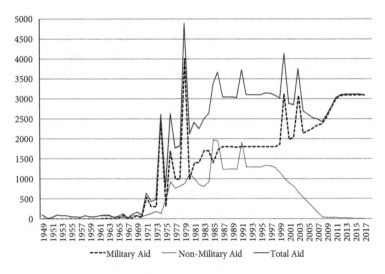

Graph 6.1   US Aid to Israel (US$ millions, current prices)

Source: Sharp (2010, 2013a, 2013b, 2014, 2015, 2016).

the total (Dagoni, 2005a, 2005b). Graph 6.1 is based on data from the US Congress. It shows a spike in aid after the wars of 1973, 1982 and after the beginning of the second Intifada in 2000, but also a spike after the peace treaty with Egypt in 1978. Egypt became a major recipient of US aid after the peace treaty, and the increased aid to Israel ensured Israel's regional military superiority even in the face of a US-supported Egyptian army (Sharp, 2013a:24). Most interestingly, the graph shows that US aid was originally distributed between military and non-military aid. Non-military aid included economic grants, loan benefits, funding to resettle Jewish refugees in Israel and funding through the American School and Hospital Association (ASHA), but since 1997 it has gradually diminished, while military aid has increased. By 2009, almost the entire US aid to Israel was military (Sharp, 2013b).

Crucially important is also the fact that the graph is given in current prices, so that the erosion of the purchasing power of the dollar is not visible in Graph 6.1. In real terms, the US aid to Israel has eroded steadily over the years, as Graph 6.2 clearly shows. By using the CPI (Consumer Price Index) provided by the US CPI agency (Bureau of Labor Statistics, 2016), one learns that the real US aid to Israel reached a peak in 1979, and stabilized in 2010 around an amount which is about a fifth of that peak. Graph 6.2 shows the differential decline in US military aid to Israel resulting from inflation, parallel to a global decline in the differential accumulation of the arms corporations (Nitzan & Bichler, 2009:390–1).

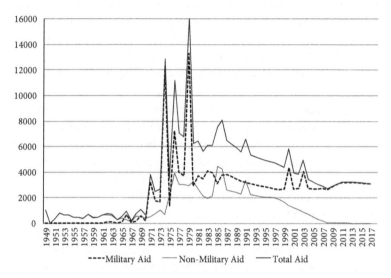

Graph 6.2   US Aid to Israel (US$ millions, 2017 prices)

6.2.2 Between self-sufficiency and specialization

Sharon Sadeh describes two schools of thought that were prominent in the Israeli military elite in the 1950s and 1960s, which I call the "self-sufficiency" and the "specialization" schools. The prominent figures in the first school were the director-general of the MOD at the time, Shimon Peres, and the chief of staff of the MOD, Zvi Tzur. The two argued that Israel must be self-reliant in military equipment, and produce as much of what the Israeli military needs locally, even combat platforms (tanks, airplanes, etc.). The second school, headed by General Yitzhak Rabin, recommended relying on imports and focusing the military industry in areas in which Israel enjoys a relative advantage.

After the 1967 War, and especially following France's reluctance to continue the arms trade with Israel as a sanction against the occupation, the Israeli government was concerned with the possibility that Israel would be subject to an arms embargo (Brigadier-General "Yud," 1995:27; Swirski, 2008). The territory occupied in the war, or at least some of it, was considered to be of strategic value (Newman, 1989:219), but an arms embargo would potentially have eroded Israel's technological advantage and weakened Israel's military. There was doubt whether the Israeli domestic arms industry would be sufficient to equip the Israeli military with sufficient arms for its needs, and the "self-sufficiency" school called for expanding the repertoire of Israel's arms production in order to ensure that any shortage could be relieved locally to prepare for a possible military embargo (Sadeh, 2001:64–77; Gordon, 2011:153–70).

US aid from the 1970s clearly decided the debate in favor of the specialization school, while the growing income from military exports in the 1980s allowed Israel to keep expanding its investment, research and development in weapon systems which it did not import (Sadeh, 2001:64–77). The US decision to provide Israel with military aid had altered the Israeli army and the military industry. Aid affected not only the military might of Israel and the diplomatic relations between Israel and the US, but also introduced a business-like culture into the arms industry (Lifshitz, 2000:372). The US offered a model of a fully private military industry, while also pursuing rapid outsourcing of security to PMSCs in the first decade of the 2000s (Markusen, 2003:480, 490–2). As a result of the aid, Israeli companies had to abandon the self-sufficiency projects and seek to integrate into cooperative and complementary projects with the US arms industry, and in the process sought to imitate the US private arms industry.

The aid to Israel was not merely a statement of support of Israeli policy by the US but also a testimony to the failure of the Israeli military industry to address the needs of the army, according to the plans of the self-sufficiency school. Israeli policymakers changed their attitude towards the military industry after they witnessed the dependence of Israel's armed forces on the US in a time of emergency. Rather than a self-relying industry, the Israeli policymakers have increasingly considered the military industry to be one tool out of several to achieve their strategic goals, instead of an indispensable strategic asset to provide the government with solutions for security problems. Therefore, privatizing military industry companies was perceived as conceding a less vital element of government sovereignty (Seidman, 2010:12).

The nature of the aid affected the process of privatization. The US government did not provide Israel with money, but with vouchers which the Israeli government could redeem by making purchases from US military producers. Thus, the aid was in fact a subsidy for promoting arms produced in the US. The Israeli government is required to spend the military aid money in the US (Toren, 2002:103–4). This is similar to the nature of US military and civilian aid to other countries, such as to Egypt (Mitchell, 2002:236). This policy has led to a rapid process of equipping the Israeli military with US-made weapons, ammunition, vehicles and other equipment. Even uniforms and combat rations, which could have been produced in Israel, were bought from the US to keep the aid from going to waste (Sadeh, 2001:64–77).

US armaments bought through the military aid system were sometimes then sold by the Israeli government to other clients (Feinstein, 2011:378–86). Israeli military companies were given an incentive to enter into joint research and development projects with US companies, in order to obtain a share of the aid money spent by the Israeli government. The cooperation between Israeli and US companies has altered the Israeli companies' priorities, encouraging these companies to develop products usable and needed by the US military. The companies sought to incorporate US-owned technologies into their products, even at the cost of seeking permission from the US government to sell the equipment to third-party countries (Bukhbut, 2009).

When cooperation of the Israeli arms companies was not forthcoming, the aid became a coercion mechanism. In certain cases (such as the development of advanced medium-range air-to-air missiles or AMRAAM), the US offered systems with similar capabilities to those developed by Israeli companies as part of the aid package. By doing so, the US encouraged the Israeli MOD to prefer free US-made systems over costly Israeli-made systems, causing the Israeli companies to lose their most important customer and putting pressure on them to discontinue production, thereby reducing the competition for the US systems worldwide (Sadeh, 2001:64–77). David Boas, a business consultant who headed several public committees, argued that the US aid pushed the Israeli MOD to abandon local suppliers in favor of US suppliers, and therefore encouraged local suppliers to sell their technologies abroad and to strengthen their ties with parallel companies abroad (Boas, 2002:106–7).

The larger Israeli weapon companies have also established subsidiaries in the US, giving these companies advantages in applying for tenders in the US, and even enabling the companies to sell their products to the Israeli government with the aid money through US-registered subsidiaries (Coren, 2009). An example of this is Orbit Technologies, an Israeli company established in 1950 that produces communication devices. It opened its first office and established two subsidiaries in the US in 1988, winning a tender in 2013 to provide a tracking and telemetry system to the Israeli MOD for NIS 3.5 million, which were taken from the US FMF to Israel (Orbit Systems, 2013; Reich, 2013a). That year US arms companies also began establishing subsidiaries in Israel (Fiske, 2013).

The Brodet Committee recommended using the US DOD as a model for budgeting security in Israel. US aid to Israel has indirectly contributed to privatization policies in Israel not only in the field of security but also in academia and industry (Brodet, 2007:175–6, 187–8). Furthermore, cooperation between companies prospers in an environment of close military and security relations between the US and Israel, in which senior US military decision-makers consider Israel to be a laboratory in which new tactics and military innovations are implemented. Those tactics and innovations are closely tied to the technologies and products produced by the arms companies and tested in the field for the benefit of both the Israeli and US governments (Kotler, 2008; Khalili, 2010:414–19; Graham, 2011:133–49).

The strategy adopted by the Israeli military industry, and supported by the government (Boas, 2002:106–7), was to promote cooperation between the Israeli and US weapon companies. Israeli arms companies commenced a process of specialization in complementary goods[2] to US military equipment. Israeli companies have reduced their focus on producing systems which were already exported by US companies, and instead increased their focus on electronic systems which can be integrated into equipment produced in the US, such as navigation systems, targeting systems, optical systems, training equipment and electronic interface systems (Sadeh, 2001:64–77). Elbit Systems, for example, produces helmets which include a heads-up display (HUD) for fighter pilots for the F-15 plane produced by McDonnel Douglas and for the F-16 plane produced by General Dynamics, both US-based companies (Elbit Systems, 2013).

This transition in the Israeli military industry began after the 1967 War, but was not a smooth process. Rather, it was fraught with friction. After the industrial boom of the 1970s, the image of Israeli state-owned military companies started deteriorating in the 1980s. The companies obtained an image of a failing, inefficient industry. The portrayal of an industry as unprofitable and inefficient lays the blame on government management and prepares the ground for privatization, even when an economic analysis of the relevant companies did not find these companies to be inefficient or unprofitable (Katz, 1997:186). In the case of government companies, however, such economic analysis is particularly difficult to conduct, especially when the deals conducted by these companies are confidential. Therefore, the image of inefficiency was generated through leaks to the press by government officials, or even by open statements such as those made by Yaron Ya'akobs, CEO of the Israeli Government Companies Authority:

> The disadvantages [for public ownership over security companies] are many. First, government companies are subjected as a rule to a long list of regulatory bodies, laws and regulations, which restrict a flexible and efficient business management. Second, government companies find it difficult to hold on to quality personnel, because of restrictions on wages, especially in light of the fact that the civilian market offers tempting conditions. ... Third, there are bureaucratic and legal limitations. Each structural change requires a long bureaucratic and legislative process, which demands several stages until the offer for sale, purchase or merger might become irrelevant (tenders, government authorisations, approvals from Knesset committees and more). One must remember that government companies, and in our case the security industries, have three fathers: the regulator (the Ministry of Defense and the Ministry of Finance), the owner (the government) and the customer (the government, the Ministry of Defense). The conflict of interests is structured into this situation. Therefore, the conclusion is that the state should not hold these companies. (Ya'akobs, 2002:121, my translation)

The aid created a dilemma for the Israeli government: it is attracted to the benefits of aid but concerned about its effect on the local arms industry. This dilemma brought about a conceptual change in the way that the Israeli government treated the Israeli arms industry. Lifshitz argued that the economic advantages offered by the military industry were considered to be secondary in the eyes of the Israeli government in the first years of the state (Lifshitz, 2000:72, 470–3), but these industries have become a significant sector in the Israeli economy after the 1967 War (Halperin, 1987, 1988:3–6; Swirski, 2008). The competition with US producers threatened an important source of income for the Israeli government and a source of employment for many Israeli workers. Yossi Ackerman, as CEO of Elbit Systems, argued that in 2000 the Israeli arms industry employed 1 percent of the Israeli workforce, compared with 0.79 percent for Germany, 0.45 percent for France and 0.42 percent for the US (Ackerman, 2002:127–8). In 2012, Minister of Defense Ehud Barak argued that it provided direct and indirect employment to 150,000 households in Israel, which means that 4.6 percent of Israeli employees relied on the arms industry, a third of the Israeli workforce in the industrial sector (Feldman, 2013; ICBS, 2013). The economic significance of the arms industry could no longer be considered secondary.

In 2016, President Obama signed a ten-year "Memorandum of Understanding" (MOU) with the Israeli government for the years 2019–28. The agreement was presented as a boon, an increase of military aid to Israel to compensate for the US deal with Iran to curb Iran's nuclear program, a deal to which Israeli Prime Minister Netanyahu strongly objected. However, the content of the deal was a further erosion of the real value of the aid. The MOU creates the illusion of a sharp increase in funding by including aid to Israel's missile program into the total amount, whereas previously the missile program aid was counted separately. More importantly, it prohibits the Israeli government from seeking ad hoc grants during the duration of the memorandum. Most importantly, the memorandum phases out the "off-shore procurement" privilege that Israel enjoyed and which allowed it to divert some of the aid money to finance its own local arms industry, a privilege which no other recipient of US aid enjoyed. Despite Israeli misgivings, the Obama administration clarified that the MOU is its "final offer" (Sharp, 2016:8–13). By signing it, the Israeli government accepted the long-term loss of a major source of income for the Israeli security elite. On the other hand, in light of the attempts to cut military aid by President Trump, the MOU has the unexpected effect of safeguarding a minimum of aid to Israel amid uncertain aid to its neighbors.

6.2.3 The Lavi project: from self-sufficiency to specialization

The "Lavi" project is the paradigmatic example of the forces which operated on the Israeli arms industry to shift its focus from competitive goods to complementary goods. During the 1980s, the Israel Aerospace Industries, which was called Israel Aircraft Industries at the time, developed a project of unprecedented size to produce an Israeli-made fighter plane. Despite the close dependency which had already been established on the US military industry, the project was in direct competition with the US fighter-plane industry. After many years of research and development and a massive investment of funds, the project was scrapped. Thousands of workers were laid off, and Israel Aerospace Industries (IAI) suffered a loss of prestige (Sadeh, 2001:64–77; Katz, 2002:126). Opinions vary regarding the reasons for the cancellation of the project. Criticism was raised by the design crew of IAI regarding the design of the aircraft. The Israeli government voted to cancel the project because of a concern over its funding, and because of US pressure to discontinue a project that could compete with US-manufactured aircraft.

In the numerous debates in the Israeli government regarding the Lavi project, the option of buying a US-manufactured fighter plane has been consistently presented as the cheaper option. The US DOD delayed the transfer of licensing for US technologies necessary for developing the Lavi plane, until pressure from Israeli Minister of Defense Moshe Arens eventually convinced the DOD to grant the licenses and the US Congress allowed Israel to use US aid funds for Lavi-related expenditures. The DOD commissioned a report by Dov Zakheim in 1986 which claimed that the Lavi is expected to cost 40 percent more than the Israeli estimates. The report was rejected by the Israeli government. The US government had also insisted that should Israel later wish to sell Lavi planes to third-party countries, the US could influence and possibly cancel export deals (State Comptroller, 1987; Brigadier-General "Yud," 1995:31–2, 34; Haimowitz, 2012).

The government decision to cancel the Lavi project was narrowly reached when Shimon Peres from the "self-sufficiency" school was convinced to withdraw support to the project, and joined the "specialization" school of Yitzhak Rabin (Friedman, 1987; Peleg, 2013). The uproar following the cancellation of the project and the waste of public funds included a media narrative describing the project as a failure of public policy (Toren, 2002:103–4; Peleg, 2013). It supported the argument of neoliberal economists that the government is incapable of running efficient projects, thereby making the privatization discourse more legitimate in the Israeli political sphere (Lifshitz, 2000:16, 394–400). The new status quo established after the scrapping of the Lavi project was that the US maintains its monopoly over the development and production of combat platforms (that is, tanks, planes, ships, etc.) while Israeli companies develop accessories which can be combined with US-made platforms (Sadeh, 2001:64–77; Katz, 2002:125–6; UPI, 2013c).

6.2.4 Israeli imitation of US policies

Israel's imitation of the US privatization of security policy fits into Sandra Destradi's theory of regional powers. Israel acts as a regional power of the "empire" type, similar to the way in which the US acts as a global power (although the US application of power relies on a more varied base, and is less narrowly focused on the use of violence, Destradi, 2010:924). Israeli imitation of US policy is not just restricted to economic policies but also to diplomatic ones. Therefore, Israeli authorities can utilize local actors and outfit them with military and other aid, in order to have them act as proxies for Israeli interests and as subcontractors, forming similar relations to those which developed between the US and Israel, as shown in case studies 6 and 7 (5.2 and 5.3).

Yair Ravid-Ravitz, a retired Israeli Mossad agent,[3] quotes Shimon Peres from a secret meeting held with senior representatives of the Lebanese Phalangists in Tel-Aviv, sometime between 1974 and 1977, when Peres was minister of defense. In the meeting, Peres said,

> There are two lakes in Israel: the Sea of Galilee and the Dead Sea. They are both fed by the same source – the Jordan River. The Sea of Galilee is abundant in life, has fish and vegetation and the water is good for drinking, but the Dead Sea has no fish or vegetation. The reason is that the Sea of Galilee takes its water from the north and gives water southwards, while the Dead Sea receives water from the north but keeps them without passing them on.

Peres explained that Israel receives aid from the US, and therefore wants to help others as well – in order to prosper like the Sea of Galilee rather than dying like the Dead Sea (Ravid-Ravitz, 2013:118–19). The reliability of the quote cannot be verified. Nevertheless, it draws a direct connection from the US aid to Israel's outsourcing of military and security operations. The quote reveals, at the very least, that senior security agents such as Ravid-Ravitz considered aid (and specifically military aid) to be a strategic tool for recruiting security subcontractors.

After the 9/11 attacks, cooperation and mutual influence between Israel and the US have intensified. The US model for a military-industrial complex is based on minimal state intervention in ownership over military production. The US military industry is part of the private sector and is therefore motivated to maximize profit. Commercial logic, unlike state or public logic, aims to achieve a constant growth in sales (Harvey, 2005:64–5). The close relationship between Israel and the US has caused this model to be gradually accepted in Israel as well, a process which is not yet completed (Lifshitz, 2002:63–5). Israel has mostly adopted US procedures and policies in the field of arms manufacture, but in the field of "homeland security" it was the US which adopted techniques and policies from Israel. President Bush announced the "War on Terror" – a global effort with large funding (Lubin, 2013). Leila Stokmarr studied the expansion of Israel's homeland security exports through the War on Terror. Israeli companies turned the Israeli colony of Ariel into a showroom for security technology, and accessed new markets on the dovetails of US companies.[4]

6.3 MILITARY EXPORT

6.3.1 Arms export figures

Israeli military companies owe their existence to contracts signed with the Israeli MOD, contracts which are renewed periodically (Sadeh, 2001:64–77). With modern production technologies, production capacity tends to outstrip demand. When the production capacity of military companies exceeds the demands of the MOD, they can sign contracts to provide military equipment to companies and institutions in the US. When arms companies suffer from a reduction in demand, they experience immediate financial difficulties. Reduced sales means that the companies might need to discharge workers, leading to resistance from unions. Companies would need to de-commission machinery, while still paying interest on their loans and administrative costs as before. This sort of difficulty puts these companies under pressure to increase sales in order to improve profits. During such times, the temptation increases to sell weapons to uncertain customers, to lower prices and even to disregard regulations prohibiting the sale of weapons to potentially hostile countries. Such policies increase the availability of weapons in the world, and can lead to an increase in conflict and to heightened feelings of insecurity, factors which contribute to the arms-race and create more demand for the products of the weapon companies (Lifshitz, 2000:339–42, 470).

This dynamic has made exports the first priority of the Israeli arms industry. As opposed to the US in which 20 percent of arms production is for exports, 80 percent of Israeli arms production is destined for export (Denes, 2011:171).

The Israeli arms export is divided among private arms dealers and both private and state-owned companies, but the Israeli MOD Sibat (acronym in Hebrew for security assistance and export) was established in the 1970s to promote the arms export. Sibat claims that arms exports contribute to Israel's national security and bolster Israel's economic strength. It publishes its goals to position Israel at the top of the world arms exporters, and to find larger markets for Israeli-made arms. Sibat confirms the estimate of Nick Denes above, with a very similar number of 75 percent of Israeli arms production for export (as of 2012), one of the highest ratios in the world (Sibat, 2013). Sibat does not address the possibility that weapon sales could lead to instability and insecurity, and continued to argue that arms sales should be perpetually increased (ibid.). In 2014 the Israeli MOD ended regulation of commissions collected by mediators in arms deals. The reciprocal nature of arms deals makes this policy relevant to both imports and exports of military supplies, but the MOD referred only to the import aspect, arguing that "The insignificant savings from cutting commissions does not justify the bureaucratic apparatus needed to supervise agents, and that purchase through such agents is conducted only on rare and financially inconsequential occasions" (Cohen & Litman, 2017).

The early retirement age in the Israeli military allows retired officers to pursue a second career after a long military service (Maman, 1988:25–6). In light of the specialized skills accumulated in the military service, officers frequently turn to the arms trade, security industry, to training of security forces or even to mercenary work as logical choices for their second career (ibid.:66–7). Daniel Maman found that 13 senior officers who retired in the years 1974–84 became arms traders or security advisors (15 percent of the retired senior officers, ibid.:67). This practice is encouraged by the MOD. Data on export permits which are issued to arms traders in recent years indicates that the ratio of retired officers seeking a second career in the arms trade has almost certainly increased from the 15 percent found by Maman.[5] Israeli lawyer Itai Mack appealed to the Israeli Supreme Court in order to obtain information about licenses for weapon export issued by the MOD to retired Israeli officers. He discovered that the legal framework for these licenses was finalized only in 2007. By 2013, the ministry issued weapon export licenses to 1006 companies and 312 independent traders. The companies and traders were issued with about 19,000 marketing permits, which allow Israeli arms technology to be presented to potential buyers, and 8716 export permits, which allow the actual sale of the weapons. There were 6784 people registered as arms exporters (Misgav, 2013).

The arms export must be considered in a global context. Especially interesting is the ranking of arms-exporting countries, which reveals much about the differential accumulation of competing industries. While the US remains unchallenged as the biggest weapons exporter in the world in terms of dollar value of the arms sold, the conditions mentioned above have pushed Israel up the ranks, making Israel the eighth biggest weapons exporter in 2012, after the US, Russia, France, Britain, Germany, China and Italy. In that year Israel's military exports peaked (after a relatively slow year in 2011), and reached an estimated $7 billion. Between 2004 and 2011, Israeli companies directed most of their exports towards developing countries, and achieved sales of $12.9 billion to developing countries during these years (Grimmett & Kerr, 2012; Coren, 2013i; Harel, 2013a). In recent years, however, the soaring exports have been checked, and even begin to falter. According to the US Congressional Research Service, Israel dropped from the eighth biggest exporter to developing countries in the years 2007–10 to ninth place in the years 2011–14. In 2014 it fell to tenth place. In terms of total arms exports, Israel fell from eighth place in 2007–10 to tenth place in 2011–14, and under twelfth place in 2014 (Theohary, 2015:35–6, 62–3).[6]

Table 6.1 Comparison of Top Arms Exporters 2008–11

Rank	Country	Total Arms Export 2008–11 (in US$, millions)	Population (2011, thousands)	Per-capita weapons export 2008–11 (US$)
1	US	145 702	311 592	467.61
2	Russia	33 500	142 961	234.33
3	France	19 600	63 294	309.66
4	Germany	9 300	81 798	113.70
5	Italy	8 800	60 739	144.88
6	China	8 300	1 344 100	6.18
7	Israel	6 900	7 759	889.26
8	Ukraine	4 100	45 779	89.56
9	UK	3 600	62 436	57.66
10	Spain	2 900	46 125	62.87
11	Sweden	2 700	9 449	285.74

Source: UN (2013), Grimmett and Kerr (2012).

Defense magazines and the Stockholm International Peace Research Institute (SIPRI) publish arms export data in absolute numbers, which is useful in identifying which countries have more influence over the global arms market. Per-capita arms export, however, is a more useful measurement of how important arms export is to each state's economy and society. Table 6.1 shows that although Israel was the seventh biggest arms exporter in the years 2008–11, it was the biggest exporter in per-capita terms, with almost twice as much per-capita arms exports than the US, indicating the centrality of arms exports to the Israeli economy.

6.3.2 Customers of Israeli arms exports

Although developed economies such as Europe and the US have a larger capacity to purchase security products than developing economies, Israeli arms companies find a significant proportion of their market in developing countries, especially in areas of extreme inequality and prolonged conflict, as shown in Table 6.2. The focus on the developing world is no accident. Two of Israel's biggest customers are Brazil and India (Dayan, 2009), both countries with extreme inequality and engaged in prolonged asymmetrical conflicts (Fernandez, 2013a). Israel has branded its military industry as an industry specializing not in conventional warfare but rather in the asymmetrical suppression of civilian resistance, which is known in military jargon as "low-intensity conflict" and is especially common in developing countries (Tinder, 1990:2–7).

It is difficult to obtain information on arms deals involving developing countries and conflict-ridden countries because trade with such countries raises both legal and moral questions and Israeli military companies are not obligated by law to release public reports on their trade with foreign countries. Military companies report to the MOD alone, which does not publish a breakdown on Israel's largest arms customers. Nevertheless, information on the extensive trade which Israeli arms companies conduct with developing countries is partially available through press releases of the companies themselves, which use such press releases to demonstrate the company's growth and attract investors (Section 2.7.1). A database on such deals (gathered mainly from press releases by Israeli companies) has been compiled by Jimmy Johnson (see below).

Media exposures of Israeli arms sales also contribute to the database, even when the companies choose not to report the deals to the public.

Examples of such deals abound. One of Israel's largest export deals in its history took place in 1988, as 60 combat planes were sold to South Africa despite a mandatory UN-imposed arms embargo on the Apartheid state (Ben, 2013b). In the Kashmir area along the India-Pakistan border, Israeli companies have installed lethal systems on Indian fences, turning them into a deadly obstacle using experience from construction of the Separation Wall in the West Bank (Scott-Clark, 2012). The Israeli mercenary company Silver Shadow operated in the Republic of the Congo, in Angola and Columbia (providing security for the British Petroleum corporation), and the Israeli company Levdan trained the Congo Brazzaville army. Levdan has also provided services in procurement of arms, demonstrating the symbiotic relations between the arms industry and the security industry. These are examples of private companies which were set up by Israeli citizens with the approval of the Israeli MOD, demonstrating how outsourcing of security creates a fertile ground for the private sector (Singer, 2003:88; War on Want, 2006:4, 9, 15). Azerbaijan signed a $1.6 billion arms deal with Israel in March 2012, for weapons which were to be developed along the Armenian border. Among the reasons for the deal was also speculation that Israel wanted to secure airfields for fueling its airplanes prior to an air-strike against Iran (Clayton, 2012).

Countries which purchase Israeli systems are not necessarily those with which Israel has friendly diplomatic relations. A document of the UK Exports Control Organization exposed some of Israel's arms exports destinations. Because Israeli companies are required to request permission before exporting military equipment which contain UK-produced or UK-licensed components, the list of approved and denied requests serves as partial evidence to Israel's export deals. The document showed that Israel received permits from the UK government to export electronic warfare systems and pilot gear to Morocco; observations systems, radar, communications and navigation systems to Algeria; missile counter-measures, fueling systems, radars and pilot gear to the United Arab Emirates; and radar systems, electronic warfare systems and pilot gear to Pakistan. These are only some examples from the report; and all three countries do not have diplomatic relations with Israel (Export Control Organization, 2013). The Israeli MOD denied that equipment was sold to Pakistan, but did not publish similar denials for the other countries. The journalists who reported the denial, Aluf Ben and Gili Cohen, speculated that the disavowal was published in response to an inquiry by India, out of concern that Israel is selling arms to its rival (Ben & Cohen, 2013).

The Israeli Arms-Deals Database compiled by Jimmy Johnson (Johnson, 2015) provides a sample of 1008 deals between Israel and other countries between 1954 and 2010. Granted that because the database is based on deals that were made public, there is a bias towards deals with Western democracies which conduct diplomatic relations with Israel, as deals with other kinds of customers are more likely to be kept a secret (Cohen, 2014b). After accumulating the value of all reported deals with each country, adjusted for the US$ CPI (based on 2010 prices), 185 deals had to be removed from the sample because insufficient data was available for them. Parts of the database are based on press releases, which offer only approximations of amounts of money involved. As an arbitrary approximation, the number "3" was substituted for the estimate "several," the number "5" for the estimate "about half a million," and the number "8" for the estimate "almost a million." Admittedly, the data cannot be considered accurate. It does, however, enable rough comparisons to be made among the largest customers of Israeli arms and even to trace trends over time. Based on the database, the average size of an arms deal was $111 million (in 2010 prices). Those deals which had no sum associated with them were assumed to be worth the average amount. It should be stressed that the totals do not represent the actual extent of Israel's deals, but merely a sample of those deals that were reported in the media.

Table 6.2 shows the results of coding Johnson's database. Arms deals are frequently arranged around a reciprocal agreement, or even barter of arms, which explains the high correlation between the recipient and supplier countries engaged in arms trade with Israel, and the dominant place of the US. Until 1967, France was Israel's largest arms supplier, which explains its position among the top ten. Israel maintained arms trade with countries suffering from severe problems of social inequality, and from prolonged asymmetrical conflict with guerrilla fighters. This explains the high places taken by India (especially after the end of the Cold War, Samaan, 2013), Turkey, South Africa (especially Apartheid-era South Africa), Chile (especially during Pinoche's regime), Mexico (in the Chiapas region) and Guatemala (during the civil war) (Fernandez, 2013b). Graph 6.3 is based on the data of Sibat (Israel's MOD arms trade department). Although Sibat has provided selective distribution by continent alone, the graph nevertheless emphasizes the shift in the arms trade in recent years towards Asia (where traditional customers of Israeli arms include India, Singapore, Taiwan and South Korea, among others).

Table 6.2 Top Ten Customers of Israeli Security and Military Products

Country	*Accumulated Deals Value (US$ millions, 2010 prices, 1950–2010)*	*Rank*
US	8 985.43	1
India	8 774.88	2
China	8 052.73	3
Turkey	3 194.28	4
Singapore	3 182.13	5
South Africa	3 120.48	6
Chile	2 739.31	7
Guatemala	2 026.06	8
Brazil	1 938.02	9
France	1 719.80	10

Source: Jimmy Johnson's Israeli Arms-Trade Database.

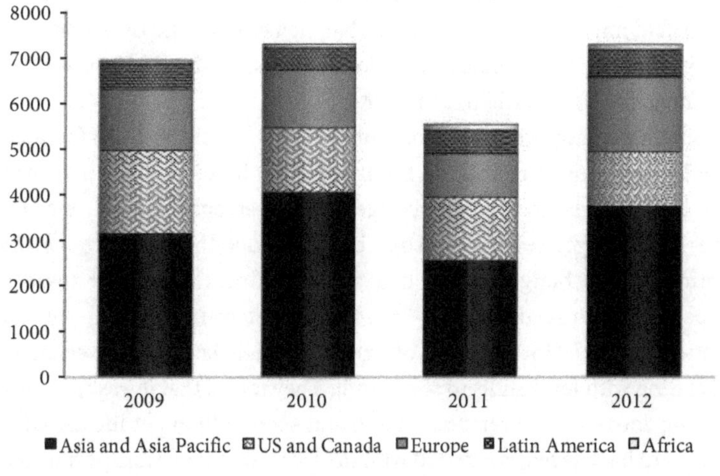
8000
7000
6000
5000
4000
3000
2000
1000
0
2009
2010
2011
2012
Asia and Asia Pacific
US and Canada
Europe
Latin America
Africa

Graph 6.3 Distribution of Israeli Military Exports by Region (millions of US$, current prices)

Source: Sibat (2013).

6.3.3 From defense to homeland security

Israeli companies became well established in the security market after the 9/11 attacks. A global market for homeland security products emerged after the attacks, and Israel attained the position of world leader in that field. The global private security market has grown further with the 2003 war in Iraq (War on Want, 2006:2–4). The products which have been in demand after the 9/11 attacks are those which enable surveillance and control over civilian populations. The demand for new kinds of security products has therefore opened the gates for private security companies to fill the void. The choice of public officials to turn to the private sector in filling this void was led by the US even before the actual 9/11 attacks. Donald Rumsfeld's speech at the DOD on September 8, 2001 (three days before the attack on the Twin Towers and the Pentagon) was an all-out attack against state intervention in defense. Rumsfeld promised to "wage an all-out campaign to shift Pentagon's resources from bureaucracy to the battlefield … I want to liberate it [the Pentagon]. We need to save it from itself" (Gómez del Prado, 2010). The War on Terror which followed was a fertile ground to implement the policy of turning the Pentagon from a central command for national forces into a central location for sourcing and managing services procured from private companies. After 2001 Rumsfeld implemented the concept that the DOD should be operated as a corporation, and as many operations as possible should be privatized (Minow, 2005:1004; Klein, 2007b:283–7).

Simultaneously with the reform of the DOD, President Bush founded the Department of Homeland Security (DHS) in 2003. Since that year, the DHS budget grew by an average of 12.7 percent annually. In 2012, the DHS budget reached $59.032 billion, about the same size as the entire defense budget of the UK, and dwarfing the entire European expenditure on security (DHS, 2013). Mark Stewart and John Mueller criticized the DHS as a case of extremely high levels of government spending with few results to show for it. They found that it was spending during 2001–06 between $64 million and $600 million per life the DHS claims to have saved, compared with the Department of Transport which was able to save one life per $3 million (Stewart & Mueller, 2008). The 20-fold difference indicates a clear bias of the US administration to fund homeland security.

The global demand for homeland security products has increased sharply, and other countries took the lead from the US. Germany, for example, has a fast-growing market for products of "civil security" worth tens of millions of euros per year. The European Union's (EU) multi-annual program for scientific research allocated €1.4 billion in funds for "civil security" research between 2007 and 2013. Israel is listed as a participating country in 29 of the projects of the EU's Security

Research Program and is the largest beneficiary of EU research funds outside of the EU itself (Groth, 2012).

Israeli security companies were quick to capitalize on the opportunity created when the US and Europe increased their spending on homeland security. They specialized in systems and technologies designed for surveillance, for control of civilian populations and for indirect use of force by soldiers, police officers and security guards who remain protected in a distant location. In 2013, the Frost & Sullivan consulting firm released a study according to which Israel had become the largest UAV exporter in the world in that year, demonstrating this point (Newsdesk, 2013). In 2009, 600 homeland security companies were estimated to be operating in Israel and exporting their products and services abroad, employing 25,000 employees (Johnston, 2009; Gordon, 2011:163).[7]

Three examples are presented here to shed light on the way that the export is structured. The examples were selected to highlight the passage of members of the Israeli security elite from public positions to the private sector, and the relations which these elite members maintain with the Israeli MOD, and how they use Israel's security policies and the occupation as economic assets.

The first example relates to the career of two Israeli retired officers, Major General Doron Almog and Brigadier-General Gal Hirsch. Both of them have attempted to convert their military experience and high rank into material gains in the private sector with mixed success, and both have decided to reverse their course and return to public service, again with mixed success.

Doron Almog is the former commander of Israel's Southern Command. He is suspected of participation in war crimes and in 2005 had escaped from London upon learning that a warrant for his arrest was waiting for him (PCHR & Hickman, 2008). Almog founded the homeland security company Athlone Global Security in 2007, and raised NIS 160 million from US investors. In the arms trade milieu, Almog's record was considered an advantage, and proved his involvement in conflict situations, and he received endorsements from senior Israeli and US security officials despite having few indications for the company's financial prospects. The company's business plan was to invest in fledging homeland security companies as a sort of venture capital fund for security companies. Athlone lost approximately 86 percent of its value within its first year of operations, and Almog resigned from his position as chairman in 2010. In 2012 the company was merged with a failed real-estate company called Ofek. Though Athlone failed, Almog was able to draw NIS 3.5 million from the company in wages, in addition to a consultancy fee of thousands of dollars per day of work (Shforer, 2012). The investors in the company demonstrated an unusual level of trust in Almog, emerging from his prestige as a retired senior Israeli military officer. After his failure in the business world, Almog returned to public service. He was appointed head of the Prawer-Begin Plan to relocate Bedouins from their lands in southern Israel, a plan which was eventually abandoned in the face of massive protests (Lis et al., 2013).

Gal Hirsch's story has many parallels. After being disgraced in the Israeli invasion of Lebanon in 2006, he proceeded to found a weapons company which came under investigation for alleged crimes. He attempted to return to public service as the police commissioner but his candidacy was withdrawn due to public scandal (Hartman, 2015). Both officers attempted to leverage their military experience in launching a business career but found themselves in stiff competition with other security companies founded by retired officers. Both have discovered that their position in the public service is not guaranteed either, and that a high military rank does not ensure a successful career in the public or the private sector, as it had before.

Another example is the company Goldschmidt & Levy International Security Group GmbH. It was founded in 2011 as a subsidiary to the Israeli Shmira Ubitakhon company (Section 5.5.1), which provides airport security in Israel's Eilat airport. The subsidiary was established in order to access the German security market. It provided security services in an airport in Berlin, emergency services for the Lufthansa airline in the Frankfurt airport, and is charged with providing security to all Israeli delegations to Germany. The company employed about 300 workers in Germany in 2012, when it won a two-year tender to provide security to about 32 courts in the Frankfurt area in Germany, a contract worth over €1.5 million (Blumenkranz, 2012b). The company employs Brigadier-General Manachem Bachrach as a CEO. Bachrach's CV is typical for a senior manager in an Israeli security company. After retiring from the army as an officer in 1972, Bachrach attained an academic degree. He served as a security officer on El-Al airplanes, and was later given various positions managing security for airlines and export companies. He was a director in the Israeli arms manufacturer Rafael. He set up his own airline security company, ICTS, and was invited to share his expertise in security in various countries, including Brazil, Cyprus, the

Dominican Republic, Greece, Hungary, Nigeria, Russia, Tajikistan and the US. Bachrach told the *Israeli Defense* magazine that "our advantage as Israelis is in analyzing risks, because we have a close knowledge with the modus operandi of terror organizations" (Ben Yosef, 2012; see also Bachrach, 2013).

The third example is the Aeronautics company, established in 1997 as a private company by two retired military officers, Colonel Haim Mandel-Shaked, who also managed Ehud Barak's office when he was prime minister, and Avi Leumi, a former intelligence officer. The company specializes in equipment for gathering intelligence through UAVs. In its early days, the company sold its UAVs to the Israeli army, which deployed them in the Gaza Strip. The company made use of that fact in its marketing, starting to grow fast and finding customers abroad. Among those customers were controversial regimes in Africa, such as the government of Equatorial Guinea. In 2005 it sold UAVs to the Ivory Coast army, in the midst of a civil war. A French military unit in the area confiscated and destroyed the Aeronautics equipment, and France issued a formal protest and demanded that the Israeli MOD respect the UN arms embargo on the Ivory Coast (the Israeli government eventually complied). Nevertheless, Aeronautics won a $260 million contract to provide UAVs to the Nigerian navy, the biggest arms deal Nigeria has ever signed with an Israeli company. The UAVs were intended to be used in the Niger River delta, where rich oil fields were discovered, and local minority groups numbering about 13 million have launched a struggle demanding a more equal distribution of the oil profits. The Nigerian navy used Israeli UAVs to suppress the civil unrest. Aeronautics also sells to Angola, Ethiopia, India, Nepal, Russia, Taiwan and the US. The Israeli MOD did not list Aeronautics as a company authorized to export weapons from Israel, but the company did not suffer sanctions for its operations because it claimed that the equipment is not a lethal weapon, but intended to gather intelligence, exploiting the distinction between military and homeland security products (Melman, 2006).

The three examples above are a small sample of the hundreds of Israeli homeland security companies accessing international markets. Their stories combine elements of success and failure. Even though the prestige of the Israeli security elites generates demand for Israeli security products, the global market is just not large enough to accommodate generation after generation of retired Israeli officers launching their own companies. The examples showcase the practices and strategies of Israeli companies in exploiting their experience with the occupation of the OPT to their advantage.

6.4 CASE STUDY: G4S

International security companies rarely find an entry point into the Israeli market, because the emphasis on Israeli expertise reduces the chance that the Israeli MOD will outsource to international companies. However, for international companies such as G4S, their efforts to gain entry into the Israeli security market bear the advantage of earning a share in the prestige of the Israeli security industry, and recruiting retired Israeli officers. G4S is a rare example of an international security company which temporarily accessed the Israeli security market, in order to gain those advantages.

Case Box 11:	G4S
Type:	Outsourcing of public security (police operations) and prison operations
Key interests:	G4S corporate interest
Opposition:	Competing Israeli security companies, anti-occupation political activists
Success:	No (temporary success)
Period:	2002–17
Similar cases:	Large Israeli security companies (such as ISS, Modi'in Ezrahi)

G4S was founded in Denmark in 1901, and eventually became the largest private security corporations in the world, operating in 125 countries and employing 620,000 workers. It offers "outsourcing solutions," especially where "security and safety risks are considered a strategic threat" (Abrahamsen & Williams, 2009:2; G4S, 2013a). G4S promotes privatization of security in the world, and at the same time plans to take part in it and profit from it. G4S's head for the UK and Africa, David Taylor-Smith, predicted that large parts of Britain's police force would be privatized by 2017 (Taylor & Travis, 2012), and indeed the *Guardian* confirmed that in many countries around the world, including the UK, this has indeed happened (Provost, 2017). The company's financial results for 2012 showed a profitable and growing corporation, with a total revenue of £8.1 billion, a profit before interest, tax and amortization of £516 million. By 2015 the total revenue had decreased to £6.9 billion, with a profit before interest, tax and amortization of £427 million. It also lost about 10,000 employees (G4S, 2013b, 2016).

The company owns 92 percent each of two subsidiaries established in Israel, G4S Secure Solutions (Israel) Limited and G4S Secure Technologies (Israel) Limited (ibid.), but relentless pressure by boycott groups convinced G4S to sell its Israeli subsidiary to Fimi Opportunity Funds in December 2016 (Gabizon, 2016). In 2002 G4S bought the Israeli Hashmira security company, and merged it into the G4S group, thereby establishing a foothold in the Israeli security market during the height of the second Intifada (G4S Israel, 2013). Through Hashmira, G4S gained the exclusive contract to operate a system of surveillance of prisoners with electronic bracelets for NIS 30 million annually (Van Leer, 2017).

The "Who Profits" project of the Israeli organization Coalition of Women for Peace studied G4S's operations for the Israeli government because of suspicions that the G4S company provides security services for the Israeli government in the OPT, and could therefore be in violation of international law. "Who Profits" found evidence that the company provided security for incarceration facilities of Palestinian political prisoners, including the Ofer Camp, an Israeli prison inside the West Bank. "Who Profits" collected reports of torture, abuse and child imprisonment in prisons for which G4S operates. G4S also provided security to businesses in the illegal colonies, and to the Israeli police headquarters in the West Bank (Who Profits, 2011a).

These findings were a blow to G4S's image, as the company makes efforts to develop a reputation as an ethical company. It established a committee for corporate social responsibility (CSR) in 2011, and distributed a DVD to all of its employees in 2012 to educate them about ethics and values (G4S, 2013a). The response of G4S to criticism for its operations in the OPT was therefore atypical. Israeli companies rarely acknowledge and engage with the criticism. G4S commissioned a legal opinion from Hjalte Rasmussen, a professor of international law at Copenhagen University, who argued that G4S's activities in the West Bank do not constitute a breach of international law. "Who Profits" challenged the legal opinion, claiming that it was based on factual inaccuracies (Who Profits, 2011a). This debate took place while in the background an international campaign against G4S and its activities in the OPT had already begun.

Protest in Denmark (the corporation's home country) and critique in the Danish media prompted Danish Minister of Foreign Affairs, Lene Espersen, to call on G4S "not to carry out activities that might help sustain illegal settlements" (Nieuwhof, 2010). G4S responded with a statement in which it promised to withdraw from some of its contracts in the West Bank (Nieuwhof, 2011). The DanWatch organization found that G4S did not commit to cancelling contracts, but only to allow them to expire between 2012 and 2015 (DanWatch, 2011). In April 2012 the European Union chose not to renew a contract with G4S in light of concerns about G4S's role in the OPT (Corporate Watch, 2012), and in March 2013 the Co-operative Asset Management disinvested from its shares in G4S (Corporate Watch, 2013). Despite this pressure, G4S announced in May 2013 that it intended to withdraw only from contracts with the Israeli government which are physically inside the West Bank, keeping contracts in prisons inside Israel containing Palestinian prisoners from the OPT, and with businesses and private customers in the West Bank (DanWatch, 2013). The international pressure continued to accumulate until in June 2014, G4S announced that it would not renew its contracts with the Israeli Prison Service, set to expire in 2017 (Plimmer, 2014), and in March 2016 it announced that all of G4S's business with Israel would end (Associated Press, 2016).

The very slow and reluctant response of G4S to the criticism against it, even at the cost of valuable contracts, demonstrates the importance to its prestige of G4S's operations in Israel/Palestine. The corporation's financial reports state that 1.6 percent of its goodwill[8] in 2012 was in Israel, a total of £34 million, increasing to 1.9 percent in 2015 worth £36 million (G4S, 2013b, 2016). According to the *Financial Times*, less than 1 percent of the company's employees are in Israel, and about 1 percent of the company's revenues and profits are generated from its activities in Israel/Palestine (Plimmer, 2013). In 2014, the company reported having 6700 employees in Israel and generating revenue of NIS 750 million (Dun & Bradstreet, 2015). As the Israeli brand is critical for success in the global homeland security market (Machold, 2015:819–21), G4S attempted to retain access to that brand, even at a cost to its reputation and to its CSR efforts. For G4S, the participation in government contracts related to the control of Palestinians opens the door for G4S to operate in the Israeli private market as a security company. It also serves G4S in tenders for which it competes in other countries.

6.5 CASE STUDY: HEWLETT PACKARD

Hewlett Packard (HP) is a large global corporation. It had a revenue of $126 billion in 2010, and $103 billion in 2015 (Who Profits, 2011b; HP, 2015). HP gained entry into Israel's security market through outsourcing of technological elements incorporated into Israeli security institutions. As its services are highly technical and complex, its participation in Israeli security projects has drawn less attention than G4S, and encountered less resistance.

Case Box 12:	Hewlett Packard (HP)
Type:	Outsourcing of police operations
Key interests:	HP
Opposition:	Competing companies, human-rights organizations
Success:	Yes
Period:	1999–
Similar cases:	L3, Microsoft

Israeli authorities have set limitations on Palestinians who seek work in Israel, and have increased the role of technology in the checkpoints stationed within the OPT (Section 5.5). As part of this control mechanism, Israeli authorities have required Palestinians to carry biometric identity cards since 2005. The cards are managed through the "Basel system," which HP has operated since October 1999 through its subsidiary EDS Israel. The contract was worth $10 million, financed by the US following the Wye River Memorandum (Who Profits, 2011b). The company that was first selected to distribute magnetic cards to Palestinians was On Time Innovations Ltd (OTI).

The reason for implementing the Basel system, according to OTI CEO Oded Bashan, is "secured and easy personal identification of people during border crossing while minimizing unnecessary contact and friction" (ibid.). This quote is a reminder about the use of technology of control by Israeli authorities to minimize human involvement in security, and as a substitute for policy. Automated control also makes a statement that contact with the Palestinian population is a peripheral and secondary function of the Israeli security organizations, and therefore can be safely privatized. Privatization is also justified through the implementation of technology because a private company such as HP has more techno-logical expertise than the Israeli military. While the checkpoints in the

West Bank have been privatized, the biometric identity card was seen as a useful way to make government regulation of the checkpoints more streamlined and centralized given the central database is controlled by the government and the local staff at the checkpoint serve a minimal function of cross-checking the data. The project was partially funded by US aid (Council for the National Interest, 2005).

After the system of biometric identity cards had been implemented for Palestinians, the Israeli police became familiar with the system, and Israeli politicians suggested that use of the system could be expanded to include labor migrants in Israel (Shadmi, 2012a:70–1). The introduction of the debate about biometric identity cards into the Israeli political discourse has created a debate about possible use of these cards against various activities which are perceived as dishonest or "cheating" the state. The person promoting the biometric database was an external consultant, who planned and managed the database for the Ministry of Public Security after receiving an exemption from applying through a tender (Paz-Fuchs & Ben-Simkhon-Peleg, 2014:48). A bill was proposed in 2012 to require labor migrants to carry biometric identity cards to prevent them from fleeing their employers, but the bill failed to pass. High-ranking officials suggested requiring welfare recipients to carry biometric identification in order to prevent them from receiving welfare unlawfully. The Likud party suggested in 2012 that yeshiva students would be forced to carry biometric identification to ensure that they are actually attending the yeshiva (Wolf, 2012). Each of these proposals is a lucrative business opportunity for HP, because the company has the advantage of experience, and can easily establish biometric identity cards compatible with the biometric database which already exists for Palestinians.

The tender for issuing biometric cards to Palestinians was launched in 2001 by the Israeli Ministry of the Interior. During the first phase of the tender, the ministry disqualified ten out of the eleven companies who applied. This allowed HP to win automatically. An appeal by three companies who lost the tender was accepted by the court and the tender was annulled. In 2005 a new tender was published, and only two submissions reached the final stage. The tender committee ruled that only HP met the requirements, although its price offer was 50 percent higher than the tender's estimate. The Ministry of Finance withdrew from the tender committee in protest and the second tender was also annulled. Following pressure by HP against the annulment of the tender, the

Ministry of Finance authorized the Ministry of the Interior to negotiate with HP without a tender selection process (Who Profits, 2011b).

Meanwhile, HP intensified its involvement with Israel's army and government by signing a contract to administer the IT infrastructure of Israel's navy from 2006, a contract which was expanded to the entire Israeli army in 2009. HP established service providers in Israel and from 1992 in an Israeli colony in the OPT called Modi'in Ilit, and from 2009 through taking part in the "Smart City" project in the Israeli colony of Ariel. The actual manufacture of the biometric cards was outsourced by HP to the Israeli company OTI (Who Profits, 2011b).

Even before legislation on the biometric database was passed, HP was contracted without a tender for NIS 270 million by the government in 2008 to produce biometric identity cards for the entire Israeli population (ibid.; Paz-Fuchs & Ben-Simkhon-Peleg, 2014:48). In December 2009, the Biometric Database Law was passed in the Israeli Knesset, decreeing a pilot period, after which (if the pilot is successful), all Israeli citizens will be required to carry a biometric identity card with information also stored on a central database with which it could be compared (Who Profits, 2011b). The Knesset members voting on the bill had to consider that if the bill failed, HP would be compensated for the cancellation of the contract with public funds (ibid.). The pilot biometric database was launched in 2013 (Paz-Fuchs & Ben-Simkhon-Peleg, 2014:48). After a long political struggle and repeated extensions of the pilot, most Knesset members were convinced that the biometric database is a costly and unnecessary measure, almost without parallels in the world, and that it creates risks for the privacy of Israeli citizens if parts of the database are hacked, leaked or sold. Nevertheless, in March 2017 HP struck gold when the Israeli Knesset approved the Biometric Database Law for the entire Israeli population, making biometric identity cards and passports obligatory, and giving HP the contract to produce those cards with tender exemption, worth about $300 million. Knesset members were forced to toe the party line and support the bill regardless of their opinion on it (Goichman & Sadeh, 2017).

6.6 INTERNATIONAL COMPARISON OF PRIVATIZATION OF SECURITY

Elke Krahmann conducted a comparative analysis of privatization in the military industry between the US, the UK and Germany. In the US, the privately owned defense industry emerged after the First World War. The US had already pursued a model of cooperation with the private sector during the Second World War, refraining from establishing factories for the production of needed arms. During the Cold War, public spending on armament fed the private arms industry's growth. The US federal government also offered various kinds of subsidies to arms producers, while allowing them to remain in private ownership (Krahmann, 2010:61–8).

6.6.1 Privatization of security in the US

The US has also led the way in the outsourcing of military and security operations. Avant estimated that the war in which the smallest participation of US civilians were involved was the First World War (in which they were 4.08 percent of the forces deployed), and the war with the highest participation of civilians prior to the invasion of Iraq in 2003 was the Korean War, in which civilians were 28.42 percent of the forces deployed (Avant, 2006:2). The use of private military firms (as opposed to civilians hired directly by government agencies) by the US government began with sending such firms to Vietnam to train Vietnamese troops before the US intervened directly. The ratio of civilians to soldiers in the Vietnam War was 16.32 percent (ibid.). Such firms were also employed in Nicaragua during the 1980s, in arming the Nicaragua Contras after Congress ended official aid. Israeli firms as well as the Israeli military have also been involved in training the Contras and arming them, at President Reagan's request (Beit-Hallahmi, 1987:90–3). The US sent private firms in the 1990s to Columbia to help the military eradicate coca crops and to repress leftist groups. In 1994, MPRI (Military Professional Resources Inc.) was contracted to provide military training to the Croatian army. Such use of private companies allowed the US government to work around US laws and around congressional opposition to sending troops and weapons. It also allowed the US government to distance itself from the activities of these private companies, which operate without US military uniforms in relative anonymity (Yeoman, 2003; Maddow, 2012:145–51).

The most famous PMSC in literature on the privatization of security was Blackwater, which served the US inside the US as well as in Iraq, Afghanistan, Bosnia and Israel (Elsea et al., 2008:7). It recruited former US soldiers and used them to train its own employees, or to offer training courses to external clients. Thus the company accumulated the experience and expertise which was developed by the military, and turned it into a company-owned asset. Former Blackwater CEO Gary Jackson mentioned that some of Blackwater's contracts with the US government are so secret that he cannot tell one government agency about business he is conducting with another. Not only does this enable the company to sell the same technology more than once to different branches of the same government, but it also places the company in a position of power, as the company has more information about government security operations than some segments of the government itself (Yeoman, 2003).

The US is considered an extreme case of privatization of security, and since the 1990s the literature on the privatization of security has focused on the US more than on any other country. Privatization of security in the US harkens to the distant past, and the role of the private sector in the US military-industrial complex had already been recognized after the Second World War (Gómez del Prado, 2010). Privatization of security in Israel emerged much later.

6.6.2 Privatization of security in the UK

Unlike the US, the UK's government nationalized much of the arms industry after the Second World War. During the economic crisis of the 1970s, the UK government nationalized additional companies in order to save them from bankruptcy. Margaret Thatcher, however, spearheaded the privatization of arms production as part of her promise to dismantle the welfare state, while US arms production was a priori privately owned. The government proceeded to sell BAE Systems, Rolls-Royce and the Royal Ordnance Factories to private investors. The operations of the Royal Dockyards at Devonport and in Rosyth were outsourced to private companies. Legislation came into effect in 1985 requiring the British MOD to perform a "market test" for various operations. Cleaning, catering, laundry, security-guarding and maintenance were to be outsourced in each case where the ministry could achieve better value for money. These operations were later expanded to include engineering, supply, training and operations support. The outsourcing of British MOD activities created further demand in the private sector, and especially for those companies capable of providing services which are not necessarily martial in nature, but which can nevertheless receive high security clearances and maintain good relations with the military and the MOD (Krahmann, 2010:60, 66, 73–4, 84–118).

6.6.3 Privatization of security in Germany

Germany's arm's industry after the Second World War was privately owned, after the Allies decided to re-arm West Germany through contracts with private companies. The West German government decided to keep the arms industry mostly private, and in 1977 only five out of the top 30 weapon companies were state-owned. However, the government employed various means to exert its control over the arms industry, through tenders, time-restricted contracts and by encouraging arms companies to diversify away from arms production. In the 1980s, the West Germany government encouraged private arms companies to increase arms exports as a mechanism to keep the companies profitable and therefore to sustain their ability to provide the West German army with armament. Outsourcing was introduced in the unified Germany only in 2002, two years after the government tasked the government-owned GEBB company to recommend strategies for privatization and outsourcing of military and security projects. Outsourcing has begun mainly through PPP projects in clothing, maintenance and repairs, and in IT (ibid.:70, 77, 156–93).

6.6.4 The growing global market for private security

The estimated total revenue of PMSCs around the world was $55.6 million in 1990, $100 million in 2000 (Leander, 2005:610; Gómez del Prado, 2010). In the following decade, however, private security spending has increased and diversified to the point that data collection is difficult. The magazine *Security Management* estimated that the global revenue of PMSCs reached $377 by 2015 (Moran, 2015).

The UN Working Group on Mercenaries estimated in 2010 that in the US alone, there were 1931 private companies in programs related to counter-terrorism, homeland security and intelligence, with about 854,000 employees (Gómez del Prado, 2010). The increasing share of private firms out of the total security expenditure is connected to the changes in modern warfare in a reciprocal loop. As the frequency and intensity of conventional wars declines, asymmetrical conflict becomes increasingly more central to military thinking and preparation (Tinder, 1990:11–12). Military preparation focuses on terrorist organizations, guerrilla groups or criminal organizations capable of crossing borders and infiltrating the civilian population. The process of securitization gradually reframes environmental, social, health and economic problems as "security problems" which are to be addressed by security measures (Buzan et al., 1998:23–9). These changes create a growing market for PMSCs, which market themselves as flexible corporate bodies which can cross borders and operate in civilian areas. The strengthening of PMSCs leads to further political and economic resources in the hands of PMSCs that help to reframe threats as security-related, appropriate for PMSC intervention.

Israel has not yet caught up to the levels of privatization of security prevalent in the US, but has already overtaken Germany. The privatization of checkpoints and the use of contractors and outsourcing of security activities are not unique to Israel, nor is Israel the first country to implement such policies, but in Israel these policies are a marked change in the structure of the security elite. A heavy emphasis on securitization and policization are also not unique to Israel. The intensive concern about security threats and the application of excessive police force in an attempt to repress social protest, or in lieu of treatment of social problems, is commonplace in the US and in Europe as well. However, although policization and securitization are prevalent in the US and in Europe, they hold a unique significance in Israel, because they are enhanced by Israel's militaristic culture (Shadmi, 2012a:124–5).

Israel's military culture, along with its relatively young retirement age from military service, and its image as a "fortress state" (Klein, 2007a) or a state in the midst of an ongoing conflict all contribute to its relative advantage in exporting the products and services produced by PMSCs, and have contributed to building Israel's image as the capital of the homeland security industry (Gordon, 2009:6).

6.7 CONCLUSION

Senior correspondent Ora Coren of the Israeli *TheMarker* economic magazine has been the most prominent journalist covering Israel's military industry for that newspaper, and her voice represents much of the discourse in the Israeli media on privatization of security. She expressed her opinion on privatization of security in an article about Israel Aerospace Industries published in May 2012. Coren argued that IAI's main shortfall is that it is a government-owned company, and must adopt a business strategy and a more business-like organizational structure in order to improve its profitability. She ended her piece with the following paragraph:

> Privatization of the company could be a force multiplier, in the sense that capital flows into the company will enable acquisitions and larger investments in research and developments, as well as by removing the restrictions which apply to a government company. The upcoming replacement of the CEO will be an added incentive to introduce changes in the company's behavior, with the almost declared goal of all involved to double the profit and triple its value. (Coren, 2012a)

Coren's text above directly engages with the resistance to the privatization policies, listing alternative advantages which can arise from privatizing the company, advantages which would apply to the future owners of IAI.

This chapter has discussed the international factors which influenced privatization of security in Israel. The adoption of privatization of security policies in Israel came later than in the US and the UK because of the strong role played by the security apparatus in Israel's political organizations. Eventually, the alliance between the US and Israel had a profound impact on Israeli security and economic policies, and brought private sector considerations into Israel's military industry. US military aid created conditions which favored differential accumulation by private Israeli investors in the arms sector, at the expense of the public sector. The Israeli military industry has therefore taken the leading role in privatization of security through sale, which has later expanded to outsourcing of security functions of state institutions and to privatization by default, culminating in privatization of some of Israel's central military operations (Chapter 5).

The privatization of security in Israel cannot be separated from the issue of security exports. Arms exports and imports, in which Israel engages disproportionately to its population size, have thrust the Israeli arms sector into the global arms market, and forced them to develop strategies in order to achieve differential accumulation, by carving a niche in the global arms market, specializing in homeland security products and in security products and services intended to pacify social unrest. Carving this niche in the global arms sector is achieved through a commodification and capitalization of security, and thereby contributes to accelerating the privatization of security in Israel. The Israeli specialization stems from Israel's security policies in the OPT, thereby creating a reciprocal feedback of economic interests, in which Israel's policies in the OPT serve the interests of exporting security companies, while the ties which are formed through Israel's arms trade influence Israel's policies in the OPT, especially the decision to privatize many security operations related to the occupation.

7
Conclusions

To my sorrow, military service as a fighter or fighting-supporter does not guarantee today success in life or access to proper employment; the change which the Israeli society has undergone led to an amazing decline in the gratitude to those fighters and fighting-supporters in recent years. (Ehud Barak, 2016)

Privatization is an economic process, and as such it cannot be separated from the social and political conditions in which it emerges. Economic interests play an undeniable role in this process. Each decision to privatize or not to privatize a security function or an arms factory has implications for the public, for the public-private relations and for the distribution of capital among different economic sectors. Those interests are attributed to institutions, such as "the state" or "the company" but are wielded in practice by individuals belonging to elite groups, such as Israel's security elite, political elite and economic elite. The privatization of security in Israel has been marked by the Israeli security elite's weakening ties with the political elite and strengthening ties with the economic elite.

The theoretical tools which have been developed to analyze privatization in general are insufficient to fully encompass the idiosyncrasies of the privatization of security. First, neoclassical economic theory holds a contradictory approach to privatization of security. It considers security to be a paradigmatic public good, a caveat to the general rule that privatization improves incentives and increases efficiency. Yet at the same time, neoclassical economists have promoted the privatization of security in Israel, using cost-cutting arguments which have been refuted by empirical evidence. Theories of Israeli militarism have similarly fallen short of explaining how privatization of Israeli security has progressed despite the importance of security to the Israeli political elites. The prolific theoretical discussion on the Israeli occupation considers the occupation of the OPT as the most important policy of the Israeli government, and the most important activity of the Israeli security forces in recent decades. However, it does not address the fact that the Israeli political and military authorities consistently consider the occupation to be a secondary matter, thereby legitimizing the outsourcing of key operations to external organizations.

The emerging field of the study of privatization of security has focused on the US case, and on the examples of the US reliance on PMSCs in Afghanistan, Iraq, Yugoslavia and elsewhere. By placing the PMSC in the center of its research, it loses the larger picture of privatized security. PMSCs are strongly tied into the arms industry, the prison industry and policing, topics which are left almost untouched by the literature on the privatization of security. Also, concentrating on the PMSCs leads to a focus on outsourcing as the only form of privatization studied, leaving sale and privatization by default unaddressed.

7.1 MAIN FINDINGS

I have attempted to draw a comprehensive picture of privatization of security in Israel, as well as to map the interests promoting and resisting the privatization of security. In addition to the twelve case studies surveyed in detail, many other policies of privatization of security and of avoiding such privatization have been systematically collected and categorized in Table A.1 in the Appendix.

The Israeli political, economic and social structures have been notoriously militaristic from the founding of the state, with security considerations penetrating every aspect of public policy and with large amounts of public resources directed to the production of security. Nevertheless, the legitimization of the privatization of security has advanced since the 1990s simultaneously in (1) outsourcing of military logistics; (2) the sale of Israel's arms companies; (3) the outsourcing of police operations and close collaboration with non-state actors in policing; (4) the outsourcing of military operations in the OPT through the establishment of the PA and through privatization of the checkpoints; (5) and the privatization of security by default, by encouraging individuals to produce or purchase security for themselves, and by allowing private security guards to wield authority close to that of police officers.

Privatization was pushed forward not just by neoliberal ideology but also by the transformation in Israel's society, namely, the individual-ism which reduced the motivation to enlist in the military, as well as by changes in the nature of armed conflicts: the end of the Cold War and political changes in the Middle East which have reduced the relevance of large conventional armies and increased the reliance of the Israeli Ministry of Defense on specialized security experts. Meanwhile, US military aid to Israel has been applied as a tool to exert pressure on Israel's arms industry to conform to a distribution of labor between the US and the Israeli arms industries. Israel had to abandon the self-sufficiency aspirations in arms production, end all armament development which could compete with the US weapon companies, and focus on complementary products for US arms. This process has been accompanied by the adoption of a business culture in the Israeli arms companies, which took on hierarchies and structures of private corporations while some of their production lines were sold off to private investors.

The privatization of security in Israel is most meaningful in the application of force for maintaining military occupations. Resulting from the crisis in Israel's security elite and its reluctance to engage in colonial policing operations, key functions of the occupation were outsourced first to the SLA and then to the PA. The outsourcing of security in occupied South Lebanon to the SLA has encountered mixed success because of the low legitimacy which the SLA had among the local population, being too closely associated with the Israeli military. The PA was formed as a quasi-sovereign body from the very group which resisted the Israeli occupation, the PLO, and therefore had more flexibility in its security operations in the OPT. The legitimization of outsourcing of security regarding the occupation began with non-corporate entities, the SLA and the PA, but has eroded the status of Israel's security institutions and opened the door to corporations to compete over the share of security in private hands. This led to further outsourcing of security, first with the reliance on private security companies in securing public spaces during the second Intifada, and then with the outsourcing of the military checkpoints in the West Bank and around the Gaza Strip to corporate entities.

7.2 INTERPRETATION AND DISCUSSION

7.2.1 Privatization of security in a capital as power framework

Theoretical frameworks have been applied which enable an alternative interpretation to the reasons for the privatization of security than those offered by conventional wisdom. Rather than considering the privatization of security an anomaly, a minor or peripheral occurrence or a rational application of incentives by the Israeli government through the free market, I adopt a political economy perspective. The commodification of security transforms symbolic capital into material capital in the Bourdieu sense, and in the analysis of Differential Accumulation Theory (DAT) it opens the arena for a race between institutions to accumulate differentially above the others.

PMSCs wield their influence to securitize the public space and to promote the culture of emergency and the commodification of security, thus opening new markets. By means of differential accumulation, those who are excluded from the public space by private security unwillingly contribute to the value of that space for those who may enter freely. This is where the DAT analytical framework comes into play, to analyze the competition between social institutions over power, and read the results of this conflict in the reallocation of differential accumulation.

The differential accumulation analysis allows for conclusions that would not otherwise have been possible to identify. We can identify that the balance of capital has shifted from the state in the direction of PMSCs and privately owned arms companies, while overall allocation of public resources to security has declined (Section 3.1.3), revealing a structural crisis in the Israeli security elite, and framing privatization as a coping mechanism with this crisis.

We can also deconstruct the sovereignty vs. mercenary dichotomy which is the main model discussed in the privatization of security literature, and see it as two separate dichotomies: public vs. private and centralized vs. decentralized. This is especially relevant to the spread of privatization by default in Israel's security operations. Although the old "nation in arms" model of large-scale mobilization for security in the Israeli public is associated with a strong public sector, it is also associated with a decentralized production of security. Neoliberal transformation has eroded the legitimacy of the public sector but did not attempt to centralize the production of security. Therefore, armed individuals suddenly switched from being a manifestation of a militaristic society (with low levels of privatization) to a manifestation of a highly privatized mode of security production by individuals, even though both modes are decentralized.

7.2.2 Crisis and resistance

Nearly every case study discussed in this book was accompanied by resistance from various elements within Israeli society. In some cases, the privatization process was structured by the private companies in a way which prevented the privatization of security, such as with the security of offshore natural-gas rigs in Section 3.2.1 or the privatization of the El-Al airline discussed in Section 3.1.5. Cases exist in which the government itself refused to forego its control over security and resisted the attempts of private companies to purchase it from them, such as the case of Lockheed-Martin's attempt to buy IMI discussed in Section 4.2.2. In some cases, the Israeli military opposed the outsourcing of security to external bodies, such as with the establishment of the Palestinian Authority discussed in Section 5.3.6. In one case the Israeli High Court overruled the privatization of a prison, as discussed in Section 4.3.5.

The embattled story of privatization of security is a struggle over the allocation of symbolic and material capital. It is a conflict not only between the state and private investors but also a fierce competition among PMSCs and arms companies over differential accumulation, a struggle that has even resulted in bloodshed between the Israeli military and the PA forces (Section 5.6.3). The various forms of resistance indicate that privatization of security in Israel was not a natural or simple development. It evolved in conditions of crisis, in which Israel's security elite had to reinvent itself. In the wake of the end of the Cold War, the rise of PMSCs on the global arena, the erosion of differential allocation of resources to security in Israel and the Palestinian resistance to the occupation, the Israeli security elite has adopted neoliberal coping mechanisms.

The strategy adopted by the Israeli security elites in order to overcome the resistance was to create the core vs. periphery framework discussed in Section 5.1. The framework avoids much of the resistance by vowing to keep the core of security operations under public control, and to privatize only peripheral functions of security organizations. This strategy has been largely successful in disguising the very existence of privatization of security as a technical issue or as a move towards cost-cutting for greater efficiency. It also disguised the high levels of dependency that were created for state institutions on private suppliers. In Section 2.2.1 I showed how "willed ignorance" is a self-destructive stance of state institutions, granting private actors unburdened by regulation a greater degree of freedom and influence over state policy.

7.3 MAIN CONCLUSIONS

The purpose of this book is to trace the reasons for the rapid transformation of Israel from a "strong state" (Hamilton & Stutton, 1989:1–5) in which the production of security is a major tool of government policy, to a state in which the private sector has expanded into the security sector to levels approaching those of the UK. These reasons are divided into three groups.

7.3.1 Allocation of public resources

The decline in the differential allocation of resources to security (see Graph 3.1), and the strong internal pressure to further cut public security spending have caused a crisis for Israel's security elite. It has restricted the career path in the political elite for many retired military and police officers, and pushed them towards the private sector. A steep decline in conscription deprived the security elite from its direct influence on the education of young Israeli citizens during their military service.

Neoliberal ideology encouraged the Israeli government to engage with private security companies staffed by former public employees rather than operate through departments of existing state institutions. The government budget is increasingly diverted to finance contracts with private companies, a move that neoliberal thinkers consider to be a cost-cutting measure. This encouraged the sale of sections of Israel's arms industry, the outsourcing of security in public spaces to PMSCs and the withdrawal of the state from providing certain security services to the public, which subsequently encourages individuals to produce or purchase security for themselves through privatization by default.

7.3.2 Responsibility for the application of force

The military occupation of the OPT has transformed Israel's security institutions, but it was an unwelcome transformation. Members of the security elite continued to consider conventional wars as the "core" activity of Israel's security institutions, regardless of the actual distribution of efforts. Maintaining the occupation, along with operations such as logistics and training, were allocated to a "secondary" role, and privatization through outsourcing has been legitimized. Although this argument is still considered controversial in the Israeli academia, the largest privatization of security has been the founding of the Palestinian Authority to oversee security operations in parts of the OPT (Section 5.3). Another part of this transformation has been the increasing reliance on technology as a labor-saving mechanism, as well as a tendency to address political and social challenges with technology tools procured from the private sector through outsourcing (Section 3.6).

7.3.3 Imitating the US and entering the global security market

These developments fit into place only when perceived in an inter-national context. Neoliberal ideology has increased its influence in Israel through US-trained economists, but the US military aid to Israel has created strong material incentives for the Israeli government and Israel's arms companies to adopt a more business-like culture in arms production and to gradually imitate the US model of a privately owned arms industry. The managers of the state-owned arms companies adopted a neoliberal ideology and called for privatization (Section 4.2). Originally, the Israeli arms industry was founded to meet the domestic needs of the Israeli security institutions, and arms exports was considered to be a pressure valve for the industry, and as a source for additional funding. As the crisis in the Israeli security elite intensified, arms exports became increasingly more important for the Israeli arms industry. Israeli arms exporters became dependent on outsourcing contracts with the Israeli government in order to promote their sales in global markets, thereby applying pressure on the Israeli government to respond to developments in the global arms trade, and in the global market for PMSCs. The government responded by utilizing technologies offered by private companies, creating opportunities for private companies to "battle-test" their technologies as part of Israeli security operations, and by allowing the Israeli Ministry of Defense to take on a role similar to the US Pentagon in supporting the private arms industry (Section 3.1.2).

*   *   *

The crisis of the Israeli security elites has not been resolved. The Palestinian resistance to the occupation has not abated, but the resistance to privatization of security inside Israel is fighting a losing battle. The more privatization progresses, the more it turns the Israeli occupation of the OPT into a question of money. When the Israeli authorities find themselves unwilling or unable to invest the resources needed to keep the contracts with countless PMSCs and arms companies in place, they will no longer be able to avoid the political issues. When that moment comes, the core function of the Israeli security elites will be revealed: the occupation and repression of Palestinians. The legal and moral consequences of this revelation are such that this elite group will no longer be able to call the shots, and it remains to be seen what political group will rise to take their place.

Appendix: Overview of Privatization of Security in Israel

A timeline summarizing the main events in privatization of security which occurred in Israel over the years is shown in Table A.1. The table mentions the events briefly, referring to the chapter in which the event was discussed. The events are ordered chronologically. The stream of events peters out in the years 2015–17 not because privatization of security has slowed, but because many of the policies for these years have not yet been reported as of the writing of this book. The type of privatization or anti-privatization involved is also mentioned: sale, outsourcing, privatization by default, preparation for privatization, resistance to privatization or regulation. Finally, each event is associated with a type of institution: "internal" for police, prisons and security; "military"; and "industry" for logistics and arms production.

Table A.1 Timeline of Privatization of Security

Chapter	Event in Privatization of Security in Israel	Type	Institution
4.2.2 1933	Establishment of IMI as a department of the MOD.	–	Industry
4.2 1937	Establishment of the private El-Op arms company.	–	Industry
4.2 1950	Establishment of the Soltam Systems company (later bought by Elbit Systems).	–	Industry
4.2 1953	Establishment of IAI arms company as a state-owned company.	–	Industry
4.2 1958	Establishment of Rafael arms company as a department of the MOD.	–	Industry
4.2 1962	Establishment of the Tadiran arms company by joining two factories owned by the MOD and Koor.	–	Industry
4.2 1966	Establishment of the private Elbit arms company (later renamed Elbit Systems).	Default	Industry
4.2 1967	Establishment of the private Elisra arms company (later bought by Elbit Systems).	Default	Industry
4.3.1 1968	Law for registering small businesses stipulates that police authorization is required, allowing the police to require security guards.	Outsourcing	Internal

Chapter	Event in Privatization of Security in Israel	Type	Institution
4.1	Bar-Lev Line of fortresses built by private construction companies (until 1969).	Outsourcing	Military
1969			
4.2	MOD sells 35% of the Tadiran arms company to a US company.	Sale	Industry
1970			
4.3.1	Establishment of the Department of Payment, which imposed on employers of Palestinians the responsibility to supervise employees and guard against security threats.	Outsourcing	Internal
1972			
4.3.6	Knesset passes the Private Investigators Law, to define the authority and rights of private investigators.	Default	Internal
1973			
6.2	The US begins to provide large-scale military aid to Israel, transforming Israel's arms industry.	–	Industry
1974			
3.1.4	Establishment of the Civil Guard, a volunteer force for internal security.	Outsourcing	Internal
1979			
5.2	SLA established to help the army control South Lebanon.	Outsourcing	Military
1984			
4.2	Establishment of the private Magal company (later traded in the US).	Default	Industry
1985			
2.5.3	The "Stabilization Plan" implements neoliberal policies and prepares the way for extensive privatizations.	–	
1986			
6.2.3	US DOD publishes a report recommending that Israel will discontinue the "Lavi" fighter-plane project.	Outsourcing	Industry

Chapter	Event in Privatization of Security in Israel	Type	Institution
1987			
6.2.3	Government cancels the "Lavi" fighter-plane project, preferring to rely on imported fighters.	Outsourcing	Industry
1990			
4.2	IMI arms company is incorporated as a state-owned company.	Preparation	Industry
4.3.6	Municipal police model developed by the government, allowing municipalities with different resources differentiated police coverage.	Default	Internal
1991			
5.1.2	Ehud Barak appointed commander in chief of the army, says "everything which doesn't shoot or directly helps to shoot – will be cut."	Outsourcing	Military
1993			
5.1.2	Assumed date of quote by Prime Minister Yitzhak Rabin that the PA will keep the OPT under control "without the High Court and without B'tselem."	Outsourcing	Military
5.3	Establishment of the Palestinian Authority which assumes partial responsibility over parts of the OPT, but is not sovereign.	Outsourcing	Military
4.1.1	Sadan Committee calls for new policies in Israel's MOD. The call is taken by Israeli authorities as a call for outsourcing and privatization.	Outsourcing	Military
1994			
5.3	Establishment of the PA.	Outsourcing	Military
4.3.6	Israeli police Chief of Staff Assaf Hefetz appointed, one of the main promoters of privatization in the police force.	Outsourcing	Internal
1996			
5.3.6	Armed conflict between the army and the PA.	Resistance	Military

Chapter	Event in Privatization of Security in Israel	Type	Institution
4.2.2	US arms company Lockheed-Martin offers to buy IMI and is refused.	–	Industry
5.1.2	US DOD document on outsourcing of military activities published. Has long-lasting impact on Israeli policies.	Outsourcing	Military
1997			
6.3.3	Establishment of the Aeronautics arms company as a private company.	Default	Military
1999			
4.3.6	Government rules that organizers and not police are responsible for securing sporting events.	Default	Internal
6.5	HP wins a tender through its EDS Israeli subsidiary to operate the Basel system for biometric identification of Palestinians.	Outsourcing	Military
5.2.2	The state claims in court that it does not bear responsibility for torture at the Khiam Detention Center, which was operated by the SLA.	Outsourcing	Military
2000			
4.3.6	"City Without Violence" project incorporates NGOs and surveillance services by private companies in police operations.	Outsourcing	Internal
5.3.6	Armed conflict between the army and the PA.	Resistance	Military
5.2.3	Israel withdraws from South Lebanon, SLA collapses. Its members flee to Israel.	–	Military
5.4.1	Police begin enforcing a law requiring businesses to hire private security guards. Rise in number of security guards and companies.	Outsourcing	Internal
2001			
6.2.4	After the 9/11 attacks, Israeli companies dominate the homeland security sector.	Default	Industry
4.1.1	Chief of staff announces that the army is adopting business elements, and that decision-making processes are derived from the private sector.	Preparation	Military

Chapter	Event in Privatization of Security in Israel	Type	Institution
6.5	HP wins the tender of the Ministry of the Interior to produce biometric identity cards, after ten out of eleven of the competing companies were disqualified.	Outsourcing	Internal
4.3.4	The army begins to obtain vehicles through leasing companies.	Outsourcing	Military
2002			
5.1.2	Commander of the air force Dan Halutz says that "the principle guiding the air force is that every theme which is not directly related to the security missions of the air force can be managed by another body."	Outsourcing	Military
6.4	G4S buys the Israeli Hashmira security company.	–	
4.2	Rafael arms company is incorporated as a state-owned company.	Preparation	Industry
2003			
3.1.5	El-Al airline is privatized, but the security functions remain under state control.	Resistance	Internal
2004			
4.1.2	Army establishes an "Israeli-Jewish Identity" department with a budget to purchase education services.	Outsourcing	Military
5.4.1	Number of private security guards peaks at 100,000.	Default	Internal
2005			
4.3.5	Evidence that the Dadash private company operates canteens in Israeli prisons.	Outsourcing	Internal
4.2.2	Government decides to sell IMI.	Sale	Industry
4.3.6	Legislation passed to allow private security guards more authority in their "close surroundings."	Default	Internal
4.3.5	Hashmira wins tender to operate system of electronic bracelets on prisoners.	Outsourcing	Internal
5.3.4	PA's security forces account for 26% of the security forces in Israeli-controlled territory.	Outsourcing	Military

Chapter	Event in Privatization of Security in Israel	Type	Institution
6.5	Five companies are selected in a tender for privatization of checkpoints in the OPT. HP wins the tender to operate the biometric system applied to Palestinians.	Outsourcing	Internal
4.2.2	The Magen factory of IMI is sold to Sami Katzav.	Sale	Industry
2006			
4.3.6	Committee convened to formulate the project for a national training center of the police. It decides to include private companies in the training program.	Outsourcing	Internal
5.3.6	Following the victory of Hamas in the PA's election, the US boosts security aid to the PA president's office of Mahmoud Abbas. Further aid was added in 2007 and 2008.	Outsourcing	Military
5.5.1	Government designates 48 checkpoints to be privatized. The Defense Ministry's Crossing Administration is established.	Outsourcing	Military
6.5	HP signs a contract to administer the navy's IT infrastructure.	Outsourcing	Military
5.3.5	Salam Fayyad appointed prime minister of the PA and promotes a policy of "good governance."	Outsourcing	Military
2007			
4.3.6	Knesset legislates addendum to the Police Law to specify conditions for hiring police officers by private individuals.	Sale	Internal
6.3.1	Legal framework for arms export licenses is finalized.	Regulation	Industry
4.3.3	MOD signs contract with McKinsey to issue an efficiency plan for the army.	Outsourcing	Military
5.3.4	PA security forces decline in number after the Gaza–West Bank split. The decline continued until 2011.	Resistance	Military
4.1.1	The Brodet Committee publishes its recommendations for restructuring the defense budget, and includes a recommendation to privatize.	Outsourcing	Military
2008			
4.3.1	"Dromi Law" passes in the Knesset, allowing civilians to use lethal force against trespassers.	Default	Internal

Chapter	Event in Privatization of Security in Israel	Type	Institution
4.3.6	Knesset legislates authority of security guards to detain and use force while securing sporting events.	Default	Internal
4.3.5	Israeli High Court rules against the establishment of a privatized prison.	Resistance	Internal
2009			
6.5	Biometric Database Law passes in the Knesset, to promote biometric identity cards produced by HP.	Outsourcing	Internal
6.5	Contract with HP to administer IT infrastructure for the navy expanded to serve the entire army.	Outsourcing	Military
4.3.5	Dadash company wins tender to operate all canteens in Israeli prisons.	Outsourcing	Internal
5.3.6	PA calls to boycott products from the colonies.	Resistance	Military
4.3.6	High Court rules that privately funded municipal police patrols are only allowed to prevent terrorism.	Resistance	Internal
4.3.3	The army reveals cut plans recommended by McKinsey, relevant to 40% of the defense budget.	Outsourcing	Military
2010			
5.4.2	Ministry of Justice gives security guards in East Jerusalem the authority to operate there, after they have been stationed there since 1987.	Outsourcing	Military
6.3.3	Shmira Ubitakhon wins a tender to operate security services in the Eilat airport for 2010–13.	Outsourcing	Internal
4.2	IAI CEO calls for an immediate privatization of IAI.	Sale	Industry
4.3.5	Israeli Prison Service issues a tender to outsource the tapping of phone conversations of prisoners, at the expense of the prisoners.	Outsourcing	Internal
4.3.6	Shikun Ubinui and G4S win the tender to build and operate the National Training Center of the police.	Outsourcing	Internal
3.4	The military acknowledges that the conscription rate fell under 50%.	Preparation	Military

Chapter	Event in Privatization of Security in Israel	Type	Institution
3.4	The military adopts marketing techniques in recruiting conscripts.	Preparation	Military
2011			
4.3.4	Army closes many military clinics and outsources soldiers' health services to two health organizations.	Outsourcing	Military
4.3.4	Despite a study demonstrating that leasing companies are more expensive than maintaining vehicles directly by the army, the army continues to rely on leasing companies.	Outsourcing	Military
4.3.6	Knesset approves order to allow privately funded police patrols in wealthy municipalities.	Outsourcing	Internal
4.1.3	MOD claims that Bahad City through BOT will save money to the ministry.	Outsourcing	Military
4.3.4	State Comptroller reports that an unnamed software company received excessive sums for a contract which was awarded through a tailored tender of the air force.	Outsourcing	Military
4.3.3	The McKinsey Report for efficiency plans for the Israeli army was supposed to be published, but was not.	Outsourcing	Military
4.2.2	Union of IMI workers prevents the privatization of the company.	Resistance	Industry
2012			
5.1.2	First PFI project signed to finance purchase of Italian training airplanes.	Outsourcing	Military
4.2	"Tor," a company formed by IAI and Elbit, receives a contract to offer flight training for the air force.	Outsourcing	Military
4.3.6	Four Israeli universities and one kibbutz employ private security companies to disperse protest actions on campus.	Default	Internal
5.3.6	Government approves the transfer of advances on taxes to the PA to stabilize it during widespread demonstrations.	Outsourcing	Military
4.3.1	Museum guides from Ariel University serving an outsourced project for the military are laid off, thereby exposing the fact that the university was used by the army as a human resources company.	Outsourcing	Military

Chapter	Event in Privatization of Security in Israel	Type	Institution
4.3.6	Legislation to expand the authority of private security guards to employ "reasonable force."	Default	Internal
4.1.2	MOD forms a special department for tenders and outsourcing.	Outsourcing	Military
5.4.1	Ministry of Public Security requires a fee whenever the person responsible for a company's weapons is replaced.	Regulation	Internal
5.3.6	PA appeals and receives member-state status in the UN.	Resistance	Military
4.3.4	Privatization of health services to soldiers expanded, civilian doctors empowered to grant leave of duty permits. MOD offers incentives to prevent soldiers from being sent to the emergency room.	Outsourcing	Military
4.2	Program for gradual privatization of IAI adopted by the government.	Sale	Industry
5.4.2	650 contractors accepted as public policewomen and policemen.	Resistance	Internal
4.1.3	Tenders for developing Bahad City issued to private companies. The MOD must compete in the tenders as a company.	Outsourcing	Military
2013			
4.2	A government plan to issue 20% of the stocks of Rafael and IAI to the public is announced.	Sale	Industry
4.2.2	Ashot Ashkelon added to IMI's privatization package.	Sale	Industry
5.5.1	MOD lists five final checkpoints in or around the OPT which are yet to be privatized. 13 already privatized.	Outsourcing	Military
6.6.5	Privatized biometric database pilot program begins.	Outsourcing	Internal
5.3.3	PA police invited by Israel into the A-Ram neighborhood in Area C.	Outsourcing	Internal
4.3.6	Application of law to expand the authority of security guards and municipal inspectors reaches 17 municipalities.	Default	Internal
4.1.3	The Minrav construction company's profit skyrockets after winning the tender to build Bahad City.	Outsourcing	Military

Chapter	Event in Privatization of Security in Israel	Type	Institution
3.1.5	The private El-Al airline is declared a monopoly because of its security services.	Regulation	Internal
4.3.6	The RAND Corporation publishes a consultancy report for the Israeli police, which was commissioned the same year.	Outsourcing	Internal
4.3.6	The Ministry of Public Security publishes a tender for long-term consultation services.	Outsourcing	Internal
4.3.5	The government halts a project to outsource phone surveillance of prisoners pending legislation.	Resistance	Internal
6.3.2	UK's Export Control Organization reveals that Israeli arms companies deal with states which Israel does not have diplomatic relations with.	Default	Industry
2014			
4.2.2	Plan for the sale of IMI finalized under a new name: "New IMI" and excluding the Givon department and the Slavin factory.	Sale	Industry
4.1.3	Negev municipalities sign agreement on the distribution of municipal taxes from Bahad City.	Outsourcing	Military
6.4	G4S announces it will not renew its contracts with the Israeli Prison Service.	Resistance	Military/ Internal
4.1.3	Shultz Group receives exclusive charter to operate restaurants and cafeterias in Bahad City.	Outsourcing	Military
4.2	State Comptroller exposes that the MOD does not register patents, allowing private companies to take possession of military intellectual property.	Default	Military
4.3.6	Ministry of Transportation launches program to train bus drivers as security guards.	Default	Internal
4.3.2	State distribution of gas masks to the public discontinued.	Default	Military
4.3.6	Volunteers in uniform authorized to issue traffic tickets.	Outsourcing	Internal
5.5.1	Only two security companies, Modi'in Ezrahi and Sheleg Lavan, remain to operate all of the privatized checkpoints in the OPT.	Outsourcing	Military
6.3.1	MOD relinquishes regulation of commissions by arms deals mediators.	Default	Industry

Chapter	Event in Privatization of Security in Israel	Type	Institution
2015			
4.3.6	Government plans stage B of the national policing training center with a tender exemption for the Policity group.	Outsourcing	Internal
5.6	Government calls on individuals to attack terrorists.	Default	Military
2016			
5.6	Elor Azaria kills Fateh al-Sharif.	Default	Military
4.3.3	MOD approves another contract with McKinsey without a tender.	Outsourcing	Military
5.6	Avigdor Lieberman appointed Minister of Defense instead of Moshe Ya'alon.	Preparation	Military
2017			
4.1.2	Attempt to move the military radio stations to the MOD fails, radio remains part of the military.	Resistance	Military
5.6	Elor Azaria sentenced and appeals.	Resistance	Military
4.3.6	Municipalities take over public transportation cameras and fines from police.	Preparation	Internal
4.1.2	Blue Flag international air force training operated by private company.	Outsourcing	Military
4.1.2	MOD plans three logistics centers through outsourcing by 2013.	Outsourcing	Military
4.3.6	Private security guards in Tel-Aviv leak racial profiling practices.	Outsourcing	Internal

Notes

CHAPTER 1

1. PMSCs will be mentioned frequently in the text that follows. It is a generic term which may include a wide variety of companies, from companies offering consultation and logistics support to those which send armed fighters to conflict areas. Such a generic term is needed because many of the companies diversify their services to cover a wide variety of security and military services, and because the distinction between military and security operations is continuously eroded (Singer, 2003:80–3; Spearin, 2008:203–6).
2. The term "institutions" is very broadly defined by Veblen, the founder of the institutional political economy school of thought, as evolving social affiliations which not only include official institutions but also social institutions such as "money," "marriage," etc. (Veblen, 1994:12–14).
3. The Washington Consensus is a set of ten policy prescriptions set forth by the World Bank and the International Monetary Fund as a universal reform package, associated with the global rise of neoliberal policies.
4. The linguist Dovid Katz explained: "*bitokhn* in Yiddish can only mean 'confidence in God's providence or fate' and, by extension, 'optimism.' Who can blame successful state builders for having to conscript the word for the new concept of 'state and military security,' which is, quite naturally, the primary meaning of *bitakhon* in Israeli [Hebrew]" (Katz, 2004:369).
5. The Ministry of Public Security is in charge of the police, the Israeli Prison Service (IPS) and fire-fighting. It is has no authority of the Israeli Security Agency (ISA) which answers to the Prime Minister's Office.

CHAPTER 2

1. Ferdinand Lassalle was a nineteenth-century jurist, activist and political thinker who promoted socialism in Prussia. He coined the concept of the "night watchman state" as a critique at the tendency to reduce the state's function to security alone (see Section 2.5.2), a metaphor for a state which has privatized all but security. Bichler and Nitzan place the temporary ownership over economic assets by the state within that framework, the state using its role as a keeper to guard those assets during a time in which direct private ownership is undesirable.
2. Public goods are defined in economic theory as goods which are not exhausted when they are used by an individual, and which are difficult or impossible to be excluded from. Examples of public goods include roads, a

clean environment, etc. The goods which are most commonly invoked as examples for public goods are public order and defense (Starr, 1988).

3. A "strong state" is understood here as an interventionist state with economically strong institutions.

4. The "Stabilization Plan" is the emergency bundle of economic reforms which the Israeli unity government adopted in 1985 in order to halt the hyperinflation and economic crisis, and which resembled the structural readjustment programs promoted by the IMF and the World Bank in developing countries during those years.

5. The literature on this transformation is quite extensive. Examples from neclassical authors are Gross (2000:1566, 1574) and Eckstein and Tsiddon (2004: 971–1002). Marxist approaches can be found with Shalev (2004:85–115).

CHAPTER 3

1. Here I am referring to two military-run radio stations, broadcasting music, news, traffic reports and interviews for the general public on civilian frequencies, and not to communications broadcasted over military frequencies.

2. The military role in the OPT has changed with the establishment of the Palestinian Authority (PA), which will be addressed extensively in Section 5.3.

3. Developing towns were designated by the government as priority areas because of their low socioeconomic conditions, high unemployment and high poverty levels.

4. In 2012, Dun & Bradstreet 100 listed the state-owned Israeli Aerospace Industries (IAI) as Israel's fifth biggest industrial company (in all sectors), while the privately owned Elbit Systems, the private arms company that was founded in 1966, was ranked as the seventh biggest, and fell to ninth place by 2014 (Dun & Bradstreet, 2012, 2015).

5. The rise of financial capitalism in those decades has created a distortion when comparing expenditures as a proportion of GDP throughout this long period. Because GDP calculations have become heavily influenced by the growth of the financial sector, it is difficult to estimate whether the impact of military costs on the average standard of living has actually declined as is the common argument (Shafir & Peled, 2004:234–5). For the purpose of our discussion here, though, the focus is on comparing Israel with other countries in different periods, rather than analyzing the global trends in military spending.

6. In 1991, Kuwait's military budget briefly raised the average proportion of military spending for the Middle East (excluding Israel) above Israel's rate of expenditure. Yet Kuwait remains a relatively small country, and a weighted average would show a lower spike for that year. A weighted average was not used for this graph, however, because of an insufficient breakdown of available data according to country, GDP and population.

7. Aluf Ben, a journalist for *Ha'aretz*, compiled an estimate for the budget of the ISA and the Mossad based on government requests for use of the budget reserve. His report found that over the period 2005–12 the combined budget of the two secret institutions ranged from NIS 4.28 billion in 2006 to NIS 6.04 billion in 2012. This report shows that Israel's intelligence organizations add more than 10 percent to the overall defense budget, and that they increase at a faster rate than the total government budget. But because the numbers are unofficial and unconfirmed, and because they cannot be compared to the expenditure on intelligence in the other countries presented here, they will not be used. The consequence of not including the intelligence budgets is that Israel's defense expenditure is further underestimated compared to the actual amounts (Ben, 2013a).

8. Major General Moshe Mizrahi in the conference, "Privatization Processes in the Police: Do They Contribute to the Citizen's Security?" in the Van Leer Institute in Jerusalem, July 17, 2012.

9. Amir Paz-Fuchs in the conference, "Privatization Processes in the Police: Do They Contribute to the Citizen's Security?" in the Van Leer Institute in Jerusalem, July 17, 2012.

10. The navy later demanded NIS 3 billion in public funds for four warships, unmanned aerial vehicles (UAVs) and surveillance mechanisms to be placed for the protection of the gas rigs (Cohen & Trilnik, 2012).

11. The Civil Administration is Israel's military government of the OPT.

12. The Separation Wall did not achieve a clear distinction between areas of the West Bank because sections of it have continuously been torn down and rebuilt in order to include additional colonies on the Israeli side or to exclude Palestinian communities on the Palestinian side, following rapid changes in policy and decisions of the Israeli High Court.

13. Ashkenazi are Jews of European descent.

14. In respecting the self-determination right of people to define themselves, the term "Palestinian" should be applied to most Arab citizens of Israel. The term "Israeli Arabs" is sometime considered offensive, as it is frequently used in the context of denying Palestinian national aspirations and history in Palestine. It also clashes with the identity of Arab Jewish citizens of Israel. Not all Adyghes, Druze and Bedouines in Israel consider themselves to be Palestinians (Amara & Schnell, 2007:175–93).

15. The figure does not refer to how many are annually exempted, but the total number of people aged 18–41 who are currently part of the agreement.

16. Additionally, people who are not recruited into the military include draft-dodgers, conscientious objectors and people with mental and physical disabilities.

17. Mizrahim are Jews of Arab, Turkish or Persian descent.

CHAPTER 4

1. As only the public sector in Israel is obligated to publish the wages of employees while the private sector may keep the wages of the employees a

secret, it is impossible to estimate whether cost-cutting in wage expenditure has been achieved in cases of privatization (Coren, 2013b).

2. In 2013 outsourcing of health services was expanded, and the companies received incentives if they avoided referring soldiers to the emergency room (Linder-Gantz, 2013). The Health Corps considered repealing the outsourcing of health services for soldiers due to a rise in medical leave of absence for soldiers (Paz-Fuchs & Ben-Simkhon-Peleg, 2014:60).

3. A "step-in clause" is a common clause in privatization contracts, which allows the state to take control of the project back from the private company or NGO, while compensating the company (New Zealand Parliament, 2015:8698).

4. Commander Ayelet Elishar in the conference, "Privatization Processes in the Police: Do They Contribute to the Citizen's Security?" in the Van Leer Institute in Jerusalem, July 17, 2012.

5. Haim Rivlin in the conference, "Privatization Processes in the Police: Do They Contribute to the Citizen's Security?" in the Van Leer Institute in Jerusalem, July 17, 2012.

6. In a PFI, private actors are invited to participate through investment in an already existing public infrastructure, creating a PPP (Hall et al., 2003:4–6).

7. Erella Shadmi in the conference, "Privatization Processes in the Police: Do They Contribute to the Citizen's Security?" in the Van Leer Institute in Jerusalem, July 17, 2012.

8. Ibid.

9. Anne Suciu in the conference, "Privatization Processes in the Police: Do They Contribute to the Citizen's Security?" in the Van Leer Institute in Jerusalem, July 17, 2012.

CHAPTER 5

1. Lecture by Brigadier-General Baruch Spiegel, consultant to the MOD, given in the Van Leer Institute in Jerusalem, February 17, 2006.

2. Amir Paz-Fuchs in the conference, "Privatization Processes in the Police: Do They Contribute to the Citizen's Security?" in the Van Leer Institute in Jerusalem, July 17, 2012.

3. PFI (Private Finance Initiative, Section 4.3.6) and BOT (Build-Operate-Transfer) are forms of privatization. BOT is an outsourcing of a project to a private contractor, which transfers the ownership of the project back to the state after it has been operated for a designated number of years (Hall et al., 2003:4–6). The first PFI contract signed by the military, however, was recorded in 2012 as Israeli and Italian banks were invited to finance the purchase of training airplanes from Italy. Further PFI projects were approved after that deal (Paz-Fuchs & Ben-Simkhon-Peleg, 2014:62).

4. B'tselem is an Israeli human-rights organization which regularly reports on human-rights violations committed by the Israeli military (www.btselem.org/).

5. Although the Israeli government does not fund the PA, the Paris Accords signed in Paris in April 1994 stipulate that Israel maintains control over the customs of the OPT, and periodically transfers to the PA the customs revenues, as well as revenues from VAT and income tax paid by Palestinians to the Israeli government. These payments comprise approximately a third of the PA's budget (Byrnen, 2005:4–6, 8, 11).

6. Wikileaks documents exposed attempts by the Israeli government to coordinate the 2008–09 invasion of the Gaza Strip with the Palestinian Authority (Ravid, 2010), a fact which was denied by the PA (Ravid & Associated Press, 2010).

7. The eight are: (1) Civilian Police, (2) National Security Forces (PNSF), (3) General Intelligence Service (GIS), (4) Civil Defense, (5) Coastal Police, (6) Preventive Security Agency (PSA), (7) Presidential Security (Force-17) and (8) Military Intelligence (Lia, 2006:310).

8. Such documents include: PNA (2009, 2011a, 2011b:24–32, 2012).

9. Moshe Ya'alon, who at the time was the commander of the general staff of the Israeli military, claimed in an interview that it was his idea to appoint Mahmoud Abbas to replace Arafat (Michael, 2010:60).

10. The cases of PMSCs operating in airport security in Israel, and the involvement of G4S in the Israeli security market (Section 6.4) can be seen as sub-cases or examples of the privatization of security companies in the public sphere, rather than similar and parallel cases.

11. Dun & Bradstreet, https://tinyurl.com/ycwpjjkg, accessed May 2013.

12. Anne Suciu in the conference, "Privatization Processes in the Police: Do They Contribute to the Citizen's Security?" in the Van Leer Institute in Jerusalem, July 17, 2012.

13. The term "civilianizing the passages" is the official term used by the Israeli MOD to describe the privatization of the checkpoints. It is less accurate than "privatizing the checkpoints" because of three reasons: (1) the checkpoints are used only for security checks and for controlling the ability of people and goods to cross, but they serve no other function of border passages such as customs, passport stamping or access to an airport or a seaport; (2) the checkpoints are not civilian, and continue to operate as a military installation by armed guards; (3) the checkpoints have been given to the management of a private company, a fact which the term "civilianizing the passages" does not convey.

14. Lecture by Brigadier-General Baruch Spiegel, consultant to the MOD, given in the Van Leer Institute in Jerusalem in February 17, 2006.

15. Ibid.

16. Ibid.

CHAPTER 6

1. Conventional arms refer to small arms, artillery, munitions, military vehicles (land, air and sea), but not to unconventional weapons (nuclear, chemical, biological) or to riot gear and surveillance equipment.

2. "Complementary goods" is a term from microeconomic theory to describe products that complement each other. An increase in the demand for one product is expected to increase demand for the other products. For example, cars and petrol are complementary goods.

3. Considering the secret nature of Israel's security operations and especially those of the Mossad, interviews are impractical as a means to obtain research information. The memoirs published by Ravid-Ravitz cannot be considered as a reliable source on the actual events which took place. However, his choice to describe the meeting, and to emphasize Peres's comment on the connection between the US-Israeli and the Israeli-Phalangists relations demonstrates that the connection was not lost on senior members of the Mossad, such as Ravid-Ravitz himself.

4. Leila Stockmarr, "The Making of Israel's Homeland Security and the Unmaking of Palestine," a lecture given in the conference, "The Israeli Homeland Security and its Global Impact" at the Dansk Institut for Internationale Studier (DIIS), March 9, 2016.

5. An exact ratio cannot be calculated without knowing the number of retired senior military officers. Maman identified 87 senior officers who retired in the years 1974–84. The number of retired officers in recent years is confidential, but the existence of 6784 registered arms exporters in 2013, even if only a minority of them were retired senior officers, is a strong indication that the ratio of retired officers who turn to the arms trade has increased.

6. These figures are for arms agreements, which include elements of arms delivery over time. Figures on arms transfers in each given year indicate a slower, but still significant, decline in arms exports, as those figures include arms delivered according to deals signed in previous years.

7. A partial list of Israeli homeland security programs which export services abroad include: Athena GS3, Ballistra, Ben International Security Consultants, Beni Tal, Cosmec Consulting, Coral Integrated Security Systems Ltd, Cortex, Counter-Terrorism Solutions Ltd, DEMCO, EMT Investigations, Energomash International, Golan Group, Global Security, Hashmira, Hawkeye International Security Consultancy (Ephod Magen), ICTS Global, International Krav-Maga Federation, International Security and Defence Systems, International Security and Marketing, International Security Consultancy, International Security Instructors, Israel Security Academy, ISP Ltd, IsraTeam, K-9 Solutions, Levdan, Max Security, Nirtal, Nitzra, Security Hashomrim, Silver Shadow, Spearhead (Hod Hahanit), Spike Security, Tandu and Team 3 (Hillary, 2007).

8. Goodwill represents the economic value of its intangible assets. It is created when assets are bought above their stated price.

Filmography

Dayan, Ilana, 2009, *Thus the Israeli Bribe Industry Operates in India*, Uvda, Channel 2, October 27.

Feldman, Yotam, 2013, *The Lab*, Gum Films, Israel.

Johnston, Nicole, 2009, *Israel 'Outsourcing' Occupation*, Al-Jazeera English, December 22, http://english.aljazeera.net/news/middleeast/2009/12/200912 2213836932226.html.

Kotler, Oshrat, 2008, *The Lords of War*, Channel 10, March 31.

Bibliography

Abrahamsen, Rita; Williams, Michael C., 2009, "Security Beyond the State: Global Security Assemblages in International Politics," *International Political Sociology*, Vol. 3, pp. 1–17.

Abu-Qarn, Aamer S., Abu-Bader, Suleiman, 2007, "Structural Breaks in Military Expenditures: Evidence for Egypt, Israel, Jordan and Syria," *Public Policy*, Vol. 14, No. 1, pp. 1–27.

Abunimah, Ali, 2007, "A Setback for the Bush Doctrine in Gaza," *The Electronic Intifada*, June 1407, https://electronicintifada.net/content/setback-bush-doctrine-gaza/7006, accessed June 2015.

Ackerman, Yossi, 2002, "Policy in Light of Private-Public Ownership of the Industry," in Tov, Imri (ed.), *Security and the National Economy in Israel: Challenges and Answers in Policy of Producing Security*, Memo No. 62, October, Tel-Aviv: Jaffee Center for Strategic Studies, pp. 127–31.

ACRI (Association for Civil Rights in Israel), 2008, "New and Illegal Collection Systems in East Jerusalem," Jerusalem: Association for Civil Rights in Israel, May 14, www.acri.org.il/he/?p=1883, accessed September 2012.

Addameer, 2011, *Violations Against Palestinian Prisoners and Detainees in Israeli Prisons and Detention Centers, Annual Report 2010*, Ramallah: Addameer Prisoner Support and Human Rights Association.

Adut, Rami; Hever, Shir, 2006, "Breaking the Labor Market – the Welfare to Work Plan in Israel, Focus on East Jerusalem," *Economy of the Occupation*, Part 7–8, The Alternative Information Center, Jerusalem, April–May.

Agmon, Tamir, 2010, "Budgets Intended for Former SLA Members," Research and Information Center at the Knesset, Jerusalem, October 12.

Akhikam, Moshe-David; Morgenstern, Ronit, 2009, "Tadiran Moves its Air Conditioning Factory to China, the Workers Go Home," *Ma'ariv*, August 6.

Al-Haq, 2008, "Torturing Each Other: The Widespread Practices of Arbitrary Detention and Torture in the Palestinian Territory," Executive Summary, Ramallah, July.

Alakhbar, 2012, "Sabra and Shatila: Escaping Justice," *Alakhbar English*, September 14, http://english.al-akhbar.com/node/12190, accessed October 2012.

Alexandra, Andrew, 2008, "Mars Meets Mammon," in Alexandra, Andrew; Baker, Deane-Peter; Caparini, Marina (eds.), *Private Military and Security Companies: Ethics, Policies and Civil-Military Relations*, London & New York: Routledge, pp. 89–101.

Allen, Lori, 2008, "Getting By the Occupation: How Violence Became Normal During the Second Palestinian Intifada," *Cultural Anthropology*, Vol. 23, No. 3, pp. 453–87.

Alsaafin, Linah, 2012, "Palestinian Authority: Running Israel's Guantanamo," *Al-Akhbar English*, September 27, http://english.al-akhbar.com/node/12668, accessed December 2013.

Alternative Information Center, 2008, "Palestine Investment Conference Opens in Bethlehem," The Alternative Information Center website, May 22, www.alternativenews.org/english/index.php/politics/politico/103-topics/news/1206-palestine-investment-conference-opens-in-bethlehem-1206, accessed December 2013.

AMAN, 2013, *Corruption Report, Palestine 2012*, Jerusalem: The Coalition for Integrity and Accountability – AMAN, April.

Amara, Muhammad; Schnell, Izhak, 2007, "Identity Repertoires among Arabs in Israel," *Journal of Ethnic and Migration Studies*, Vol. 30, No. 1, pp. 175–93.

Amir, Merav, 2010, *Borders Beyond Territory: Population Management through Border-Making and the Borders of Israel*, PhD Thesis, Tel-Aviv University, October.

Amirav, Moshe, 2007, *The Jerusalem Syndrome; Israel's Unification Policy Delusions 1967–2007* [*Syndrom Yerushalayim: Kakh Karsa Hamediniyut Leikhud Yerushalaim*], Jerusalem: Carmel.

Amit, Hagai, 2013, "Israel Military Industries: Powerful Arms but Feet of Clay," *Ha'aretz*, September 29, www.haaretz.com/business/.premium-1.549562, accessed November 2013.

—— 2017a, "Hizkiyahu was Recruited to Satisfy Lieberman and the Privatization of Taas is on its Way Again," *TheMarker*, June 20, www.themarker.com/news/macro/1.4181665, accessed July 2017.

—— 2017b, "Cost of New IDF Supply Center; NIS 3–4 Billion," *TheMarker*, August 15, www.themarker.com/allnews/1.4352560, accessed September 2017.

Amnesty International, 1992, The Khiam Detainees: "Torture and Ill-Treatment," Amnesty International, AI Index: MDE 15/8/92, May.

—— 2013, "'Shut Up We are the Police': Use of Excessive Force by Palestinian Authority in the Occupied West Bank," Amnesty International, AI Index: MDE 21/006/2013, September 23.

Amrov, Sabrien; Tartir, Alaa, 2014, "Subcontracting Repression in the West Bank and Gaza," *New York Times*, November 26, www.nytimes.com/2014/11/27/opinion/subcontracting-repression-in-the-west-bank-and-gaza.html?_r=0, accessed July 2015.

Amsterdamsky, Shaul, 2016, "The IDF Hires the McKinsey Consulting Firm Again with Tender Exemption," *Calcalist*, May 9, www.calcalist.co.il/local/articles/0,7340,L-3687852,00.html, accessed January 2017.

Arlozerov, Merav, 2013a, "Is the Israeli Police Efficient? A Research Institute Will Check for NIS 1.6 Million," *TheMarker*, October 3, www.themarker.com/misc/1.570305, accessed January 2014.

—— 2013b, "The Dangerous Precedents of Taas's Privatization," *TheMarker*, September 9, www.themarker.com/news/macro/1.2115511, accessed January 2014.

—— 2014, "The Jews Have Distributive Justice Among Themselves, and the Bedouins are Left on the Side," *TheMarker*, May 21, www.themarker.com/news/1.2327025, accessed July 2014.

Arnon, Arie, 2007, "Israeli Policy towards the Occupied Palestinian Territories: The Economic Dimension, 1967–2007," *Middle East Journal*, Vol. 61, No. 4, pp. 573–95.

Arnove, Anthony, 2012, "Palestine and the Intifada," *Socialist Worker*, December 6, http://socialistworker.org/2012/12/06/palestine-and-the-intifada, accessed January 2014.

Arouri, Fadi, 2012, "Repressive PA Police Trained, Equipped by Western Donors," *The Electronic Intifada*, July 7, http://electronicintifada.net/content/repressive-pa-police-trained-equipped-western-donors/11473, accessed December 2013.

Associated Press, 2006, "Abbas' Presidential Guard is Getting Bigger Role as Tension with Rival Hamas Intensified," *7News*, May 10, www1.whdh.com/news/articles/world/BO30324/, accessed October 2012.

—— 2016, "Security Firm G4S Pulling Out of Israel, Denies BDS Influence," *Haaretz*, March 10, www.haaretz.com/israel-news/1.708110, accessed March 2016.

Avant, Deborah D., 2005, *The Market for Force*, New York: Cambridge University Press.

—— 2006, "The Privatization of Security: Lessons from Iraq," *Orbis*, Vol. 50, No. 2, Spring, pp. 1–15.

Azoulay, Ariella; Ophir, Adi, 2013, *The One-State Condition: Occupation and Democracy in Israel/Palestine*, Stanford: Stanford University Press.

Azoulay, Yuval, 2008, "Peres Composes a Plan that will Grant Free Academic Studies to Each IDF Soldier," *Haaretz*, September 16.

—— 2012, "IMI Reports Breakthrough in Privatization Talks," *Globes*, October 23, www.globes.co.il/serveen/globes/docview.asp?did=1000792234&fid=1725, accessed January 2013.

—— 2013, "Taas Board of Directors Approves the Firm's Privatization Scheme," *Globes*, September 11, www.globes.co.il/news/article.aspx?did=1000878739, accessed January 2014.

—— 2014, "Privatization in IAI and Rafael? 'Nothing Will Come Out of this Idea,'" *Globes*, October 6, www.globes.co.il/news/article.aspx?did=1000976486.

Bachrach, Menachem, 2013, "Menachem – Mena – Bachrach: CV Summary," Tandu Security Systems Ltd website, www.tandu.co.il/Pics/mena_bachra.doc, accessed March 2013.

Bamahane, 2007, "Precedent: UAVs will Replace Pilots in Defending the State's Sea Shores," *Bamahane*, November 22.

Bar-Eli, Avi, 2012, "The Secret Tender of the Ministry of Defense," *TheMarker*, July 31, www.themarker.com/dynamo/1.1789920, accessed January 2013.

Bar-Eli, Avi; Arlozerov, Merav, 2015, "The First Privatized Base: Swimming Pool, Museum and Barbershop: Meet the New and Comfortable College of the Israeli Police," *TheMarker*, April 10, www.themarker.com/markerweek/1.2610445, accessed August 2015.

Bar-Siman-Tov, Yaacov, 2007, "Dialectic between Conflict Management and Conflict Resolution," in Bar-Siman-Tov, Yaacov (ed.), *The Israeli-Palestinian Conflict; From Conflict Resolution to Conflict Management*, New York: Palgrave, pp. 9–41.

Barak, Ehud, 2016, "Why I Donated to the General Staff Reconoissance Unit," *Ha'aretz*, March 27, www.haaretz.co.il/opinions/1.2895622, accessed March 2016.

Barak, Oren; Sheffer, Gabriel, 2010, "The Study of Civil-Military Relations in Israel: A New Perspective," in Sheffer, Gabriel; Barak, Oren (eds.), *Militarism and Israeli Society*, Bloomington: Indiana University Press, pp. 14–41.

Barak-Erez, Dafna, 2008, "Public Trial of Privatization: Models, Norms and Challenges," *Court Debates [Iyunei Mishpat]*, Vol. 30, No. 3, February, pp. 461–515.

Barzilai, Amnon, 2006, "IAI and Elbit Collaborate on Unmanned Patrol Vehicle," *Globes*, July 3.

Bassok, Moti, 2013, "Van Leer Institute: The Government Pursued Unprecedented Privatization in Security," *TheMarker*, January 8, www.themarker.com/news/1.1902974, accessed March 2016.

—— 2016, "Ministry of Defense Hires the Services of the McKinsey Company with Exemption from a Tender Again," *TheMarker*, June 15, www.themarker.com/news/1.2976675, accessed June 2016.

Bauman, Zygmunt, 1998, *Globalization, the Human Consequences*, Cambridge: Polity Press.

Beaumont, Peter, 2016, "Israeli Military Chief Backtracks from 1930s Germany Comparison," *Guardian*, May 5, www.theguardian.com/world/2016/may/05/israeli-military-chief-yair-golan-nazi-germany-comparison, accessed August 2016.

Beit-Hallahmi, Benjamin, 1987, *The Israeli Connection, Who Israel Arms and Why*, New York: Pantheon Press.

Bell, Daniel, 1973, *The Coming of Post-Industrial Society: A Venture in Social Forecasting*, New York: Basic Books.

Ben, Aluf, 2013a, "The Mossad and Shabak Budget Increased by Tens of Percent Points During Netanyahu's Reign," *Ha'aretz*, June 3, www.haaretz.co.il/news/politics/.premium-1.2036241, accessed June 2013.

—— 2013b, "Thus Saved the Dying Apartheid the Israeli Security Industry," *Ha'aretz*, December 10, www.haaretz.co.il/news/politics/.premium-1.2187339, accessed February 2014.

Ben, Aluf; Cohen, Gili, 2013, "Ministry of Defense: We Did Not Sell Military Equipment to Pakistan, We Will Demand Clarifications from the British," *Ha'aretz*, June 12, www.haaretz.co.il/news/politics/1.2044484, accessed June 2013.

Ben Meir, Yehuda, 1995, *Civil-Military Relations in Israel*, New York: Columbia University Press.

Ben-Israel, Rut, 2002, *Labor Law [Dinei Avoda]*, Jerusalem: Open University.

Ben Yosef, Moria, 2012, "In Seven Israeli Eyes," *Israel Defense*, May 24, www.israeldefense.co.il/en/node/11341, accessed September 2017.

Berda, Yael, 2012, *The Bureaucracy of the Occupation: The Permit Regime in the West Bank, 2000–2006 [Birokratyat Hakibush, Mishtar Heyterei Hatnu'a Bagada Hama'aravit]*, Jerusalem: Hakibutz Hameukhad.

Bergen, Peter, 2012, "A Dangerous New World of Drones," *CNN*, October 8, http://edition.cnn.com/2012/10/01/opinion/bergen-world-of-drones, accessed April 2013.

Bichler, Shimshon; Nitzan, Jonathan, 2001, *From War Profits to Peace Dividends* [*Merivkhei Milkhama Ledividendim Shel Shalom*], Jerusalem: Carmel.

Bigo, Didier, 2001, "The Möbius Ribbon of Internal and External Security(ies)," in Albert, Mathias; Jacobson, David; Lapid, Yosef (eds.), *Identities Borders Orders: Rethinking International Relations Theory*, London: University of Minnesota Press, pp. 91–116.

Binyamin, Bat-El, 2016, "Barkat: 'During a Terror Event – Jerusalemites Seek to Engage,'" 20, September 18, https://tinyurl.com/y8dyfxvb, accessed March 2017.

Bisharat, George E., 1994, "Land, Law and Legitimacy in Israel and the Occupied Territories," *The American University Law Review*, Vol. 43, pp. 467–561.

Biur, Khaim, 2012, "The Histadrut Appeals to Court: Don't Privatize Security in East Jerusalem," *TheMarker*, November 28, https://tinyurl.com/ybab7ck8, accessed November 2012.

Blau, Uri, 2012, "Jewish Army for Israel," *Ha'aretz*, May 2, www.haaretz.co.il/magazine/1.1698256, accessed December 2012.

Blumenkranz, Zohar, 2012a, "El-Al Pilots: Firing the Veteran Security Guards Will Harm Security," *TheMarker*, June 19, www.themarker.com/consumer/tourism/1.1735283, accessed October 2012.

—— 2012b, "A Subsidiary of the Israeli Shmira Ubitakhon Won a Tender to Secure Frankfurt's Courts," *TheMarker*, December 20, www.themarker.com/news/1.1890548, accessed March 2013.

—— 2013, "The State Will Increase the Participation in Security Costs of Israeli Airlines," *TheMarker*, December 19, www.themarker.com/news/aviation/1.2194518, accessed February 2014.

Blumenkranz, Zohar; Coren, Ora, 2013, "El-Al Appeals its Classification as a Monopoly: Each Company Should Take Care of Security on its Own," *TheMarker*, February 12, www.themarker.com/consumer/tourism/1.1928272, accessed February 2013.

Boas, David, 2002, "Economic Consequences of Increasing the Security Aid to Israel," in Tov, Imri (ed.), *Security and the National Economy in Israel: Challenges and Answers in Policy of Producing Security*, Memo No. 62, October, Tel-Aviv: Jaffee Center for Strategic Studies, pp. 106–7.

Bourdieu, Pierre, 1985, "The Social Space and the Genesis of Groups," *Theory and Society*, Vol. 14, No. 6, November, pp. 723–44.

Branović Željko, 2011, "The Privatization of Security in Failing States – a Quantitative Assessment," Geneva Center for the Democratic Control of Armed Forces (DCAF), Occasional Paper No. 24.

Breznitz, Dan, 2005, "Collaborative Public Space in a National Innovation System: A Case Study of the Israeli Military Impact on the Software Industry," *Industry and Innovation*, Vol. 12, No. 1, pp. 31–64.

Brigadier-General "Yud," 1995, "The 'Lavi' Project: Decision-Making Process, 1980–1987," *Campaigns* [*Ma'arakhot*], June, Vol. 341, pp. 26–35.

Broad, William J., 2012, "Israel's Antimissile System Attracts Potential Buyers," *New York Times*, November 29, www.nytimes.com/2012/11/30/world/ middleeast/israeli-success-in-downing-hamas-rockets-has-worlds-attention. html?_r=0, accessed February 2013.

Brodet, David, 2005, "The Stabilization Plan – from Then Until Today," *TheMarker*, July 1, www.themarker.com/markets/1.311335, accessed May 2013.

—— 2007, *Report of the Committee to Examine the Defense Budget* [*Dokh Hava'ada Lebkhinat Taktziv Habitakhon*], State of Israel, Jerusalem, May 17.

Brohman, John, 2010, "Economism and Critical Silences in Development Studies: A Theoretical Critique of Neoliberalism," *Third World Quarterly*, Vol. 16, No. 2, pp. 297–318.

Brooks, Doug; Chorev, Matan, 2008, "Ruthless Humanitarianism, Why Marginalizing Private Peacekeeping Kills People," in Alexandra, Andrew; Baker, Deane-Peter; Caparini, Marina (eds.), *Private Military and Security Companies: Ethics, Policies and Civil-Military Relations*, London & New York: Routledge, pp. 116–30.

Brown, John, 2016, "What Does the Police Conceal? Gag Order on the Killing of the Kalandia Siblings Extended," *Local Call* [*Sikha Mekomit*], August 29, https://tinyurl.com/y83s5u6v, accessed September 2016.

Bukhbut, Amir, 2009, "Security Source: We Can Do Without U.S. Aid," *NRG*, July 23, www.nrg.co.il/online/1/ART1/920/330.html, accessed June 2013.

—— 2016, "Crowded Rooms and Prolonged Training: 'Bahad City' Doesn't Live Up to Expectations," *Walla*, March 13, http://news.walla.co.il/item/2942914, accessed March 2016.

Bureau of Labor Statistics, 2016, "CPI Inflation Calculator," United States Department of Labor, https://data.bls.gov/cgi-bin/cpicalc.pl, accessed September 2017.

Burnham, James, 1941, *The Managerial Revolution*, Bloomington: Indiana University Press.

Buso, Nimrod, 2013, "Dania Cybus to Build 12 Structures in Bahad City Costing NIS 200 Million," *TheMarker*, July 30, www.themarker.com/realestate/ 1.2084417, accessed January 2014.

—— 2014, "Cost of Moving the IDF Bases to the Negev: NIS 23 Billion," *TheMarker*, December 18, www.themarker.com/realestate/1.2515274, accessed August 2015.

Buzan, Barry; Wæver, Ole; de Wilde, Jaap, 1998, *Security: A New Framework for Analysis*, Boulder: Lynne Rienner Publishers.

Byrnen, Rex, 2005, "Public Finance, Conflict, and Statebuilding: The Case of Palestine," Prepared for the project on Public Finance in Post-Conflict Statebuilding, Center on International Cooperation, NYU, www.mcgill.ca/ icames/files/icames/PalestinePublicFinance2.pdf, accessed June 2015, pp. 1–33.

Cahana, Ariel, 2003, "Fence at All Costs," *Besheva*, Vol. 48, July 26, www.inn.co.il/ Besheva/Article.aspx/1700, accessed November 2015.

Channel 2, 2010, "45% of Mental State Exemptions are Ultra-Orthodox," *Channel 2*, December 20, www.mako.co.il/news-military/security/Article-396b25f63 dood21004.htm, accessed September 2017.

Chiki-Arad, Roee, 2012, "When the Inspector Becomes a Detective on the Coast: Hunt after Palestinians in the Tel-Aviv Beach," *Ha'aretz*, August 5, www.haaretz. co.il/news/education/1.1793940, accessed January 2013.

Clayton, Nicholas, 2012, "Drone Violence Along Armenian-Azerbaijani Border Could Lead to War," *Minnpost*, October 23, www.minnpost.com/global-post/ 2012/10/drone-violence-along-armenian-azerbaijani-border-could-lead-war, accessed January 2013.

Cockayne, James, 2007, "Make or Buy? Principal-Agent Theory and the Regulation of Private Military Companies," in Chesterman, Simon; Lehnardt, Chia (eds.), *From Mercenaries to Market: The Rise and Regulation of Private Military Companies*, New York: Oxford University Press, pp. 196–216.

Cohen, Gili, 2012a, "The Ministry of Public Security Will Collect a Fee from Security Companies that Replace those Responsible for Weapons," *Ha'aretz*, August 16, www.haaretz.co.il/news/education/1.1802654, accessed October 2012.

—— 2012b, "Comptroller: The IDF Does Not Prepare to Assimilate the Control System of the Land Units," *Ha'aretz*, October, www.haaretz.co.il/news/ politics/1.1844530, accessed January 2013.

—— 2013a, "The Security System Pays NIS 2.8 Million Annually for Private Investigations," *Ha'aretz*, May 7, www.haaretz.co.il/news/politics/.premium-1.2013859, accessed May 2013.

—— 2013b, "One Out of Every Six Soldiers Drops Out Before the End of the Military Service," *Ha'aretz*, June 9, www.haaretz.co.il/news/politics/.premium-1.2041209, accessed July 2013.

—— 2013d, "The Security Apparatus Will Hire a Private Company to Convince Intelligence People to Move to the Negev," *Ha'aretz*, October 10, www.haaretz. co.il/news/politics/.premium-1.2133097, accessed February 2014.

—— 2014a, "Protection of the Drilling Platforms is Partial, Despite Substantial Threats to the Facilities," *Ha'aretz*, March 12, www.haaretz.co.il/news/ mevaker/1.2267139, accessed March 2014.

—— 2014b, "Despite the Court's Request: The State Conceals Destinations of Arms Exports," *Ha'aretz*, January 9, www.haaretz.co.il/news/politics/.premium-1.2212358, accessed April 2014.

—— 2017a, "Lieberman Decdied that Galei Tsahal Will Transform from a Military Unit to a Part of the Ministry of Defense," *Ha'aretz*, January 24, www.haaretz. co.il/news/politics/1.3429472, accessed January 2017.

—— 2017b, "For the First Time: The Airforce will Privatize Management of the Internatioanl Flag Training in Israel," *Ha'aretz*, February 26, www.haaretz.co.il/ news/politics/.premium-1.3882030, accessed July 2017.

Cohen, Gili; Litman, Shani, 2017, "On the Eve of the Ships Deal, the Ministry of Defense Willingly Relinquished Supervision of Arms Agents," *Ha'aretz*, February 8, www.haaretz.co.il/news/politics/.premium-1.3738097, accessed February 2017.

Cohen, Gili; Trilnik, Itai, 2012, "Guarding the Tycoons: The Navy Demands NIS 3 Billion to Protect the Gas Rigs in the Mediterranean," *Ha'aretz*, July 9, www. haaretz.co.il/news/politics/1.1751818, accessed January 2013.

Cohen, Gili; Kobovitz, Yaniv; Lis, Jonathan, 2013, "300 Thousand Citizens Hold Guns, But Life in Israel are No Safer," *Ha'aretz*, April 25, www.haaretz.co.il/news/law/.premium-1.2003492, accessed May 2013.

Cohen, Stuart, 1995, "The Israel Defense Force (IDF): From a 'People's Army' to a 'Professional Military' – Causes and Implications," *Armed Forces & Society*, Vol. 21, pp. 237–54.

Collard, Rebecca, 2012, "Clashes in West Bank as Anger Over Gaza is Directed at Mahmoud Abbas," *Guardian*, November 18, www.theguardian.com/world/2012/nov/18/west-bank-palestinian-gaza-abbas, accessed December 2013.

Cook, Jonathan, 2013, "Why Israel Wanted Arafat Dead," *Global Research*, November 13, www.globalresearch.ca/why-israel-wanted-arafat-dead/5358030, accessed December 2013.

Coren, Ora, 2009, "CEO of IAI: American Companies Will Eat US – the Tiger is Awake and Tries to Sell Whatever He Can," *TheMarker*, August 21.

—— 2010a, "Change in IMI's Privatization Plan – No Stock Issue, Will be Sold Whole to an Israeli Investor," *TheMarker*, January 17.

—— 2010b, "IMI Workers Agree to Privatization – and Want NIS 2 Billion Layoff Compensations in Exchange," *TheMarker*, February 7.

—— 2010c, "Ministry of Finance Offers to the IAI: Freedom in Wages and Purchases, in Exchange for Issuing 25% of the Company," *Ha'aretz*, May 23, www.haaretz.co.il/misc/1.1203007, accessed March 2014.

—— 2010d, "Apparently: IMI Will be Merged with the IAI or Rafael," *Ha'aretz*, December 26, www.haaretz.co.il/misc/1.1237108, accessed March 2014.

—— 2012a, "IAI Needs Corporate Recovery," *TheMarker*, May 1, www.themarker.com/career/1.1697323, accessed December 2012.

—— 2012b, "Rafael Transferred a Dividend of NIS 316.4 Million to the State," *TheMarker*, June 4, www.themarker.com/markets/1.1723028, accessed December 2012.

—— 2012c, "UAV Control and Monitoring Station Given to Ort Pupils by IAI," *TheMarker*, October 29, www.themarker.com/news/1.1852352, accessed January 2013.

—— 2012d, "The Security Industries Must Stop Competing with Each Other," *TheMarker*, November 11, www.themarker.com/news/1.1869702, accessed February 2013.

—— 2013a, "Ministry of Defence CEO to Sanmina: Don't Close the Factory in Israel," *TheMarker*, January 1, www.themarker.com/news/macro/1.1897993, accessed March 2013.

—— 2013b, "Highest Wage Cost in the Security Industries: 106,500 NIS," *TheMarker*, January 6, www.themarker.com/career/1.1901237, accessed March 2013.

—— 2013c, "Corruption Index: Israel Doesn't Have Enough Supervision of the Army – High Risk of Corruption," *TheMarker*, January 29, www.themarker.com/news/1.1917217, accessed April 2013.

—— 2013d, "Rafael Will Present and Offer Iron Dome for Sale for the First Time in an Indian Trade Show," *TheMarker*, February 3, www.themarker.com/news/macro/1.1920960, accessed April 2013.

—— 2013e, "Taas Owes the Government NIS 2.17 Billion," *TheMarker*, May 20, www.themarker.com/news/macro/1.2024756, accessed July 2013.

—— 2013f, "The Privatization of Taas Will Include the Sale of the Public Ashot Ashkelon," *TheMarker*, May 20, www.themarker.com/news/1.2024805, accessed July 2013.

—— 2013g, "Major General Udi Adam Appointed Taas Chairman and will Promote its Privatization," *TheMarker*, July 10, www.themarker.com/news/macro/1.2068076, accessed December 2013.

—— 2013h, "Taas will be Privatized in One Piece Except the Givon Department which will be Transferred to the Ministry of Defense," *TheMarker*, September 8, www.themarker.com/news/macro/1.2114828, accessed January 2014.

—— 2013i, "The Weapons Test of the Security Industries," *TheMarker*, September 21, www.themarker.com/magazine/1.2109815, accessed January 2014.

—— 2013j, "The Billionaire Rennert Will Not be Able to Control Taas," *TheMarker*, October 2, www.themarker.com/news/1.2130931, accessed January 2014.

—— 2013k, "Bad News for Elbit: The Government Will Consider Capital Concentration in Taas's Privatization," *TheMarker*, December 28, www.themarker.com/news/macro/1.2201839, accessed February 2014.

—— 2014a, "Thus Our Billions Were Funnelled to Connected People in the Security Industries," *TheMarker*, March 13, www.themarker.com/news/macro/1.2269468, accessed May 2014.

—— 2014b, "Taas Privatization: Deals Between the State, the Firm and the Workers Signed this Evening," *TheMarker*, April 9, www.themarker.com/news/macro/1.2293317, accessed June 2014.

—— 2014c, "Did You Try to Eat in the Same Restaurant for 22 Years Straight? IDF Soldiers are About to Experience this Soon," *TheMarker*, May 1, www.themarker.com/news/macro/1.2310231, accessed July 2014.

—— 2015, "Why are Hundreds of Low Security Deals Censored from the Suppliers Report of the Ministry of Defense?" *TheMarker*, August 5, www.themarker.com/news/macro/1.2701035, accessed November 2015.

—— 2016a, "Taas Tender: Elbit Remains the Only Contender – and the Ministry of Finance Re-examines the Minimum Price," *TheMarker*, January 24, www.themarker.com/news/1.2828835, accessed April 2016.

—— 2016b, "Severe Flaw in Taas's Tender: One of the Evaluating Companies, Prometheus, Works for Elbit," *TheMarker*, March 27, www.themarker.com/news/1.2895258, accessed March 2016.

Cornes, Richard; Sandler, Todd, 1996, *The Theory of Externalities, Public Goods and Club Goods*, Cambridge: Cambridge University Press.

Corporate Watch, 2012, "G4S: Palestine," Corporate Watch website, September 10, https://corporatewatch.org/company-profiles/g4s-palestine, accessed May 2016.

—— 2013, "Co-operative Asset Management Confirms it has Dropped G4S," Corporate Watch website, March 22, http://corporateoccupation.org/cooperative-asset-management-confirms-it-has-dropped-g4s/, accessed June 2013.

Council for the National Interest, 2005, "More on US Aid for Checkpoint Crossing," *The Electronic Intifada*, February 11, http://electronicintifada.net/content/more-us-aid-checkpoint-crossings/5465, accessed June 2013.

Cronin, David, 2010, *Europe's Alliance with Israel: Aiding the Occupation*, London: Pluto Press.

Dabdoub, Leila, 1995, "Palestinian Public Opinion Polls on the Peace Process," *Palestine-Israel Journal*, Vol. 2, No. 1, pp. 60–3.

Dagoni, Ran, 2005a, "Worries that Aid to Israel Will Suffer in 2006–2007 from the Katrina Damages," *Globes*, September 11–12.

—— 2005b, "The IMF Predicts a 3.9% Growth Rate for Israel in 2006," *Globes*, September 21.

—— 2006, "Israel's Rafael Markets 'Protector' Unmanned Boat in US," *Globes*, June 25.

Dahan Kalev, Henriette, 1999, "The Wadi Salib Events," *Theory and Criticism* [*Teoria Ubikoret*], Vol. 12–13, Winter, pp. 149–58.

DanWatch, 2011, "G4S Retreat from Settlements Drags Out," *DanWatch*, October 17, www.danwatch.dk/en/articles/g4s-retreat-settlements-drags-out/105, accessed June 2013.

—— 2013, "G4S: We'll Stay in Prisons and Settlements," *DanWatch*, May 30, www.danwatch.dk/en/articles/g4s-well-stay-prisons-and-settlements/258, accessed June 2013.

Dayton, Keith, 2009, "Program of the SOREF Symposium Michael Stein Address on U.S. Middle East Policy," Washington Institute for Near East Policy, May 7.

Denes, Nick, 2011, "From Tanks to Wheelchairs: Unmanned Aerial Vehicles, Zionist Battlefield Experiments, and the Transparence of the Civilian," in Zureik, Elia; Lyon, David; Abu-Laban, Yasmeen (eds.), *Surveillance and Control in Israel/Palestine: Population, Territory and Power*, New York: Routledge, pp. 171–95.

Destradi, Sandra, 2010, "Regional Powers and their Strategies: Empire, Hegemony, and Leadership," *Review of International Studies*, Vol. 36, No. 4, October, pp. 903–30.

DHS (Department of Homeland Security), 2013, *Budget in Brief*, Fiscal Year 2013, Washington, DC.

Director, Amnon, 2011, "Moving the IDF to the Negev Will Create an Income of Six Billion NIS Per Year," *IDF Spokesman*, January 2011, http://dover.idf.il/IDF/News_Channels/today/2011/01/2001.htm, accessed January 2013.

Dobbing, Mary; Cole, Chris, 2014, "Israel and the Drone Wars: Examining Israel's Production, Use and Proliferation of UAVs," *Drone Wars UK*, January.

DOD (Department of Defense), 1996, "Improving the Combat Edge Through Outsourcing," *Defense Issues*, Volume 11, No. 30, March.

Dori, Oren, 2017, "Public Transportation Lane Cameras in Tel-Aviv Pass to Municipal Authority," *TheMarker*, February 27, www.themarker.com/dynamo/cars/1.3885844, accessed July 2017.

Doron, Assaf, 2010, "IDF: 50% of the Jewish Population Aged 18–40 Do Not Serve in Any Capacity," Knesset Committee for Foreign Relations and Security, November 9, http://portal.knesset.gov.il/Com4bitachon/he-IL/Messages/9.10.10.htm, accessed July 2013.

Doron, Gideon; Rosenthal, Maoz, 2013, "Intradomestic Bargaining Over the Lands and the Future: Israel's Policy Toward the 1967 Occupied Territories," in Bar-Tal, Daniel; Schnell, Izhak (eds.), *The Impacts of Lasting Occupation; Lessons from Israeli Society*, New York: Oxford University Press, pp. 250–72.

Dror, Yekhezkel, 2014, "'Conflict Management' is Dangerous for Israel," *Ha'aretz*, August 5, www.haaretz.co.il/opinions/.premium-1.2398051, accessed March 2015.

Dun & Bradstreet, 2012, "Largest Industrial Companies, by Sales Volume," Dun's100 Israel's Largest Enterprises, http://duns100.dundb.co.il/ts.cgi?tsscript=/2011e/e59a1, accessed August 2012.

—— 2015, "Largest Industrial Companies, by Sales Volume," Dun's100 Israel's Largest Enterprises, http://duns100.globes.co.il/rating?did=1000961355, accessed December 2015.

Ebo, Adedeji, 2008, "Private Actors and the Governance of Security in West Africa," in Alexandra, Andrew; Baker, Deane-Peter; Caparini, Marina (eds.), *Private Military and Security Companies: Ethics, Policies and Civil-Military Relations*, London & New York: Routledge, pp. 143–58.

Eckstein, Zvi; Tsiddon, Daniel, 2004, "Macroeconomic Consequences of Terror: Theory and the Case of Israel," *Journal of Monetary Economics*, Vol. 51, No. 5, July, pp. 971–1002.

Economist, The, 2008, "The Next Generation," *The Economist*, Vol. 387, No. 8574, April 5, www.economist.com/node/10909916, accessed November 2015.

Efraim, Omri; Morag, Gilad; Azoulay, Moran, 2016, "The Government Will Send Security Guards Home with Weapons: 'To Put Out a Fire with Flame,'" *Ynet*, January 4, www.ynet.co.il/articles/0,7340,L-4748222,00.html, accessed August 2016.

Ehrlich, Avishai, 1993, "Society at War: The National Conflict and the Social Structure," in Ram, Uri (ed.), *Israeli Society: Critical Aspects*, Tel-Aviv: Breirot, pp. 253–74.

Elad, Moshe, 2012, "Who Wants an Arab Combat Soldier?" *Ha'aretz*, July 23, www.haaretz.co.il/opinions/1.1782681, accessed May 2013.

Elbit Systems, 2013, Elbit Systems website, www.elbitsystems.com/elbitmain/, accessed June 2013.

Eli, Yossi, 2015, "Barkat Calls on the Residents to Carry their Personal Weapons: 'A Force Multiplier,'" *Walla*, October 8, http://news.walla.co.il/item/2895438, accessed August 2016.

Elmer, Jon, 2009, "The 'Green Zone' Called Jordan," *The Electronic Intifada*, November 18, http://electronicintifada.net/content/green-zone-called-jordan/8540, accessed June 2013.

Elsea, Jennifer K.; Schwartz, Moshe; Nakamura, Kennon H., 2008, *Private Security Contractors in Iraq: Background, Legal Status, and Other Issues*, CRS Report for Congress, August 25.

Export Control Organization, 2013, "Strategic Export Controls, Country Pivot Report 1st. January 2008–31st. December 2012, Israeli Requests," UK Export Control Organization, www.haaretz.co.il/st/inter/Hheb/images/ab.pdf, accessed June 2013.

European Commission, 2010, "Occupied Palestinian Territory," *Countries*, http://ec.europa.eu/trade/creating-opportunities/bilateral-relations/countries/palestine/, accessed May 2010.

FAOSTAT, 2014, "Resources: Population," Food and Agriculture Association of the United Nations, http://faostat.fao.org/site/550/DesktopDefault.aspx?PageID=550#ancor, accessed January 2014.

Farr, Warner D., 1999, "The Third Temple's Holy of Holies: Israel's Nuclear Weapons," *The Counterproliferation Papers*, Future Warfare Series No. 2, Alabama, September.

Feigenbaum, Harvey B.; Henig, Jefrey R., 1994, "The Political Underpinnings of Privatization, a Typology," *World Politics*, Vol. 46, January, pp. 185–208.

Feinstein, Andrew, 2011, *The Shadow World*, New York: Farrar, Straus and Giraux.

Fernandez, Belen, 2013a, "Israel's Insecurity Industry," *Al Jazeera*, January 16, www.aljazeera.com/indepth/opinion/2013/01/201311216555732158.html, accessed April 2013.

—— 2013b, "Death by 'Security': Israel's Services in Latin America," *Al Jazeera*, July 7, www.aljazeera.com/indepth/opinion/2013/07/20137717429632532.html, accessed December 2013.

Fiske, Gavriel, 2013, "Lockheed-Martin to Open Major Subsidiary in Israel," *Times of Israel*, November 3, www.timesofisrael.com/lockheed-martin-to-open-major-subsidiary-in-israel/, accessed February 2014.

FMEP (Foundation for Middle East Peace), 2002, "Sharon Declares Arafat Irrelevant – the End of the Oslo Era," *Report on Israeli Settlement in the Occupied Territories*, Vol. 12, No. 1, January–February, p. 1.

Friedman, Milton, 1982, *Capitalism and Freedom*, Chicago: University of Chicago Press.

Friedman, Thomas, 1987, "Israelis Decide Not to Construct Lavi Jet Fighter," *New York Times*, August 31, www.nytimes.com/1987/08/31/world/israelis-decide-not-to-construct-lavi-jet-fighter.html, accessed March 2016.

G4S, 2013a, "Who We Are," G4S website, www.g4s.com/en/Who%20we%20are/, accessed June 2013.

—— 2013b, "G4S Security Your World, G4S plc Annual Report and Accounts 2012," G4S website, www.g4s.com/~/media/Files/Annual%20Reports/g4s_annual_report_2012.ashx, accessed June 2013.

—— 2016, "Securing Your World, Integrated Report and Accounts 2015," G4S website, www.annualreport.g4s.com/documents/G4S_2016IR_Final_PDF.pdf, accessed March 2017.

G4S Israel, 2013, "About G4S Israel," G4S website, www.g4s.co.il/he-IL/Who_we_ are/, accessed June 2013.

Gabai, Shlomi, 2012, "The Social Outpost in the Sharon was Evacuated Tonight by Security Guards," *Walla*, July 27, http://news.walla.co.il/?w=/90/2553620, accessed December 2012.

Gabizon, Yoram, 2011, "CEO of Palsan Sasa: The Workers in IMI Will Lose Their Jobs Faster than they Think," *TheMarker*, January 21.

—— 2016, "Fimi Fund Buys G4S Israel According to Operations Value of NIS 400 Million," *TheMarker*, December 2, www.themarker.com/markets/1.3140442, accessed September 2017.

Gal, Einat, 2004, "Crime and Punishment – Privatization of Prisons," Physicians for Human Rights, Position Paper, November.

Galatz, 2015, "Minister of Defense: Recommend Citizens with Weapons to Carry it with Them in These Days," *Galatz*, August 17, http://glz.co.il/1064-69974-he/ Galatz.aspx, accessed August 2016.

Ghanem, As'ad, 2010, *Palestinian Politics After Arafat: A Failed National Movement*, Bloomington: Indiana University Press.

Ghantous, Wassim, 2012, *Privatization of the Israeli Military Checkpoints in the Occupied Territories, from the Humanitarian International Law Perspective*, MA Dissertation, Haifa University, November.

Gil, Yasmin, 2011, "El-Al Updates: We Signed an Agreement with the State to Increase Funding of Security Costs," *Calcalist*, August 15, www.calcalist.co.il/ local/articles/0,7340,L-3528117,00.html, accessed April 2013.

Glanz, James; Pazner Garshowitz, Irit, 2016, "Moshe Yaalon, Israeli Defense Minister, Resigns," *New York Times*, May 20, www.nytimes.com/2016/05/21/ world/middleeast/moshe-yaalon-israeli-defense-minister-resigns.html?_r=0, accessed August 2016.

Goichman, Refaela; Sadeh, Shuki, 2017, "Fingerprint in the Bedroom, Terror and Bribery: The Horror Scenarios of the Biometric Database," *TheMarker*, March 3, www.themarker.com/markerweek/1.3902077, accessed March 2017.

Goldstein, Tani, 2005, "New CEO for Taas: Avi Feldar," *Ynet*, May 30, www.ynet. co.il/articles/0,7340,L-3092542,00.html, accessed March 2016.

Gómez del Prado, José L., 2009, "Private Military and Security Companies and the UN Working Group on the Use of Mercenaries," *Journal of Conflict and Security Law*, Vol. 13, No. 3, pp. 429–50.

—— 2010, "The Privatization of War: Mercenaries, Private Military and Security Companies (PMSC)," *Globalresearch*, November 8, www.globalresearch.ca/ the-privatization-of-war-mercenaries-private-military-and-security- companies-pmsc/21826, accessed February 2013.

Gordon, Neve, 2002, "Outsourcing Violations: The Israeli Case," *Journal of Human Rights*, Vol. 1, No. 3, September, pp. 321–37.

—— 2005, "Outsourcing the Occupation," *Ha'aretz*, April 30.

—— 2008, *Israel's Occupation*, Berkeley, Los Angeles, London: University of California Press.

—— 2009, "The Political Economy of Israel's Homeland Security/Surveillance Industry," *The New Transparency*, Working Paper, April 28.

—— 2011, "Israel's Emergence as a Homeland Security Capital," in Zureik, Elia; Lyon, David; Abu-Laban, Yasmeen (eds.), *Surveillance and Control in Israel/Palestine: Population, Territory and Power*, New York: Routledge, pp. 153–70.

Gouldner, Alvin, 1979, *The Future of Intellectuals and the Rise of the New Class*, New York: Macmillan Press.

Government Bills Register, 2007, "Bill: Police Law (Disciplinary Law, Arbitration of Police Complaints and Various Regulations) (Correction No. 22) (Employing Police for Wages), Hatashsav-2007," Israeli Government, Jerusalem, June 4.

Government Company Authority, 2012, "Report on Government Companies: Israeli Military Industries," Government Company Authority website, www.gca.gov.il/GCA, accessed August 2012.

—— 2014, "Report on Government Companies: Israeli Military Industries," Government Company Authority website, www.gca.gov.il/NR/exeres/DB26DCB5-B0FA-4E84-B52D-0ED5F8432EE7, accessed July 2014.

—— 2015, "Report on Government Companies: Israeli Military Industries," Government Company Authority website, http://mof.gov.il/GCA/Reports/DocLib3/Taas_FinancialReport_2016.pdf, accessed January 2016.

Graham, Stephen, 2011, "Laboratories of War: Surveillance and US-Israeli Collaboration in War and Security," in Zureik, Elia; Lyon, David; Abu-Laban, Yasmeen (eds.), *Surveillance and Control in Israel/Palestine: Population, Territory and Power*, New York: Routledge, pp. 133–52.

Greenberg, Hannan, 2011, "Thus the Navy Defends the Drilling Facilities," *Ynet*, April 24, www.ynet.co.il/articles/0,7340,L-4059998,00.html, accessed January 2013.

Grimmett, Richard F.; Kerr, Paul K., 2012, "Conventional Arms Transfers to Developing Nations, 2004–2011," Congressional Research Service, 7-5700, August 24.

Gronau, Reuven, 2002, *Security Threat and Economic Crisis*, Jerusalem: Israeli Institute for Democracy, July.

Gross, Oren, 2000, "Mending Walls: The Economic Aspects of Israeli-Palestinian Peace," *American International University International Law Review*, Vol. 1539, No. 16, pp. 1539–626.

Groth, Anette, 2012, "German Aid to Israel's War Machine is an Invitation to Abuse Human Rights," *The Electronic Intifada*, May 25, http://electronicintifada.net/content/german-aid-israels-war-machine-invitation-abuse-human-rights/11329, accessed December 2012.

Guata, Yasmeen, 2014, "Tel-Aviv's Municipality New Yax: The Residents Will Pay a Fee for a Security Patrol," *TheMarker*, November 4, www.themarker.com/law/1.2476993, accessed January 2017.

Gurvitz, Yossi, 2014, "Abandoning Responsibility," *Yesh Din Blog*, September 18, http://blog.yesh-din.org/en/?p=896, accessed April 2016.

Gutman, Lior, 2009, "Cancelling the Establishment of the Private Prison: Leviev and Kuzinski May Sue NIS 1.6 Billion from the State," *Calcalist*, November 19, www.calcalist.co.il/local/articles/1,7340,L-3368107,00.html, accessed August 2014.

—— 2012, "The State Will Establish a Fund to Absorb the Gas and Oil Profits," *Calcalist*, February 19, www.calcalist.co.il/local/articles/0,7340,L-3562619,00.html, accessed January 2013.

Ha'aretz Editorial, 2015, "The Dangerous Rush to Arm Israeli Civilians," *Ha'aretz*, October 9, www.haaretz.com/opinion/1.679458, accessed August 2015.

Haimowitz, Mordechai, 2012, "Why Did the Lavi Project Really Fail?" *NRG*, September 1, www.nrg.co.il/online/1/ART2/399/505.html, accessed April 2014.

Hall, David; de la Motte, Robin; Davies, Steve, 2003, "Terminology of Public-Private Partnerships (PPPs)," European Public Services Union (EPSU), March, www.epsu.org/sites/default/files/article/files/PPPs-defs.doc, accessed June 2015.

Halper, Jeff, 2008, "The Palestinians; Warehousing a 'Surplus People,'" *Znet*, September 7, www.zcommunications.org/the-palestinians-warehousing-a-surplus-people-by-jeff-halper, accessed January 2013.

—— 2009, *Obstacles to Peace: A Reframing of the Israeli-Palestinian Conflict*, Jerusalem: ICAHD.

—— 2015, *War Against the People: Israel, the Palestinians and Global Pacification*, London: Pluto Press.

Halperin, Ariel, 1987, "Military Power Building and Economic Growth," *Economic Quarterly* [*Riv'on Lecalcala*], Vol. 37, No. 131, February, pp. 990–1010.

—— 1988, *Military Industry and Economic Growth* [*Hata'asiya Habitkhonit Vehatsmikha Hacalcalit*], Jerusalem: Jerusalem Center for Israel Studies.

Halutz, Dan, 2002, "Building Air Might, Strategic Changes and Resource Limitation," in Tov, Imri (ed.), *Security and the National Economy in Israel: Challenges and Answers in Policy of Producing Security*, Memo No. 62, October, Tel-Aviv: Jaffee Center for Strategic Studies, pp. 49–55.

Hamilton, Gary G.; Stutton, John R., 1989, "The Problem of Control in the Weak State: Domination in the United States, 1880–1920," *Theory and Society*, Vol. 18, pp. 1–46.

Handels, Shuki, 2003, "Guards and Security Guards in Israel 1995–2003" [*Meavtekhim Veshomrim Beyisrael 1995–2003*], Ministry of Industry, Trade and Labour, Planning, Research and Economics Administration.

Harders, Cilja, 2015, "Provincializing and Localizing Core-Periphery Relations," *Middle East Topics and Arguments (META)*, Vol. 5, pp. 36–45.

Harel, Amos, 2003, "The IDF in the Service of the Settlers," *Ha'aretz*, September 23, www.haaretz.co.il/misc/1.912539, accessed August 2014.

—— 2013a, "Israel's Arms Exports Increased by 20 Percent in 2012," *Ha'aretz*, January 10, www.haaretz.com/news/diplomacy-defense/israel-s-arms-exports-increased-by-20-percent-in-2012.premium-1.492990, accessed April 2013.

—— 2013b, "The Saturday of Bahad 1 Cadets: Tours by a Right Wing NGO," *Ha'aretz*, May 16, www.haaretz.co.il/news/education/.premium-1.2021168, accessed February 2015.

—— 2016, "Netanyahu and Lieberman Will Seek to Reeducate Israel's Military Brass," *Ha'aretz*, May 20, www.haaretz.com/israel-news/.premium-1.720658, accessed August 2016.

Harel, Amos; Issacharoff, Avi, 2012, "Israel Forms a Plan to Prevent the Collapse of the Palestinian Authority," *Ha'aretz*, September 24, www.haaretz.co.il/news/politics/1.1829496, accessed January 2013.

Hareuveni, Eyal, 2014, *The Lawless Zone: The Transfer of Policing and Security Powers to the Civilian Security Coordinators in the Settlements and Outposts*, Tel-Aviv: Yesh Din.

Hartman, Ben, 2015, "Gal Hirsch Withdrawn as Candidate to Lead Police after Weeks of Controversy," *Jerusalem Post*, September 23, www.jpost.com/Israel-News/Former-IDF-officer-Gal-Hirsch-wont-be-next-police-chief-Erdan-says-417907, accessed November 2015.

—— 2016, "Thousands at Tel Aviv Rally Call for Release of IDF Soldier Charged in Hebron Shooting," *Jpost*, April 19, www.jpost.com/Israel-News/Activists-gather-for-controversial-Tel-Aviv-rally-to-support-IDF-shooter-451709, accessed August 2016.

Haruti-Sover, Tali, 2017, "Yair Shamir Presents: The French UAVs, the Chinese Cars, the Dubius Advisor and the Conflicts of Interest," *TheMarker*, January 30, www.themarker.com/career/1.3462828, accessed January 2017.

Harvey, David, 2005, *A Brief History of Neoliberalism*, New York: Oxford University Press.

Hasson, Nir, 2012, "The Ministry of Defense Used Ariel University as a Human Resources Company," *Ha'aretz*, December 30, www.haaretz.co.il/news/education/1.1896655, accessed March 2013.

—— 2015, "Jerusalem Mayor Calls on Civilians to Carry Weapons in Wake of Terror Attacks," *Ha'aretz*, October 8, www.haaretz.com/israel-news/.premium-1.679383, accessed August 2016.

Hasson, Nir; Khoury, Jack, 2013, "Extraordinary Operation of the Palestinian Police Against Criminals in A-Ram Neighborhood," *Ha'aretz*, November 11, www.haaretz.co.il/news/politics/1.2162301, accessed February 2014.

Hasson, Nir; Hoval, Revital; Cohen, Gili, 2013, "For the Fifth Time This Year: Murder with a Security Guard's Personal Firearm," *Ha'aretz*, July 24, www.haaretz.co.il/news/law/1.2079612, accessed July 2013.

Hasson, Yael, 2006, *Three Decades of Privatization* [*Shlosha Asorim Shel Hafrata*], Tel-Aviv: Adva Center, November.

Hattem, Ben, 2014, "Israel Security Conference: Data Overload," *Al-Jazeera*, March 20, www.aljazeera.com/indepth/features/2014/03/israel-security-conference-data-overload-20143198520109460.html, accessed May 2014.

Havkin, Shira, 2014, "Privatization of the Checkpoints in the West Bank and Gaza Strip," Position Paper, Van Leer Institute, February.

Hever, Shir, 2009, "Cast Lead: Israel Attacks Gaza," *Economy of the Occupation*, Part 21–22, The Alternative Information Center, Jerusalem, June.

—— 2011a, "Elbit Systems," in Winstanley, Asa; Barat, Frank (eds.), *Corporate Complicity in Israel's Occupation; Evidence from the London Session of the Russell Tribunal on Palestine*, London: Pluto Press, pp. 148–54.

—— 2011b, "Flammable Politics: Political-Economic Implications of Israel's Natural Gas Find," *Economy of the Occupation*, Part 27–28, The Alternative Information Center, Jerusalem, December.

—— 2013, "Private Funding of Right-Wing Ideology in Israel," *Economy of the Occupation*, Part 29–30, The Alternative Information Center, Jerusalem, May.

Hillary, John, 2007, "War on Want Letter to the UN on PMSCs," War on Want, London, May 25.

Hofstetter, Noam; Yavne, Lior, 2016, *Matter of Access: Obstacles to Public Accessibility to Government Archives*, Tel-Aviv: Akevot Institute for the Study of the Israeli-Palestinian Conflict, April.

Hoval, Revital, 2012, "Private Security Guards Would be Allowed to Use 'Reasonable Force,'" *Ha'aretz*, July 18, www.haaretz.co.il/news/law/1.1778950, accessed December 2012.

—— 2013, "The Prison Walls Have Ears," *Ha'aretz*, April 19, www.haaretz.co.il/news/education/.premium-1.1998004, accessed May 2013.

HP (Hewlett Packard), 2015, *Form 10-K, HP INC – HPQ*, Filed December 16.

Human Rights Council, 2009, *Human Rights in Palestine and Other Occupied Arab Territories: Report of the United Nations Fact-Finding Mission on the Gaza Conflict*, Geneva: United Nations, September 25.

Human Rights Watch, 1996, "Civilian Pawns: Laws of War Violations and the Use of Weapons on the Israel-Lebanon Border," Human Rights Watch Arms Project, Human Rights Watch/Middle East.

—— 2017, "Israel/Palestine: Some Officials Backing 'Shoot-to-Kill,'" Human Rights Watch website, January 2, www.hrw.org/news/2017/01/02/israel/palestine-some-officials-backing-shoot-kill, accessed March 2017.

Human Security Unit, 2016, "Human Security Approach," United Nations, Geneva, www.un.org/humansecurity/human-security-unit/human-security-approach, accessed April 2016.

Huysmans, Jef, 1998, "Security! What Do You Mean? From Concept to Thick Signifier," *European Journal of International Relations*, Vol. 4, No. 2, pp. 226–55.

ICBS (Israeli Central Bureau of Statistics), 2006, "Public Order," *Statistical Annual Yearbook 2005*, www.cbs.gov.il/reader/shnaton/shnatonh_new.htm?CYear=2005&Vol=56&CSubject=11/, accessed March 2017.

—— 2008, "Statistical Abstract of Israel 2007," www.cbs.gov.il/reader/shnatonhnew_site.htm, accessed March 2017.

—— 2010, "Population Census 2010," www.cbs.gov.il/census/census/pnimi_page_e.html?id_topic=11, accessed March 2017.

—— 2012, "Table 12.11: Employed Persons, Percentage of Employees and Percentage of Part-Time Employed Persons, by Industry (Division) 2011," *Statistical Annual Yearbook 2012*, www.cbs.gov.il/reader/shnaton/shnatonh_new.htm?CYear=2011&Vol=62&CSubject=12, accessed March 2017.

—— 2013, "Table B/1: Population by Population Group," *Statistical Monthly Journal of Statistics*, No. 12, 2012.

—— 2015, "B1: Population, by Population Group," *Statistical Annual Yearbook 2014*, www1.cbs.gov.il/reader/?MIval=cw_usr_view_SHTML&ID=629, accessed November 2015.

—— 2017, "B1: Population, by Population Group," *Statistical Annual Yearbook 2016*, www.cbs.gov.il/reader/?MIval=cw_usr_view_SHTML&ID=629, accessed January 2017.

IDF (Israel Defence Force), 2014, "IDF Soldiers Educate the Next Generation," IDF website, October 16, www.idfblog.com/blog/2014/10/16/idf-soldiers-educate-next-generation/, accessed November 2015.

INN TV (Israel National News TV), 2009, "Israel Defense Exhibition 2009," *Arutz Sheva 7*, October 13, www.israelnationalnews.com/News/News.aspx/133831#. Vaoi1_mqqkp, accessed July 2015.

Institute for National Security Studies, 2010, "Middle East Balance Files," *Military Balance Files*, www.inss.org.il/weapons.php?cat=283, accessed May 2011.

—— 2011, "Middle East Balance Files," *Military Balance Files*, www.inss.org.il/weapons.php?cat=283, accessed September 2012.

Inter-Departmental Tender Committee, 2006, "National Training Center Project," Ministry of Public Security, Israeli Police and the Ministry of Finance, November.

Israel Aerospace Industries, 2011, Israel Aerospace Industries website, www.iai.co.il/22031-en/Homepage.aspx, accessed February 2011.

Israeli Government, 2013a, "Definition of Communities and Areas as National Priorities," Decision Proposal, *Ha'aretz*, August 8, Jerusalem.

—— 2013b, "Issue of 20% of Rafael and IAI Stocks," Decision 175 of the Israeli Government from May 13th, 2013, 33rd Government, www.pmo.gov.il/SECRETARY/GOVDECISIONS/2013/Pages/des175.aspx, accessed February 2014.

Israeli High Court of Justice, 1999, "Al-Khiam Prison," Case HCJ 1951/99, translated by Hamoked.

—— 2009, "Case of the Academic Center for Justice and Business against State of Israel," Case HCJ 2605/05.

—— 2015, "Case of the Academic Center for Justice and Business," Case HCJ 2779/13.

Israeli Military Industries, 2015, "About IMI," IMI website, www.imi-israel.com/home/doc.aspx?mCatID=63195&mCatID2=0, accessed November 2015.

Israeli Ministry of Finance, 2013a, *Budget Proposal for the Fiscal Year 2013–2014: and Explanations, Presented to the Nineteenth Knesset: Various Security Paragraphs* [*Hatsa'at Taktziv Lishnat Haksafim 2013–2014 Vedivrey Hesber Mugashim Lakneset Hatsha-Esre*], Jerusalem, June.

—— 2013b, "Insurance Coverage Due to War or Hostilities," Israeli Ministry of Finance website, http://ozar.mof.gov.il/hon/2001/insurance/war.asp, accessed August 2013.

Israeli Ministry of Public Security, 2006, "The Process of Constructing a National Training Center for the Israeli Police in Beit Shemesh was Approved," Press release, November 20, http://147.237.72.72/BP/BPNews/Press2006/IPTrainingCenter20_11_06.htm, accessed May 2013.

—— 2010, "Constructing the Israeli Police Training Center in Beit Shemesh – Winning of Policity Group," Press release, January 13, http://mops.gov.il/ PolicingAndEnforcement/NationalTrainingCenter/Pages/IPTrainingCenter Policity.aspx, accessed May 2013.

Israeli Prime Minister's Office, 2011, "Adoption of the Recommendations of the Committee for Examining Fiscal Policy Regarding Oil and Gas Resources in Israel (Sheshinski Report)," Government Decision No. 2762, of January 23, 2011.

IPS (Israeli Prison Service), 2006, *Summary of Work Year 2005*, Jerusalem.

—— 2009, "Tender with Dadash Company for Operating Prison Canteens," received by fax, September 20, 2011.

—— 2015, "Prisoner Numbers Over the Years," www.ips.gov.il/Web/He/Research/ Statistics/Prisoners/Default.aspx, accessed December 2015.

Johnson, Jimmy, 2010, "India Employing Israeli Oppression Tactics in Kashmir," *The Electronic Intifada*, August 19, http://electronicintifada.net/content/india-employing-israeli-oppression-tactics-kashmir/8985, accessed September 2012.

—— 2015, "Israeli Arms-Deals Database," privately shared.

Jpost.com Staff, 2016, "IDF General in Bombshell Speech: Israel Today Shows Signs of 1930s Germany," *Jpost*, April 5, www.jpost.com/Israel-News/Politics-And-Diplomacy/IDF-general-in-bombshell-speech-Israel-today-shows-signs-of-1930s-Germany-453142, accessed August 2016.

Kam, Ze'ev, 2016, "Ya'alon on the Shooting Soldier Storm: 'Do You Want a Beastly Army?'" *NRG*, March 28, www.nrg.co.il/online/1/ART2/764/238.html, accessed August 2016.

Katz, Dovid, 2004, *Words of Fire: The Unfinished Story of Yiddish*, New York: Basic Books.

Katz, Haim, 2002, "The Industrial Policy from the Perspective of the Workers," in Tov, Imri (ed.), *Security and the National Economy in Israel: Challenges and Answers in Policy of Producing Security*, Memo No. 62, October, Tel-Aviv: Jaffee Center for Strategic Studies, pp. 125–6.

Katz, Yitzhak, 1997, *Privatization in Israel and the World [Hafrata Beyisrael Ubaolam]*, Tel-Aviv: Pecker.

Kershner, Isabel, 2016, "Debate Over Role of 'People Army' in Israel Reflects Wider Fissures," *New York Times*, May 29, www.nytimes.com/2016/05/30/ world/middleeast/israel-idf-netanyahu-lieberman-yaalon.html, accessed August 2016.

Khalili, Laleh, 2010, "The Location of Palestine in Global Counterinsurgencies," *International Journal of Middle East Studies*, Vol. 42, pp. 413–33.

Khalidi, Rashid, I., 2009, *Sowing Crisis: The Cold War and American Dominance in the Middle East*, Boston: Beacon Press.

Kinsey, Christopher, 2006, *Corporate Soldiers and International Security: The Rise of Private Military Companies*, London & New York: Routledge.

Klein, Naomi, 2007a, "Laboratory for a Fortress World," *The Nation*, July 2, www.thenation.com/article/laboratory-fortressed-world/, accessed November 2015.

—— 2007b, *The Shock Doctrine: The Rise of Disaster Capitalism*, New York: Metropolitan Books.

Knesset Committee for Domestic and Environmental Affairs, 2005, "Protocol 495 of the Committee for Domestic and Environmental Affairs, Wednesday 27.7.2005, 10:00," 16th Knesset, Third Seat, July 27.

Knesset Committee for Labor, Welfare and Health, 2013, "Protocol No. 39 from the Session of the Knesset Committee for Labor, Welfare and Health," 19th Knesset, First Seat, June 24.

Knesset Committee for State Comptroller Matters, 2008, "Protocol No. 179 from the Session of the Committee for State Comptroller Matters," 17th Knesset, Third Seat, February 6.

Knesset Library, 2003, "Democracy in Times of War," Israeli Knesset Publications, Jerusalem, www.knesset.gov.il/library/heb/docs/sif002.htm, accessed April 2013.

Kobowich, Yaniv, 2015, "Deregulation on Carrying Arms: The State Will Allow Municipalities to Approve Possession of Firearms," Ha'artz, October 14, www.haaretz.co.il/news/politics/1.2751641, accessed August 2016.

Kobowitz, Yaniv, 2013, "At the Expense of the Periphery: The Police Funds Security Officers in Small Communities," Ha'aretz, September 2, www.haaretz.co.il/news/education/.premium-1.2111942, accessed January 2014.

Kobowitz, Yaniv; Idelman, Ofra, 2016, "Police Volunteers Authorities Expanded: Can Conduct Arrests and House Searches," Ha'aretz, March 31, www.haaretz.co.il/news/law/.premium-1.2899998, accessed March 2016.

Koriel, Ilana, 2009, "Because of the Benefit of the Doubt: Shai Dromi Acquitted from Killing the Burglar," Ynet, July 15, www.ynet.co.il/articles/0,7340, L-3746751,00.html, accessed August 2014.

Korin-Liber, Stella, 1999, "Now the IDF is Taking Everything Out," Globes, July 28.
—— 2010, "IMI is in a State of Emergency," Globes, January 20–21.

Krahmann, Elke, 2007, "Transitional States in Search of Support: Private Military Companies and Security Sector Reform," in Chesterman, Simon; Lehnardt, Chia (eds.), From Mercenaries to Market: The Rise and Regulation of Private Military Companies, New York: Oxford University Press, pp. 94–112.
—— 2008, "The New Model Soldier and Civil-Military Relations," in Alexandra, Andrew; Baker, Deane-Peter; Caparini, Marina (eds.), Private Military and Security Companies: Ethics, Policies and Civil-Military Relations, London & New York: Routledge, pp. 247–61.
—— 2010, States, Citizens and the Privatization of Security, New York: Cambridge University Press.

Kretzmer, David, 2013, "The Law of Belligerent Occupation as a System of Control: Dressing Up Exploitation in Respectable Garb," in Bar-Tal, Daniel; Schnell, Izhak (eds.), The Impacts of Lasting Occupation; Lessons from Israeli Society, New York: Oxford University Press, pp. 31–60.

Landau, Idan, 2012, "The Israeli Gas and the Chronicles of its Disappearance in the Jaws of Capital-Government-Security," Not to Die Stupid [Lo Lamut Tipesh], September 24, http://idanlandau.com/2012/09/24/how-israeli-gas-was-swallowed-up/, accessed August 2013.

Landau, Pinhas, 2008, "Dealing with the Wealth," Eretz Aheret, Vol. 43, pp. 42–6.

Laor, Tal, 2014, "The Ticket was Not Written by a Police Officer," *Ha'aretz*, May 4, www.haaretz.co.il/magazine/tozeret/.premium-1.2310450, accessed February 2015.

Lazzarini, Philippe, 2009, "The Crisis in the West Bank," *Humanitarian Exchange*, No. 44, September, pp. 2–4.

Le More, Anne, 2005, "Killing with Kindness: Funding the Demise of a Palestinian State," *International Affairs*, Vol. 81, No. 5, pp. 983–1001.

Leander, Anna, 2005, "The Market for Force and Public Security: The Destabilizing Consequences of Private Military Companies," *Journal of Peace Research*, Vol. 42, No. 5, pp. 605–22.

Leibowitz-Dar, Sarah, 2009, "Journey After the Capital Nobility: The Seventies. Getting Rich from Bar Lev," *NRG*, April 29, www.nrg.co.il/online/16/ART1/884/160.html, accessed September 2015.

LeVine, Mark, 2012, "Stratfor and Geopolitical Instruments of Our Demise," *Al-Jazeera*, March 8, www.aljazeera.com/indepth/opinion/2012/03/20123684 94858921.html, accessed November 2012.

Levinson, Chaim, 2010, "Paper Jam: Bureaucracy Causes Checkpoint Chaos," *Ha'aretz*, November 12, www.haaretz.com/print-edition/news/paper-jam-bureaucracy-causes-checkpoint-chaos-1.324235, accessed September 2012.

—— 2013, "The Private is the Public," *Ha'aretz*, January 4, www.haaretz.co.il/magazine/tozeret/1.1899840, accessed March 2013.

Levy, Daniel, 2008, "A Move Private Occupation," *Ha'aretz*, April 13.

Levy, Yagil, 2003, *Another Army for Israel: Materialistic Militarism in Israel* [*Tsava Akher Leyisrael: Materialism Khomrani Beyisrael*], Tel-Aviv: Yedioth Ahronot.

—— 2008, "Military-Society Relations: The Demise of the 'People's Army,'" in Ben-Port, Guy; Levy, Yagil; Mizrahi, Shlomo; Naor, Arye; Tzfadia, Erez (eds.), *Israel Since 1980*, Cambridge: Cambridge University Press, pp. 117–45.

—— 2012, *Israel's Death Hierarchy: Casualty Aversion in a Militarized Democracy*, New York: NYU Press.

—— 2015, "On the Way to Cancel the Obligatory Conscription," *Ha'aretz*, July 23, www.haaretz.co.il/opinions/.premium-1.2689833, accessed March 2016.

Li, Darryl, 2006, "The Gaza Strip as Laboratory: Notes in the Wake of Disengagement," *Journal of Palestine Studies*, Vol. 35, No. 2, Winter, p. 38.

Lia, Brynjar, 2006, *A Police Without a State: A History of the Palestinian Security Forces in the West Bank and Gaza*, Reading: Garnet Publishing.

Lifshitz, Ya'akov, 2000, *Security Economy, the General Theory and the Case of Israel*, Jerusalem: Ministry of Defense Publishing and the Jerusalem Center for Israel Studies.

—— 2002, "Defense Exports as a Source of Funding," in Tuv, Imri (ed.), *Security and the National Economy in Israel: Challenges and Answers in Policy of Producing Security*, Memo No. 62, October, Tel-Aviv: Jaffee Center for Strategic Studies, pp. 61–5.

—— 2011, "The Strategic and Economic Role of the Security Industries in Israel," Begin-Sadat Center for Strategic Studies, Bar-Ilan University, *Middle East Security Essays*, No. 92, December.

Linder-Gantz, 2013, "Monetary Incentives to a Private Company to Avoid Referring Soldiers to Emergency Rooms," *TheMarker*, June 27, www.themarker. com/consumer/health/1.2056718, accessed December 2013.

Lior, Ilan, 2017, "Tel-Aviv Central Station Security Instructed to Demand ID from those of Arab Appearance," *Ha'aretz*, August 23, www.haaretz.co.il/news/local/. premium-1.4383063, accessed August 2017.

Lis, Jonathan; Khouri, Jack; Seidler, Shirly, 2013, "Netanyahu's Point Man on Bedouin Relocation Says Plan Still on Track," *Ha'aretz*, December 17, www. haaretz.com/israel-news/.premium-1.563930, accessed November 2015.

Little, Douglas, 2008, *American Orientalism: The United States and the Middle East Since 1945*, Chapel Hill: University of North Carolina Press.

Loader, Ian, 2000, "Plural Policing and Democratic Governance," *Social & Legal Studies*, Vol. 9, No. 3, pp. 323–45.

Locker Committee, 2015, *Committee Report to Examine the Defense Budget*, June, Jerusalem.

Lovering, John, 2000, "Loose Cannons: Creating the Arms Industry of the Twenty-First Century," in Kaldor, Mary (ed.), *Global Insecurity*, London: Continuum International Publishing Group, pp. 147–76.

Lubin, Alex, 2013, "The Disappearing Frontiers of US Homeland Security: Mapping the Transit of Security Across the US and Israel," *Jadaliyya*, February 26, www.jadaliyya.com/pages/index/10365/the-disappearing-frontiers-of-us-homeland-security, accessed May 2013.

Machold, Rhys, 2015, "Mobility and the Model: Policy Mobility and the Becoming of Israeli Homeland Security Dominance," *Environment and Planning*, Vol. 47, pp. 816–32.

Mackey, Robert, 2016, "Israeli Rights Group Releases Video of Army Medic Executing Wounded Palestinian Suspect," *The Intercept*, March 25, https:// theintercept.com/2016/03/24/israeli-rights-group-releases-video-soldier-executing-wounded-palestinian-suspect/, accessed August 2016.

Maddow, Rachel, 2012, *Drift: The Unmooring of American Military Power*, New York: Crown Publishers.

Maman, Daniel, 1988, *The Second Career of Top Military Officers and the Civilian Elites in Israel: 1974–1988* [*Hakaryera Hashniya shel Haktzuna Habkhira Vehaelitot Haezrakhyot Beyisrael: 1974–1984*], Jerusalem: Levy Eshkol Institute for Economic, Social and Political Research.

Mann, Itamar, 2017, "Israel and the Forever War," Gunneflo Book Symposium: Part 1, March 8, https://voelkerrechtsblog.org/gunneflo-book-symposium-part-1/, accessed March 2017.

Maoz, Eilat, 2008, "Privatization of the Checkpoints and the Late Occupation," *Hagada Hasmalit*, October 10.

Maranda, Amnon, 2008, "'Dromi Law' was Approved: Shooting is Permissible to Chase Off a Burglar," *Ynet*, June 24, www.ynet.co.il/articles/0,7340, L-3559858,00.html, accessed August 2014.

Markusen, Ann R., 2003, "The Case Against Privatizing National Security," *Governance*, Vol. 16, pp. 471–501.

Marom, Dror, 2001, "Taas had a Net Loss of US$ 48.8 in 2000, a 28% Reduction," *Globes*, March 22, www.globes.co.il/news/article.aspx?did=478459, accessed July 2014.

Megginson, William L.; Netter, Jeffry M., 2001, "From State to Market: A Survey of Empirical Studies on Privatization," *Journal of Economic Literature*, Vol. 39, No. 2, June, http://papers.ssrn.com/sol3/papers.cfm?abstract_id=262311.

Melman, Yossi, 2006, "Israeli UAVs in Africa's Skies," *Ha'aretz*, April 30, www.haaretz.co.il/news/uav/1.1102078, accessed January 2013.

Menahem, Sarit, 2010, "Commander, Cut!," *TheMarker*, May 7.

MFA (Israeli Ministry of Foreign Affairs), 1994, Agreement on Preparatory Transfer of Power and Responsibilities, Israeli Ministry of Foreign Affairs website, August 29, www.mfa.gov.il/mfa/foreignpolicy/peace/guide/pages/agreement%20on%20preparatory%20transfer%20of%20powers%20and%20re.aspx, accessed June 2015.

—— 1995a, "Article XIII: Security," *The Israeli-Palestinian Interim Agreement on the West Bank and Gaza Strip*, Israeli Ministry of Foreign Affairs website, September 28, www.mfa.gov.il/mfa/foreignpolicy/peace/guide/pages/the%20israeli-palestinian%20interim%20agreement.aspx, accessed June 2015.

—— 1995b, "Annex I: Protocol Concerning Redeployment and Security Arrangements," *The Israeli-Palestinian Interim Agreement on the West Bank and Gaza Strip*, Israeli Ministry of Foreign Affairs website, September 28, www.mfa.gov.il/MFA/ForeignPolicy/Peace/Guide/Pages/THE%20ISRAELI-PALESTINIAN%20INTERIM%20AGREEMENT%20-%20Annex%20I.aspx#article2, accessed June 2015.

—— 2000, "Major Palestinian Violations of Agreements – October 2000," Israeli Ministry of Foreign Affairs website, October 11, www.mfa.gov.il/mfa/foreignpolicy/peace/guide/pages/major%20palestinian%20violations%20of%20agreements-%20octobe.aspx, accessed June 2015.

—— 2009, *Supporting Palestinian Capacity Building: Israel's Effort in Supporting the Palestinian Economy, Security Reforms and Civil Affairs*, Report of the Government of Israel to the Ad Hoc Liaison Committee, Oslo, June 7–8.

Michael, Kobi, 2010, "Military Knowledge and Weak Civilian Control in the Reality of Low Intensity Conflict – the Israeli Case," in Sheffer, Gabriel; Barak, Oren (eds.), *Militarism and Israeli Society*, Bloomington: Indiana University Press, pp. 42–66.

Michaels, Daniel; Gauthier-Villars, David; Cimilluca, Dana; Walker, Marcus, 2012, "Government Discord Derails Massive European Merger," *Wall Street Journal*, October 11, http://online.wsj.com/article/SB10000872396390443294904578048180379906930.html, accessed January 2013.

Mills, C. Wright, 1956, *The Power of Elites*, New York: Oxford University Press.

Minow, Martha, 2005, "Outsourcing Power: How Privatizing Military Efforts Challenges Accountability, Professionalism, and Democracy," *Boston College Law Review*, Vol. 46, pp. 989–1026.

Mirovski, Arik, 2008, "News for Reservists? Proposal: Discounts for Up to 50 Thousand NIS When Buying ILA Lands," *TheMarker*, December 31.

Misgav, Uri, 2013, "The Golden Club of the Israeli Weaponry," *Ha'aretz*, June 13, www.haaretz.co.il/opinions/.premium-1.2044960, accessed November 2013.

Mitchell, Timothy, 2002, *Rule of Experts: Egypt, Techno-Politics, Modernity*, London: University of California Press.

Mizrahi, Shelli, 2010, *Weapon Permits for Private Citizens – Policy and Numerical Data*, Report for the Committee of Domestic Affairs and Environmental Protection, Research and Information Center at the Knesset, July.

MOD Online (Ministry of Defense Online), 2016, "Entry for Registered User," Ministry of Defense website, www.online.mod.gov.il/Online2008/Pages/General/Info/Login.aspx?ReturnUrl=/Online2008/pages/Personal/Balam/BalamResultsListNew.aspx, accessed February 2016.

MOITAL (Ministry of Industry, Trade and Labor), 2009, "National Priority to the Periphery," *Main Budget Elements 2009–2010*, Jerusalem, www.mof.gov.il/BudgetSite/StateBudget/Lists/201020092/Attachments/4/B4.pdf, accessed April 2013.

Mombelli, Gabriele, 2014, "The Palestinian National Authority Security Sector: An Operational Review," Paper presented at the Middle East Studies Association 2014 Annual Meeting, Washington, DC, November 22–25.

Moran, Michael, 2015, "Security Market Growth Continues," *SM*, May 15, https://sm.asisonline.org/Pages/Security-Market-Growth-Continues.aspx, accessed March 2017.

Myre, Greg, 2006, "Israel Economy Hums Despite Annual Tumult," *New York Times*, December 31, www.nytimes.com/2006/12/31/business/worldbusiness/31iht-israelecon.4059101.html?_r=0, accessed August 2013.

Na'aman, Oded, 2012, "The Checkpoint, Terror, Power and Cruelty," *Boston Review*, July–August, www.bostonreview.net/BR37.4/oded_naaman_israeli_defense_forces_palestinians_occupation.php, accessed September 2012.

Naor, Ravit, 2011, "Check-up: What Changed in the Security Checks in Airports?" *NRG*, September 11, www.nrg.co.il/online/55/ART2/283/051.html, accessed April 2013.

NII (National Insurance Institute), 2010, *The Poverty Rates and the Social Gaps, Annual Report 2009*, The National Insurance Institute, Administration of Research and Planning, Jerusalem, November.

—— 2011, *The Poverty Rates and the Social Gaps, Annual Report 2010*, The National Insurance Institute, Administration of Research and Planning, Jerusalem, November.

—— 2012, *The Poverty Rates and the Social Gaps, Annual Report 2011*, The National Insurance Institute, Administration of Research and Planning, Jerusalem, November.

—— 2013, *The Poverty Rates and the Social Gaps, Annual Report 2012*, The National Insurance Institute, Administration of Research and Planning, Jerusalem, November.

—— 2014, *The Poverty Rates and the Social Gaps, Annual Report 2013*, The National Insurance Institute, Administration of Research and Planning, Jerusalem, November.

—— 2016, *The Poverty Rates and the Social Gaps, Annual Report 2015*, The National Insurance Institute, Administration of Research and Planning, Jerusalem, December.

Neuman, Nadav, 2012, "IAI CEO: 'We Will Get to Privatization Eventually,'" *Globes*, December 10, www.globes.co.il/news/article.aspx?did=1000805187, accessed July 2014.

New Zealand Parliament, 2015, "Urgent Debates – Serco – Decision to End Contract for Mt Eden Corrections Facility," *New Zealand House of Representatives*, Vol. 710, December 9, p. 8698, www.parliament.nz/en-nz/pb/debates/debates/51HansD_20151209_00000016/urgent-debates-%E2%80%94-serco%E2%80%94decision-to-end-contract-for-mt, accessed March 2016.

Newman, David, 1989, "Civilian and Military Presence as Strategies of Territorial Control: The Arab-Israel Conflict," *Political Geography Quarterly*, Vol. 8, No. 3, July, pp. 215–27.

Newsdesk, 2013, "Frost & Sullivan: Israel is the World's Largest Exporter of Unmanned Aircraft," *IHLS*, May, http://i-hls.com/2013/05/frost-sullivan-israel-is-the-worlds-largest-exporter-of-unmanned-aircraft/, accessed December 2013.

Nieuwhof, Adri, 2010, "Outcry in Denmark over Firm's Involvement in Occupation," *The Electronic Intifada*, December 15, http://electronicintifada.net/content/outcry-denmark-over-firms-involvement-occupation/9142, accessed June 2013.

—— 2011, "Security Firm G4S Partly Withdraws from West Bank," *The Electronic Intifada*, March 18, http://electronicintifada.net/content/security-firm-g4s-partly-withdraws-w-bank/9273, accessed June 2013.

Nitzan, Jonathan, 2001, "Regimes of Differential Accumulation: Mergers, Stagflation and the Logic of Globalization," *Review of International Political Economy*, Vol. 8, No. 2, Summer, pp. 226–74.

Nitzan, Jonathan; Bichler, Shimshon, 2002, *The Global Political Economy of Israel*, London: Pluto Press.

—— 2006, "Cheap Wars," *The Economy of the Occupation*, No. 10, The Alternative Information Center, Jerusalem, July.

—— 2009, *Capital as Power: A Study of Order and Creorder*, New York: Routledge.

Norton, Richard, 2000, "Hizballah and the Israeli Withdrawal from Southern Lebanon," *Journal of Palestine Studies*, Vol. 30, No. 1, Autumn, pp. 22–35.

OCHA (Office for Coordination of Humanitarian Affairs), 2016, "Movement and Access Restrictions," in *Fragmented Life, Humanitarian Overview 2015*, www.ochaopt.org/content/2015-overview-movement-and-access-restrictions#WestBank, accessed February 2017.

—— 2017, *Protection of Civilians Report, 2–15 May 2017*, May 18, www.ochaopt.org/content/protection-civilians-report-2-15-may-2017, accessed September 2017.

Ochs, Juliana, 2011, *Security and Suspicion: An Ethnography of Everyday Life in Israel*, Philadelphia: University of Pennsylvania Press.

Opall-Rome, Barbara, 2012, "Elbit Sues Israeli Gov't Over Turkish Contract Default," *Defense News*, November 9, http://rpdefense.over-blog.com/article-elbit-sues-israeli-gov-t-over-turkish-contract-default-112417971.html, accessed August 2017.

—— 2013, "Interview: Joseph Weiss," *Defense News*, June 24, www.defensenews.com/article/20130624/DEFREG04/306240021/, accessed December 2013.

Orbit Systems, 2013, "Looking Back," Orbit-CS website, www.orbit-cs.com/looking-back, accessed June 2013.

Oren, Ami; Newman, David, 2006, "Competing Land Uses: The Territorial Dimension of Civil-Military Relations in Israel," *Israel Affairs*, Vol 12, No. 3, pp. 561–77.

Otsari, Shye; Itzik, Ohad; Ze'evi, Guy, 2009, "Verdict of the Month: December, High Court Decision 2605/05," *He'arat Din*, Vol. 6, No. 1, pp. 1–4.

Owen, Roger, 2007, "Willed Ignorance, Misplaced Assumptions: Explaining US/UK Pre-Invasion Iraq Policy and its Contradictory Consequences," Paper presented at the workshop on Power, Rule and Governmentality in Zones of Emergency: The Israeli Occupation in Global Perspective, Jerusalem, June 3–5.

Pauzner, Shye, 2012, "'Apartment Prices in the Center Without a Mamad Dropped by 5%,'" *Calcalist*, November 20, www.calcalist.co.il/real_estate/articles/0,7340,L-3588159,00.html, accessed April 2013.

Paz-Fuchs, Amir, 2011, "Who Moved My Knowledge," *Eretz Akheret [Another Country]*, Vol. 63, November–December, pp. 62–6.

Paz-Fuchs, Amir; Ben-Simkhon-Peleg, Sarit, 2013, *On the Seam between the Public and the Private: Privatization and Nationalization in Israel, Annual Report 2012 [Bein Hatziburi Laprati: Hafratot Vehalamot Beyisrael]*, Jerusalem: The Van Leer Institute in Jerusalem.

—— 2014, *On the Seam between the Public and the Private: Privatization and Nationalization in Israel, Annual Report 2013 [Bein Hatziburi Laprati: Hafratot Vehalamot Beyisrael]*, Jerusalem: The Van Leer Institute in Jerusalem.

Paz-Fuchs, Amir; Leshem, Elad, 2012, *On the Seam between the Public and the Private: Privatization and Nationalization in Israel, Annual Report 2011 [Bein Hatziburi Laprati: Hafratot Vehalamot Beyisrael]*, Jerusalem: The Van Leer Institute in Jerusalem.

PCHR (Palestinian Center for Human Rights; Hickman, Rose, 2008, "British Police Failed to Arrest Israeli War Criminal," *The Electronic Intifada*, February 21, http://electronicintifada.net/content/british-police-failed-arrest-israeli-war-criminal/3321, accessed October 2012.

Peleg, Yariv, 2013, "Billions of Dollars in the Trash: The Great Israeli Failures," *Mako*, May 27, www.mako.co.il/men-money/Article-3559eb1de75ee31006.htm, accessed March 2016.

Peri, Yoram, 2006, *Generals in the Cabinet Room: How the Military Shapes Israeli Policy*, Washington, DC: United States Institute of Peace Press.

Peters, Heidi M.; Schartz, Moshe; Kapp, Lawrence, 2017, *Department of Defense Contractor and Troop Levels in Iraq and Afghanistan: 2007–2017*, Congressional Research Service, CRS Report for Congress 7-5700, April 28.

Pfeffer, Anshel, 2009, "Head of the IDF's Manpower Department, Major General Zvi Zamir: The Number of Non-Enlisted Has Grown, Obligatory Service Will Not be Shortened," *Ha'aretz*, March 1.

—— 2010a, "Colonel Gadi Agmon, is There Still Such a Thing as Bakum Shock?" *Ha'aretz*, July 25, www.haaretz.co.il/news/politics/1.1213597, accessed November 2015.

—— 2010b, "IDF: Half of Jewish Men Under 40 Don't Serve in the Army, Within a Decade They will be 60%," *Ha'aretz*, November 19.

—— 2016, "This is the Age of the 'Individual's *Intifada*,'" *The Jewish Chronicle Online*, June 16, www.thejc.com/comment-and-debate/analysis/159410/this-age-individuals-intifada, accessed August 2016.

Phares, Walid, 2001, "Are Christian Enclaves the Solution? Disappearing Christians of the Middle East," *Middle East Quarterly*, Winter, pp. 61–70.

Plimmer, Gill, 2013, "G4S to Quit Key Contracts in Israel," *Financial Times*, April 21, www.ft.com/intl/cms/s/0/14e992ca-aa7a-11e2-9a38-00144feabdc0.html#axzz2WqP3fW00, accessed June 2013.

—— 2014, "G4S to End Israeli Jail Contracts Within Three Years," *Financial Times*, June 6, www.ft.com/cms/s/0/06e06252-ecc9-11e3-8963-00144feabdc0.html#axzz33qmfuiEh, accessed June 2014.

PNA (Palestinian National Authority), 2009, "Ending the Occupation, Establishing the State," Program of the Thirteenth Government, Ramallah, August.

—— 2011a, *Building Palestine: Achievements and Challenges*, Report of the Palestinian National Authority to the Ad Hoc Liaison Committee, Brussels, April 13.

—— 2011b, *National Development Plan 2011–13: Establishing the State, Building our Future*, Ramallah, April.

—— 2012, *Moving Beyond the Status-Quo: Safeguarding the Two-State Solution*, Report of the Palestinian National Authority to the Ad Hoc Liaison Committee, New York, September 23.

Program on Humanitarian Policy and Conflict Research, 2008, "Private Security Companies in the Occupied Palestinian Territory (OPT): An International Humanitarian Law Perspective," Policy Brief, Program on Humanitarian Policy and Conflict Research, Harvard University, March.

Provost, Claire, 2017, "The Industry of Inequality: Why the World is Obsessed with Private Security," *Guardian*, May 12, www.theguardian.com/inequality/2017/may/12/industry-of-inequality-why-world-is-obsessed-with-private-security, accessed July 2017.

Prusher, Ilene R., 2010, "Palestinian Authority Steps up Boycott of Goods Made in Israeli Settlements in West Bank," *Christian Science Monitor*, February 25, www.csmonitor.com/World/Middle-East/2010/0225/Palestinian-Authority-steps-up-boycott-of-goods-made-in-Israeli-settlements-in-West-Bank, accessed January 2014.

Pumranz-Zurin, Limor, 2014, "On Sociology of Logistics in Fighting," *Campaigns* [*Ma'arakhot*], Vol. 453, February, pp. 40–7.

Rafael Advanced Defense Systems Ltd, 2016, Rafael Advanced Defense Systems Ltd website, www.rafael.co.il/Marketing/197-en/Marketing.aspx, accessed March 2016.

RAND, 2013, *Effective Policing for 21st-Century Israel*, various cities: RAND Corporation.

Rapoport, Meron, 2007, "Outsourcing the Checkpoints," *Haaretz*, October 2, www.haaretz.com/weekend/week-s-end/outsourcing-the-checkpoints-1.230416, accessed February 2013.

Ravid, Barak, 2010, "WikiLeaks Exposé: Israel Tried to Coordinate Gaza War with Abbas," *Haaretz*, November 28, www.haaretz.com/news/diplomacy-defense/wikileaks-expose-israel-tried-to-coordinate-gaza-war-with-abbas-1.327487, accessed December 2013.

—— 2016, "Netanyahu Reassures Father of Soldier Who Shot to Death Prone Palestinian," *Haaretz*, March 31, www.haaretz.com/israel-news/.premium-1.712093, accessed August 2016.

Ravid, Barak; Associated Press, 2010, "Palestinians: Gaza War Claim Exposed by WikiLeaks is Untrue," *Haaretz*, November 29, www.haaretz.com/news/diplomacy-defense/palestinians-gaza-war-claim-exposed-by-wikileaks-is-untrue-1.327669, accessed December 2013.

Ravid, Barak; Cohen, Gili, 2014, "The Cabinet Decided to Stop Distribution of Protective Kits to Citizens," *Haaretz*, January 19, www.haaretz.co.il/news/politics/1.2221098, accessed January 2016.

Ravid, Barak; Pfeffer, Anshel; Issacharoff, Avi; News Agencies, 2011, "Netanyahu: Palestinians, World Must Condemn Settlement Attack 'Unequivocally,'" *Haaretz*, March 12, www.haaretz.com/news/diplomacy-defense/netanyahu-palestinians-world-must-condemn-settlement-attack-unequivocally-1.348763, accessed June 2015.

Ravid-Ravitz, Yair, 2013, *Window to the Back Yard: The History of Israel's Ties with Lebanon, Facts and Illusions* [*Khalon Lakhatzer Ha'akhorit: Toldot Kishrei Yisrael Im Levanon, Uvdot Veashlayot*], Yahood: Ofir Bichurim.

Reich, Dror, 2012, "The Hever Organization Joins Keren Noy as a Franchise Owner for the Bahad City in the Negev," *TheMarker*, September 18, www.themarker.com/markets/1.1825908, accessed January 2013.

—— 2013a, "Orbit Will Supply the Ministry of Defense Systems for 3.5 Million Nis," *TheMarker*, January 13, www.themarker.com/wallstreet/stock/1.1905910, accessed April 2013.

—— 2013b, "Thanks to Bahad City: A 530% Rise in the Net Profit of Minrav in 2012," *TheMarker*, March 17, www.themarker.com/markets/reports/1.1967906, accessed May 2013.

Rimon, Ran, 2012, "650 Contractors Join the Police as Part of the Staff," *Ynet*, July 18, www.ynet.co.il/articles/0,7340,L-4257126,00.html, accessed July 2017.

Roded, Batia; Tzfadia, Erez, 2012, "Recognition of Native People's Rights to Land: The Case of the Arab-Bedouins in the Negev from a Comparative Perspective," *The Public Space* [*Hamerkhav Hatziburi*], Vol. 7, Autumn, pp. 66–99.

Rosenberg, David, 2016, "Amid Terrorism Fears, Israelis Avoid Old City of Jerusalem," *Arutz Sheva*, April 24, www.israelnationalnews.com/News/News.aspx/211352, accessed August 2016.

Rozner, Rivka, 2011, "Someone to Think for Us," *Eretz Akheret* [*Another Country*], Vol. 63, November–December, pp. 24–31.

Rubin, Barry, 1998, "External Influences on the Israeli Elections," in Elazar, Daniel J.; Sandler, Shmuel (eds.), *Israel at the Polls, 1996*, New York: Routledge, pp. 149–66.

Sadan, Ezra, 2004, "How is Israel's Economy Affected by the Security Situation?" *Jerusalem Issue Brief*, Vol. 4, No. 11, www.jcpa.org/brief/brief004-11.htm, accessed August 2013.

Sadeh, Sharon, 2001, "Israel's Beleaguered Defense Industry," *Middle East Review of International Affairs Journal*, Vol. 5, No. 1, March, pp. 64–77.

Samaan, Jean-Loupe, 2013, "The Pakistani Test of the Israel-India Partnership," *Al Monitor*, June 23, www.al-monitor.com/pulse/originals/2013/06/pakistantest-israel-india.html#, accessed December 2013.

Schmil, Daniel, 2014, "Suspicious Passenger on the Bus? The Driver Could Conduct a Search," *TheMarker*, August 17, www.themarker.com/dynamo/1.2408229, accessed March 2015.

Schroeder, Ursula C.; Chappuis, Fairlie; Kocak, Deniz, 2013, "Security Sector Reform from a Policy Transfer Perspective: A Comarative Study of International Interventions in the Palestinian Territories, Liberia and Timor-Leste," *Journal of Intervention and Statebuilding*, Vol. 7, No. 3, pp. 381–401.

Scott-Clark, Cathy, 2012, "The Mass Graves of Kashmir," *Guardian*, July 9, www.guardian.co.uk/world/2012/jul/09/mass-graves-of-kashmir, accessed January 2013.

Securities and Exchange Commission, 2010, "Magal Security Systems LTD.," Commission file number: 0-21388, Washington, DC.

Segev, Tom, 2005, *1967: And the Land Changed its Face* [*1967: Veha'aretz Shinta et Paneyha*], Jerusalem: Keter.

Seidman, Guy, 2010, "From Nationalization to Privatization: The Case of the IDF," *Armed Forces & Society*, Vol. 36, No. 4, July, pp. 1–34.

Selby, Jan, 2013, "Cooperation, Domination and Colonisation: The Israeli-Palestinian Joint Water Committee," *Water Alternatives*, Vol. 6, No. 1, pp. 1–24.

Seliktar, Ofira, 2009, *Doomed to Failure: The Politics and Intelligence of the Oslo Peace Process*, Santa Barbara: Greenwood.

Shadmi, Erella, 2010, "Privatization State," *Ha'aretz*, February 28.

—— 2012a, *The Fortified Land; Police and Policing in Israel* [*Eretz Meuvtakhat: Mishtara, Shitur Vehapolitika Shel Habitakhon Ha'ishi*], Tel-Aviv: Hakibutz Hameukhad.

—— 2012b, "Bullying Freedom Instead of Academic Freedom," *Haoketz*, October 30, https://tinyurl.com/yaunjwo5, accessed February 2013.

Shafir, Gershon; Peled, Yoav, 2004, *Being Israeli: The Dynamics of Multiple Citizenship*, Cambridge: Cambridge University Press.

Shahak, Israel, 1991, "The Israeli Occupation Three Years after the Intifada," *Washington Report on Middle East Affairs*, March, p. 27.

Shalev, Michael, 1984, "Labor, State, and Crisis: An Israeli Case Study," *Industrial Relations*, Vol. 23, No. 3, Fall, pp. 362–86.

—— 2004, "Did Globalization and Liberalization 'Normalize' Israeli Political Economy?" in Ram, Uri; Filc, Dani (eds.), *The Power of Property: Israeli Society in the Global Age* [*Shilton Hahon: Hakhevra Hayisraelit Ba'idan Haglobali*], Van-Leer Institute, Jerusalem, pp. 85–115.

Shapira, Anita, 2001, *A State on the Way* [*Medina Baderekh*], Jerusalem: Zalman Shazar Center for Israel's History.

Shapiro, Shlomo, 2011, "Armed Civilians and Fighting Terror," *NRG*, July 29, www.nrg.co.il/online/1/ART2/265/137.html, accessed August 2014.

Sharabi, Linda, 2002, "Israel's Economic Growth: Success Without Security," *Merida: Middle East Review of International Affairs*, Vol. 6, No. 3, www.gloria-center.org/2002/09/sharaby-2002-09-03/, accessed August 2013.

Sharp, Jeremy M., 2010, *U.S. Foreign Aid to Israel*, Congressional Research Service, CRS Report for Congress 7-5700, September 16.

—— 2013a, *Egypt: Background and U.S. Relations*, Congress Research Service, CRS Report to Congress, 7-5700, February 26.

—— 2013b, *U.S. Foreign Aid to Israel*, Congressional Research Service, CRS Report for Congress 7-5700, April 11.

—— 2014, *U.S. Foreign Aid to Israel*, Congressional Research Service, CRS Report for Congress 7-5700, April 11.

—— 2015, *U.S. Foreign Aid to Israel*, Congressional Research Service, CRS Report for Congress 7-5700, June 10.

—— 2016, *U.S. Foreign Aid to Israel*, Congressional Research Service, CRS Report for Congress 7-5700, December 22.

Sheffer, Gabriel; Barak, Oren, 2010, "Introduction," in Sheffer, Gabriel; Barak, Oren (eds.), *Militarism and Israeli Society*, Bloomington: Indiana University Press, pp. 1–13.

—— 2013, *Israel's Security Networks*, New York: Cambridge University Press.

Shenfeld, Yoni, 2007, "25% of 18 Year-Olds Don't Conscript to the IDF," *MSN*, July 17.

Shforer, Sharon, 2012, "The Retired General Assaulted the Business World – and Burnt Tens of Millions of NIS," *TheMarker*, May 11, www.themarker.com/markerweek/1.1705583, accessed October 2012.

Shiffer, Zalman, 2010, "The Debate Over the Defense Budget in Israel," in Sheffer, Gabriel; Barak, Oren (eds.), *Militarism and Israeli Society*, Bloomington: Indiana University Press, pp. 213–37.

Sibat, 2013, "Sibat: Security Exports, Press-Release 2013," Israeli Ministry of Defense website, Jerusalem.

Sikolar, Na'ama, 2011, "Ministry of Defense Paid McKinsey NIS 100 Million, Five Times More than the Contract," *Calcalist*, December 27, www.calcalist.co.il/local/articles/0,7340,L-3556611,00.html, accessed August 2014.

Sikolar, Na'ama; Amsterdamsky, Shaul, 2009, "The Targets Bank of IDF Economists Updates in the Crisis: 'We Cannot Implement Efficiency Unto Death,'" *Calcalist*, July 5, www.calcalist.co.il/local/articles/0,7340,L-3320044,00.html, accessed December 2013.

Singer, Peter Warren, 2003, *Corporate Warriors: The Rise of Privatized Military Industry*, Ithaca: Cornell University Press.

SIPRI (Stockholm International Peace Research Institute), 2014, "The SIPRI Top 100 Arms-Producing and Military Service Companies, 2012," *SIPRI*, January, www.sipri.org/sites/default/files/files/FS/SIPRIFS1401.pdf, accessed September 2017.

—— 2015, *SIPRI Yearbook 2015: Armaments, Disarmament and International Security*, Stockholm.

—— 2017, "SIPRI Military Expenditure Database 1988–2015," *SIPRI*, www.sipri.org/databases/milex, accessed January 2017.

Skhayek, Dafna, 2003, "Security Guards in Public Institutions and in Private Businesses," Introduction Paper, Knesset Research Center, December.

Space War, 2013, "Israel Builds up its War Robot Industry," *Space War*, June 3, www.spacewar.com/reports/Israel_builds_up_its_war_robot_industry_999.html, accessed June 2013.

Spearin, Christopher, 2008, "Privatized Peace?" in Alexandra, Andrew; Baker, Deane-Peter; Caparini, Marina (eds.), *Private Military and Security Companies: Ethics, Policies and Civil-Military Relations*, London & New York: Routledge, pp. 203–16.

Spiegel, Udi, 2001, "Youth Motivation to Serve in the IDF," Research and Information Center at the Knesset," Jerusalem, June 26.

Starr, Paul, 1988, "The Meaning of Privatization," *Yale Law & Policy Review*, Vol. 6, No. 1, pp. 6–41.

State Comptroller, 1987, *The "Lavi" Project – Decision Making Process*, Annual Report 37 for 1986 and the Fiscal Year 1985, Jerusalem, pp. 1288–325.

—— 2010, *Passages Activity Between Israel and Judea and Samarea Area*, Annual Report 61a for 2010, Jerusalem, pp. 13–38.

—— 2012, *Industrial Zones in Judea and Samaria and the Rural Sector*, State Comptroller Report 2012, Jerusalem, pp. 1661–700.

State of Israel, 1986, "Law of Security Service (Combined Version) Hatashmav-1986," Jerusalem.

—— 2005, "Law of Authorities for Protecting Public Security, Hatashsah-2005," Jerusalem.

Steinman, Tamir, 2014, "Ya'alon Stopped the IDF Move to the Negev," *Reshet*, November 30, http://reshet.tv/News_n/heb/news/Politics/Security/articlenews,10349/, accessed September 2017.

Stewart, M.G.; Mueller, J., 2008, "Assessing the Costs and Benefits of United States Homland Security Spending," Centre for Infrastructure Performance and Reliability, Research report No. 265.04.08, Newcastle: University of Newcastle.

Stiglitz, Joseph, 2002, *Globalization and its Discontents*, New York: W.W. Norton & Co.

Stockmarr, Leila, 2014, "Seeing is Striking: Selling Israeli Warfare," *Jadaliyya*, January 18, www.jadaliyya.com/pages/index/16044/seeing-is-striking_selling-israeli-warfare, accessed April 2014.

Swift, Robert, 2016, "This *Intifada* is Worse than the Last," *Jerusalem Post*, March 30, www.jpost.com/Arab-Israeli-Conflict/This-Intifada-is-worse-than-the-last-449648, accessed August 2016.

Swirski, Shlomo, 2008, "1967: Political-Economic Shift in Israel," *Tarabut*, October 2, www.tarabut.info/he/articles/article/turningpoint/, accessed November 2012.

Tal-Sapiro, Uri, 2009, "Establishing a Privately-Managed Prison: State of Affairs," Research and Information Center at the Knesset, Jerusalem, August 3.

Tartir, Alaa, 2015, "The Evolution and Reform of Palestinian Security Forces 1993–2013," *Stability: International Journal of Security & Development*, Vol. 4, No. 1, pp. 1–20.

Taylor, Matthew; Travis, Alan, 2012, "G4S Chief Predicts Mass Police Privatization," *Guardian*, June 20, www.guardian.co.uk/uk/2012/jun/20/g4s-chief-mass-police-privatisation, accessed June 2013.

The Second Authority for Television & Radio; Midgam, 2006, "Survey of Listening to Local and National Radio Stations Broadcasted in the State of Israel," December.

Theohary, Catherine A., 2015, "Conventional Arms Transfers to Developing Nations 2007–2014," Congressional Research Service, document 7-5700.

TI (Transparency International), 2013, "Government Defense Anti-Corruption Index 2013," London: Transparency International UK.

Tilly, Charles, 1990, *Coersion, Capital and European States, AD 990–1990*, Cambridge: Basil Blackwell.

Tinder, Alan J., 1990, *Low Intensity Conflict*, Air War College Research Report, A Defense Analytical Study submitted to the Faculty, Maxwell Air Force Base, Alabama, April, pp. 1–60.

Toker, Nati, 2017, "Lieberman has Second Thoughts: Galatz Will Stay in the IDF, Will Not Move to the Ministry of Defense," *TheMarker*, February 5, www.themarker.com/advertising/1.3627496, accessed February 2017.

Toren, Ya'akov, 2002, "Effects of the Defense Aid on the Industrial Policy," in Tov, Imri (ed.), *Security and the National Economy in Israel: Challenges and Answers in Policy of Producing Security*, Memo No. 62, October, Tel-Aviv: Jaffee Center for Strategic Studies, pp. 103–4.

Tran, Pierre, 2012, "Little Movement Seen on Nexter Privatization," *Defense News*, November 21, www.defensenews.com/article/20121121/DEFREG01/311210005/Little-Movement-Seen-Nexter-Privatization, accessed February 2013.

Trivedi, Anjani, 2013, "How the American Privatized Prison is Spreading Overseas," *Time*, August 23, http://world.time.com/2013/08/23/crime-pays-at-least-if-youre-a-private-prison-operator/, accessed August 2014.

Tuv, Imri (ed.), 2002, *Security and the National Economy in Israel: Challenges and Answers in Policy of Producing Security*, Memo No. 62, October, Tel-Aviv: Jaffee Center for Strategic Studies.

Tzur, Nadir, 2011, "The Third Lebanon War," *Reshet Bet*, July 17, www.iba.org.il/bet/?entity=748995&type=297, accessed December 2013.

UN (United Nations), 2012, "General Assembly Votes Overwhelmingly to Accord Palestine 'Non-Member Observer State' Status in United Nations," General Assembly, GA/111317, www.un.org/News/Press/docs/2012/ga11317.doc.htm, accessed August 2014.

—— 2013, "5. Estimates of Mid-Year Population: 2002–2011," *Demographic Yearbook*, http://unstats.un.org/unsd/demographic/products/dyb/dyb2011.htm, accessed June 2013.

Una, Yair, 2011, "A Matter Without Rating," *Eretz Akheret* [*Another Country*], Vol. 63, November–December, pp. 32–35.

UPI, 2013a, "Israel Sends Turks EW Systems Despite Rift," *UPI.com*, February 19, www.upi.com/Business_News/Security-Industry/2013/02/19/Israel-sends-Turks-EW-systems-despite-rift/UPI-64261361301814/#ixzz2LThVZtLa, accessed February 2013.

—— 2013b, "Israeli Navy Seeks Gas Field Defense Force," *UPI.com*, April 2, www.upi.com/Business_News/Security-Industry/2013/04/02/Israeli-navy-seeks-gas-field-defense-force/UPI-47581364929327/, accessed May 2013.

—— 2013c, "In Israel, Lingering Bitterness Over a Failed Fighter Project," *UPI.com*, October 15, www.upi.com/Business_News/Security-Industry/2013/10/15/In-Israel-lingering-bitterness-over-a-failed-fighter-project/78961381856103/, accessed March 2016.

Van Leer, 2017, "Privatizations and Nationalizations in Israel," Van Leer Institute in Jerusalem, Ya'akov Chazan Center for Social Justice and Democracy, https://tinyurl.com/y8htuskb, accessed January 2017.

Veblen, Thorstein, 1921, *The Engineers, and the Price System*, Kitchener: Batoche Books.

—— 1994, *Theory of the Leisure Class*, Dover Thrift Editions, originally published in 1899.

Wade, Lisa, 2013, "Race, Rehabilitation and the Private Prisons Industry," *Sociological Images*, January 25, http://thesocietypages.org/socimages/2013/01/25/race-rehabilitation-and-the-private-prison-industry/, accessed May 2013.

War on Want, 2006, *Corporate Mercenaries: The Threat of Private Military and Security Companies*, London: War on Want.

Weber, Max, 1970, *From Max Weber: Essays in Sociology*, London: Routledge and Kegan Paul.

Wehrey, Frederic M., 2002, "A Clash of Wills: Hizballah's Psychological Campaign Against Israel in South Lebanon," *Small Wars & Insurgencies*, Vol. 13, No. 3, pp. 53–74.

Weisberg, Hilla, 2012, "MK Katz to Modi'in Ezrakhi: 'Bring Back the Fired Security Guards,'" *TheMarker*, March 19, www.themarker.com/career/1.1667285, accessed November 2012.

—— 2013, "'A Business Without Security Which Will have a Terror Attack in It – Will Go Bankrupt,'" *TheMarker*, November 26, www.themarker.com/career/1.2174721, accessed February 2014.

Weisblei, Eti, 2006, "Data on Equal Opportunities in Education from Kindergarten Age to University," Knesset: Center for Research and Information, Jerusalem, October.

Weisman, Lilach, 2010, "60 Thousand Exemptions," *Globes*, August 2, www.globes.co.il/news/article.aspx?did=1000578518, accessed September, 2012.

Weizman, Eyal, 2007, *Hollow Land: Israel's Architecture of Occupation*, London & New York: Verso.

Who Profits, 2011a, "The Case of G4S: Private Security Companies and the Israeli Occupation," *Who Profits: The Israeli Occupation Industry*, March, http://

whoprofits.org/sites/default/files/WhoProfits-PrivateSecurity-G4S.pdf, accessed June 2013.

—— 2011b, "Technologies of Control: The Case of Hewlett Packard," *Who Profits: The Israeli Occupation Industry*, December, www.whoprofits.org/sites/default/files/hp_report-_final_for_web.pdf, accessed October 2012.

Wikipedia, 2017, "Soltam Systems," https://en.wikipedia.org/wiki/Soltam_Systems, accessed September 2017.

Wolf, Klaus Dieter; Deitelhoff, Nicole; Engert, Stefan, 2007, "Corporate Security Responsibility: Towards a Conceptual Framework for a Comparative Research Agenda," *Cooperation and Conflict*, Vol. 42, pp. 294–320.

Wolf, Pinkhas, 2012, "Biometric Database Will Ensure that Yeshiva Students Study?" *Walla*, July, http://news.walla.co.il/?w=/9/2550398, accessed June 2013.

World Bank, 2014, "Data: Population (Total)," The World Bank, http://data.worldbank.org/indicator/SP.POP.TOTL?page=5, accessed January 2014.

Ya'acobi-Keller, Uri, 2008, "The False Rhetoric of the 'True Israelis' Campaign and Counter-Campaign," The Alternative Information Center, February 24, www.alternativenews.org/english/index.php/news/news/1086-the-false-rhetoric-of-the-qtrue-israelisq-campaign-and-counter-campaign.html, accessed September 2012.

Ya'akobs, Yaron, 2002, "Desirable Structure and Ownership of Security Industries," in Tov, Imri (ed.), *Security and the National Economy in Israel: Challenges and Answers in Policy of Producing Security*, Memo No. 62, October, Tel-Aviv: Jaffee Center for Strategic Studies, pp. 121–4.

Ya'alon, Moshe, 2002, "Building Power Under Restrictions of Resources and Time," in Tov, Imri (ed.), *Security and the National Economy in Israel: Challenges and Answers in Policy of Producing Security*, Memo No. 62, October, Tel-Aviv: Jaffee Center for Strategic Studies, pp. 94–9.

Yaron, Amos, 2002, "The Ministry of Defense's Industrial Policy," in Tov, Imri (ed.), *Security and the National Economy in Israel: Challenges and Answers in Policy of Producing Security*, Memo No. 62, October, Tel-Aviv: Jaffee Center for Strategic Studies, pp. 117–20.

Yates, Sally Q., 2016, "Memorandum for the Acting Director Federal Bureau of Prisons: Reducing Our Use of Private Prisons," US Department of Justice, Office of the Deputy Attorney General, August 18.

Yeoman, Barry, 2003, "Soldiers of Good Fortune," *Mother Jones*, May/June, www.motherjones.com/politics/2003/05/soldiers-good-fortune, accessed November 2012.

Yiftachel, Oren, 2005, "Neither Two States Nor One: The Disengagement and 'Creeping Apartheid' in Israel/Palestine," *The Arab World Geographer/Le Géographe du monde arabe*, Vol. 8, No. 3, pp. 125–9.

Ynet, 2006, "The Ministers Ezra and Olmert Signed a Contract to Found a Private Prison," *Ynet*, January 2, www.ynet.co.il/articles/0,7340,L-3193850,00.html, accessed June 2015.

Zandberg, Esther, 2013, "Fear and Privatization in Every Home," *Ha'aretz*, April 15, www.haaretz.com/culture/fear-and-privatization-in-every-home.premium-1.515539, accessed April 2013.

Zansh, Yaffa, 2011, "Your Appeal for Information on 'Canteen' and Funds Regarding Security Prisoners in Jails," Letter from the department of the spokesperson of the IPS, Ramle, September 11.

Zertal, Idith; Eldar, Akiva, 2009, *Lords of the Land: The War Over Israel's Settlement in the Occupied Territories, 1967–2007*, New York: Nation Books.

Zitun, Yoav, 2016, "Hebron Soldier Charged with Manslaughter, Named," *Ynet*, April 18, www.ynetnews.com/articles/0,7340,L-4793155,00.html, accessed August 2016.

Zohar, Hanna; Hever, Shir, 2010, "Israel Owes Billions of Shekels to Palestinian Workers," *Economy of the Occupation*, No. 25, Kav Laoved and The Alternative Information Center, Jerusalem, December.

Zureik, Elia, 2011, "Colonialism, Surveillance, and Population Control: Israel/Palestine," in Zureik, Elia; Lyon, David; Abu-Laban, Yasmeen (eds.), *Surveillance and Control in Israel/Palestine: Population, Territory and Power*, New York: Routledge, pp. 3–46.

Zwobener, Sarah, 2005, "Border Passes from Gaza and from the West Bank," Knesset: Center for Research and Information, Jerusalem, November 15.

Index